LEARNING ISLAM 3

Islamic Studies Textbook Series
Level Three

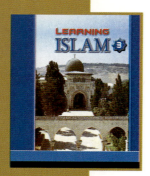

Learning Islam 3

بسم الله الرحمن الرحيم

In the Name of Allah, Most Compassionate, Most Merciful

Learning Islam © is a series of Islamic studies textbooks that introduces Muslim students to the essentials of their faith, and brings to light the historic and cultural aspects of Islam in elaborate manner. The series may be used for middle school and/or highschool grades. Each level is served by a student textbook and workbook, as well as a teacher's guide. This series builds upon the ISF's primary series "I Love Islam" which covers grades one through five.

The Islamic Services Foundation is undertaking this project in collaboration with Brighter Horizons Academy in Dallas, Texas. Extensive efforts have been made to review the enclosed material. However, constructive suggestions and comments that would enrich the content of this work are welcome.

All Praise is due to Allah (God), for providing us with the resources that have enabled us to complete the first part of this series. This is an ongoing project, and it is our sincere wish and hope that it will impact our Muslim children today, and for many years to come.

Copyright © 2020 by Islamic Services Foundation

ISBN 1-933301-42-6

All rights reserved. No part of this publication may be reproduced or transmitted in any form or by any means, electronic or mechanical, including photocopy, recording, or any information storage and retrieval system, without permission in writing from the publisher.

PROGRAM DIRECTOR *

Nabil Sadoun, Ed.D.

WRITING TEAM

Suad Abu Amarah
Ummukulthum Al-Maawiy
Lena Dirbashi
Nabil Sadoun, Ed.D.
Omar Tarazi

REVIEWERS AND ADVISORS

Freda Shamma, Ph.D.
Jerald Dirks, Ph.D.

CONTRIBUTORS

Dianna Abdul-Qadir
Kacem Ayachi
Lana Baghal Dasti
Nicholas Howard
Sarah Islam
Sophia Jetpuri
Kamla Milad

CURRICULUM DESIGN

Majida Salem
Nabil Sadoun, Ed.D.

ENGLISH EDITOR

Sumaiya Susan Gavell

GRAPHIC DESIGN

Mohammed Eid Mubarak

ILLUSTRATIONS

Raed Abdulwahid

PHOTOGRAPHY

Al-Anwar Designs
Khadija Bin Lahoucine

PUBLISHER AND OWNER

ISF PUBLICATIONS

Islamic Services Foundation
P.O. Box 451623
Garland, Texas 75045
U.S.A
Tel: +1 972-414-5090
Fax: +1 972-414-5640
www.myislamicbooks.com

* Names are in alphabetical order of the last names.

UNIT A

Allah Controls the World

Chapter One	Allah Controls the World	A2
Chapter Two	Only Allah Gives Life and Death	A12
Chapter Three	Allah Gives and Deprives Wealth	A20
Chapter Four	The Prophet of Patience and Thankfulness	A26
Chapter Five	Patience and Perseverance	A32
Chapter Six	Patience and Perseverance in Daily Life	A42
Chapter Seven	Shukr: Thankfulness to Allah	A56
Chapter Eight	Surat-ul-Qiyamah	A66
Lesson 1	Surat-ul-Qiyamah: Verses (1-15)	A66
Lesson 2	Surat-ul-Qiyamah: Verses (16-25)	A70
Lesson 3	Surat-ul-Qiyamah: Verses (26-40)	A74
Lesson 4	Tajweed: Types of Madd	A78

Portraits of Faith

Chapter One	Two Martyrs: The Stories of Prophets Zakariyya and Yahya	B4
Chapter Two	Purity of Faith: The Story of Maryam	B14
Chapter Three	The Miracle of Miracles: The Story of Prophet Isa	B24

Beautiful Worship: The Rules of Siyam and Hajj

Chapter One	Ramadan: A Month of Blessings	C2
Chapter Two	Ahkam-us-Siyam, The Rules of Fasting	C10
Chapter Three	Mubtilaat-us-Siyam, The Nullifiers of Fasting	C20
Chapter Four	Hajjat-ul-Wadaa' (Part I)	C28
Chapter Five	Hajjat-ul-Wadaa' (PartI II)	C36

UNIT D

Islam Prevails over Arabia

Chapter One	Ghazwat Tabook	D2
Chapter Two	Honesty Saves: The Story of the Three Who Missed Tabook	D10
Chapter Three	Surat-ul-Munafiqoon	D16
Lesson 1	Surat-ul-Munafiqoon: Verses (1-4)	D17
Lesson 2	Surat-ul-Munafiqoon: Verses (5-8)	D21
Lesson 3	Surat-ul-Munafiqoon: Verses (9-11)	D25
Chapter Four	Prophet Muhammad Passes to Jannah	D28

UNIT E

As-Sunnah: The Other Divine Revelation

Chapter One	As-Sunnah: The Prophet's Way	E2
Chapter Two	The Basics of Uloom-ul-Hadeeth	E10
Chapter Three	The Recording of the Hadeeth	E16
Chapter Four	The Major Books of Hadeeth (Part I)	E22
Chapter Five	The Major Books of Hadeeth (Part II)	E30

Leading A Pure Lifestyle

Chapter One	Surat-ul-Hujuraat سورة الحجرات	F2
Lesson 1	Surat-ul-Hujuraat: Verses (1-5)	F2
Lesson 2	Surat-ul-Hujuraat: Verses (6-8)	F8
Lesson 3	Surat-ul-Hujuraat: Verses (9-10)	F16
Lesson 4	Surat-ul-Hujuraat: Verses (11-13)	F24
Lesson 5	Surat-ul-Hujuraat: Verses (14-18)	F32
Chapter Two	Alcoholic Beverages, The Mother of All Evils	F36
Chapter Three	Pork and Other Haram Meats	F46
Chapter Four	Gambling and Lottery	F54
Chapter Five	Other Addictions	F62

UNIT A

Allah Controls the World

Chapter One	Allah Controls the World	A2
Chapter Two	Only Allah Gives Life and Death	A12
Chapter Three	Allah Gives and Deprives Wealth	A20
Chapter Four	The Prophet of Patience and Thankfulness	A26
Chapter Five	Patience and Perseverance	A32
Chapter Six	Patience and Perseverance in Daily Life	A42
Chapter Seven	Shukr: Thankfulness to Allah	A56
Chapter Eight	Surat-ul-Qiyamah	A66
Lesson 1	Surat-ul-Qiyamah: Verses (1-15)	A66
Lesson 2	Surat-ul-Qiyamah: Verses (16-25)	A70
Lesson 3	Surat-ul-Qiyamah: Verses (26-40)	A74
Lesson 4	Tajweed: Types of Madd	A78

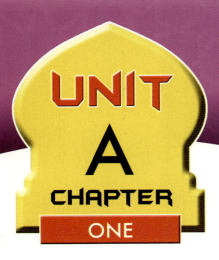

Unit A — Chapter One

Allah Controls the World

CHAPTER OBJECTIVES

1. Understand the concept of Al-Qadar in Islam.
2. Internalize that nothing happens in the universe without Allah's permission and knowledge.
3. Understand that man has free will to choose good or evil actions.

VOCABULARY

- Al-Qadar (Divine Fate) القدر
- Al-Ilm (Knowledge) العلم
- Kitabah (Written Destiny) الكتابة
- Mashee'ah (Divine Will) المشيئة
- Al-Khalq (Creation) الخلق

Belief in Al-Qadar

As you learned in your elementary years, there are six pillars of i-man (faith). These pillars are to believe in Allah, His angels, His messengers, His Books, the Day of Judgment, and to believe in Al-Qadar (divine fate).

Pillars of Faith

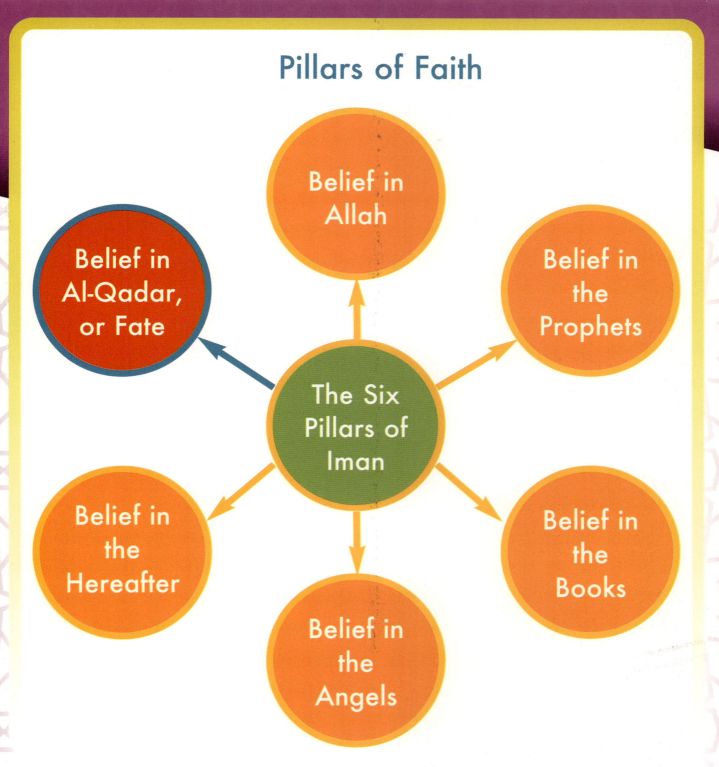

In this unit, you will have ample opportunity to learn about the sixth pillar of faith: the belief in Al-Qadar.

The universe is Allah's property, and nothing happens in His Kingdom without His knowledge and permission. The Arabic term for divine fate, or destiny, is Al-Qadar. Everything in the world has a predetermined and set course. The destiny of every element of creation and the outcome of every situation, whether major or minor, is already known to Allah.

The original meaning of the word Al-Qadar is "exact measure" or amount. The Arabic verb "yuqaddir" means, among other things, to measure or decide the quantity, quality, or position of something before you actually make it.

There are many references to Al-Qadar in the Holy Qur'an. Allah says:

﴿ إِنَّا كُلَّ شَيْءٍ خَلَقْنَٰهُ بِقَدَرٍ ﴾ القمر : ٤٩

Verily, We have created all things with Qadar. (54:49)

﴿ وَخَلَقَ كُلَّ شَيْءٍ فَقَدَّرَهُۥ تَقْدِيرًا ﴾ الفرقان : ٢

He has created everything, and has measured it exactly according to its due measure. (25:2)

﴿ أَلَمْ نَخْلُقكُّم مِّن مَّآءٍ مَّهِينٍ ﴿٢٠﴾ فَجَعَلْنَٰهُ فِى قَرَارٍ مَّكِينٍ ﴿٢١﴾ إِلَىٰ قَ
مَعْلُومٍ ﴿٢٢﴾ فَقَدَرْنَا فَنِعْمَ ٱلْقَٰدِرُونَ ﴿٢٣﴾ ﴾ المرسلات : ٢٠-٣

Did we not create you with a fluid of no value? Then We placed it in a place of safety (womb), for a known period? So We did measure, and We are the best to measure. (77:20-23)

﴿ قُل لَّن يُصِيبَنَآ إِلَّا مَا كَتَبَ ٱللَّهُ لَنَا هُوَ
مَوْلَىٰنَا وَعَلَى ٱللَّهِ فَلْيَتَوَكَّلِ ٱلْمُؤْمِنُونَ ﴿٥١﴾ ﴾ التوبة : ١

Say: "Nothing shall ever happen to us except what Allah has ordained for us. He is our Lord and Protector. And in Allah let the believers put their trust." (9:51)

The belief in Al-Qadar is one of the six pillars of faith in Islam. In a famous hadeeth of Jibreel, we understand the true meaning of faith. "Now tell me about iman," the Angel Jibreel once said to Prophet Muhammad ﷺ .

The Prophet replied, "It means that you should believe in Allah, His angels, His books, His messengers, and the Last Day; and that you should believe in fate, both good and evil."

Scholars have defined Al-Qadar as "that [which] Allah has ordained and permitted, both good and evil, before creating His creation, and that all what has happened and will happen are through Allah's knowledge and will."

Scholars of Islam also say that there are four aspects of Al-Qadar that help us understand how Al-Qadar happens in our world:

1 Al-Ilm العلم Divine Knowledge: Allah first knows what will happen.

2 Al-Kitabah الكتابة Written Destiny: The angels write what will happen.

3 Al-Mash'eeah المَشِيئة Divine Will: Allah wills and permits what is written to happen when its time comes.

4 Al-Khalq الخَلَق Creation: Allah creates and makes His will happen in the real world.

Let us learn in some detail about the above aspects of Al-Qadar:

1. Al-Ilm

Knowledge - A Muslim believes that Allah has full knowledge of everything in the universe, whether major or minor. This amazing knowledge encompasses all the actions of Allah and the actions of all His creation. Allah says:

﴿ أَلَمۡ تَعۡلَمۡ أَنَّ ٱللَّهَ يَعۡلَمُ مَا فِى ٱلسَّمَآءِ وَٱلۡأَرۡضِ ۗ إِنَّ ذَٰلِكَ فِى كِتَٰبٍ ۚ إِنَّ ذَٰلِكَ عَلَى ٱللَّهِ يَسِيرٌ ﴾ الحج: ٧٠

Didn't you know that Allah knows all that is in heaven and on earth? Surely this is in a book; surely this is easy to Allah. [22:70]

2. Kitabah

Written Destiny – A Muslim believes that Allah recorded everything in a Book that was kept with Him in Heaven. This Book is called "Al-Lawh'-ul-Mah'foodh," the Preserved Book. Allah says in Surat-ul-An'aam,

﴿ وَعِندَهُۥ مَفَاتِحُ ٱلۡغَيۡبِ لَا يَعۡلَمُهَآ إِلَّا هُوَ ۚ وَيَعۡلَمُ مَا فِى ٱلۡبَرِّ وَٱلۡبَحۡرِ ۚ وَمَا تَسۡقُطُ مِن وَرَقَةٍ إِلَّا يَعۡلَمُهَا وَلَا حَبَّةٍ فِى ظُلُمَٰتِ ٱلۡأَرۡضِ وَلَا رَطۡبٍ وَلَا يَابِسٍ إِلَّا فِى كِتَٰبٍ مُّبِينٍ ﴾ الأنعام: ٥٩

And with Him are the keys of (all that is hidden); none knows them but He. And He knows whatever there is in (or on) the Earth and in the sea; not a leaf falls, but he knows it. There is not a grain in the darkness of the Earth, nor anything fresh or dry, but is written in a clear record. (6:59)

Abdullah Ibn Amr Ibn Al-Aas رضي الله عنه said that he heard Prophet Muhammad ﷺ say, "Allah recorded the measurement of all matters pertaining to Creation fifty thousand years before He created the Heavens and Earth." [Reported by Imam Muslim]

3. Mashee'ah

Divine Will- Mashee'ah is the belief that nothing, whether related to Allah's actions or actions taken by His slaves, can happen without His permission. Allah says in the Qur'an:

﴿ وَرَبُّكَ يَخۡلُقُ مَا يَشَآءُ وَيَخۡتَارُ ﴾ القصص: ٢٨

And your Lord creates whatsoever He wills and chooses. (28: 68)

﴿ وَيَفۡعَلُ ٱللَّهُ مَا يَشَآءُ ﴾ إبراهيم: ٢٧

And Allah does what He wills. (14: 27)

﴿ هُوَ ٱلَّذِى يُصَوِّرُكُمۡ فِى ٱلۡأَرۡحَامِ كَيۡفَ يَشَآءُ ۚ لَآ إِلَٰهَ إِلَّا هُوَ ٱلۡعَزِيزُ ٱلۡحَكِيمُ ﴾ آل عمران: ٦

He it is Who shapes you in the wombs as He pleases. (3:6)

4. Al-Khalq

The Creation - The final aspect of Al-Qadar is the belief that Allah is the sole Creator of all creation, and that He endowed us with our attributes and all our actions. Allah says in the Qur'an:

﴿ ٱللَّهُ خَٰلِقُ كُلِّ شَىۡءٍ ۖ وَهُوَ عَلَىٰ كُلِّ شَىۡءٍ وَكِيلٌ ﴾ الزمر: ٦٢

Allah is the Creator of all things, and He is the Guardian over all things. (39:62)

﴿ وَخَلَقَ كُلَّ شَىۡءٍ فَقَدَّرَهُۥ تَقۡدِيرًا ﴾ الفرقان: ٢

He has created everything, and has measured it exactly according to its due measurements. (25: 2)

Also, Prophet Ibraheem said to his people, as mentioned in the Qur'an,

﴿ وَٱللَّهُ خَلَقَكُمۡ وَمَا تَعۡمَلُونَ ﴾ الصافات: ٩٦

"And Allah has created you and what you make." (37:96)

Aspects of Al-Qadar

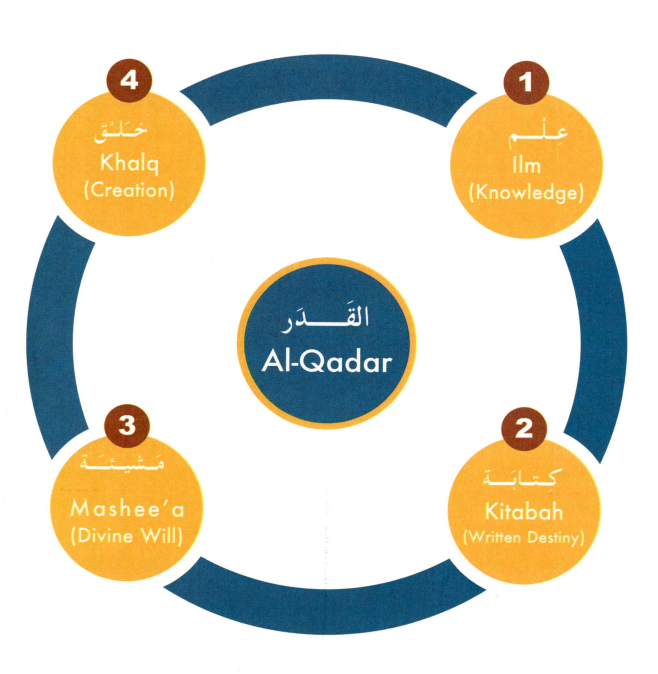

Do We Have Free Will?

Some people think that since Allah controls our lives and decides everything that happens in the world, we do not have free will, or any control over our actions. This is far from the truth. The belief in Al-Qadar does not mean that we are passive individuals who have no part to play in our lives. Al-Qadar does not prevent a person from exercising free will to choose a course of action.

Allah does not force people to do anything. He only encourages His servants to do the good and avoid the bad. It is entirely up to the individual as to whether he or she chooses to obey or disobey. Allah gave man free will to choose his actions, whether good or evil.

To make things more understandable, human actions can be categorized into three types:

1. Actions within you (blood circulation, heart beats, etc.)

2. Actions upon you (weather, accidents, environment, attacks, etc.)

3. Actions from you (praying, helping others, harming others, etc.)

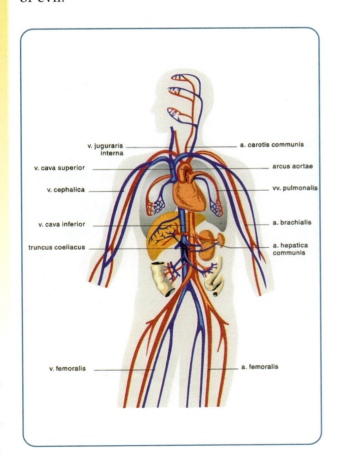

While man cannot fully control the actions within him or upon him, he still can control the actions that come out of him. God gave humans the brain and other faculties to choose their actions and decide to do good or evil. Therefore, man has free will when it comes to the actions that come out of him; thus he is responsible for these actions. On the other hand, he has no control over those actions that happen within him or upon him. Therefore, he is not responsible for these actions. Only Allah controls these types of actions.

Indeed, Allah has given us ample information through His prophets and messengers to guide us so that we may lead good, obedient lives. The responsibility now lies within each individual to make the right choices. Allah says in the Qur'an:

﴿ وَمَا نُرْسِلُ ٱلْمُرْسَلِينَ إِلَّا مُبَشِّرِينَ وَمُنذِرِينَۖ فَمَنْ ءَامَنَ وَأَصْلَحَ فَلَا خَوْفٌ عَلَيْهِمْ وَلَا هُمْ يَحْزَنُونَ ﴿٤٨﴾ وَٱلَّذِينَ كَذَّبُوا بِـَٔايَـٰتِنَا يَمَسُّهُمُ ٱلْعَذَابُ بِمَا كَانُوا يَفْسُقُونَ ﴿٤٩﴾ الأنعام: ٤٨-٤٩ ﴾

Messengers give good news and warnings to mankind. Those who believe and mend their ways will have nothing to fear nor regret. But those who deny Allah's revelations will be punished for their sins. [Suratul-Anaam 6:48-49]

﴿ فَمَن شَآءَ ٱتَّخَذَ إِلَىٰ رَبِّهِۦ مَـَٔابًا ﴿٣٩﴾ النبأ: ٣٩ ﴾

So, whosoever wills, let him take a return to his Lord [by obeying His commandments. [Surat-un-Naba' 78:39]

However, Allah knows the choices we will make, even before we decide. We do not know what our destiny is, but surely Allah knows the fate of all things.

Of course, one might ask: "What can man do, if Allah has already decreed for him to go astray with no possibility of guidance?" The answer to this question is that Allah guides whoever sincerely wants guidance and leads astray whoever deliberately and continuously chooses to disobey. Allah says in Surat-us-Saff

﴿ فَلَمَّا زَاغُوٓا أَزَاغَ ٱللَّهُ قُلُوبَهُمْۚ وَٱللَّهُ لَا يَهْدِى ٱلْقَوْمَ ٱلْفَـٰسِقِينَ ﴿٥﴾ الصف: ٥ ﴾

Then when they deviated [on their own], Allah let their hearts go wrong. For Allah guides not those who are rebellious transgressors. [Surat-us-Saff 61: 5]

Therefore, Allah, in His infinite wisdom, wills guidance to the one He knows is seeking the truth and striving toward the right path. On the other hand, Allah prescribes misguidance to the one who insists on remaining disobedient and deviant even after he knows the truth.

Of course, there are many things that occur in life over which one has no control. Natural disasters like hurricanes or afflictions such as serious illness or death are completely out of our hands. Those with firm faith understand that whatever befalls them in this life is according to the will of Allah, and it only occurs with His full knowledge. When things that we do not understand happen, as true Muslims, we must trust that Allah has wisdom behind all things. Therefore, we should accept the outcome as Al-Qadar.

The Benefits of the Belief in Al-Qadar

There are so many great benefits of the belief in Al-Qadar, that one cannot them, count. These benefits have profound effects on man's personality and behavior. Here are some important benefits of the belief in Al-Qadar.

1. Believers in Al-Qadar Receive Allah's Mercy. This mercy is bestowed upon them because they turn to Allah alone during any calamity. Allah says in the Qur'an:

﴿ وَلَنَبْلُوَنَّكُم بِشَيْءٍ مِّنَ ٱلْخَوْفِ وَٱلْجُوعِ وَنَقْصٍ مِّنَ ٱلْأَمْوَالِ وَٱلْأَنفُسِ وَٱلثَّمَرَاتِ وَبَشِّرِ ٱلصَّابِرِينَ ﴿١٥٥﴾ ٱلَّذِينَ إِذَآ أَصَابَتْهُم مُّصِيبَةٌ قَالُوٓا۟ إِنَّا لِلَّهِ وَإِنَّآ إِلَيْهِ رَاجِعُونَ ﴿١٥٦﴾ أُو۟لَٰٓئِكَ عَلَيْهِمْ صَلَوَاتٌ مِّن رَّبِّهِمْ وَرَحْمَةٌ ۖ وَأُو۟لَٰٓئِكَ هُمُ ٱلْمُهْتَدُونَ ﴿١٥٧﴾ ﴾ البقرة: ١٥٥-١٥٧

Be sure we shall test you with something of fear and hunger, some loss in goods or lives or the fruits (of your toil), but give glad tidings to those who patiently persevere. (They are those) who, when afflicted with calamity, say: 'Truly! to Allah we belong and truly, to Him shall we return'. They are those on whom are the blessings from their God, and (they are those) who receive His mercy; and it is they who are the guided ones. [Surat-ul-Baqarah 2:155-157]

2. Believing in Al-Qadar teaches acceptance of pain and courage in times of calamity. All incidents that happen to a person are a result of Allah's Qadar. We should accept the will of Allah when harm happens to us and we can not protect ourselves from it. All this takes place according to the Qadar of Allah. Let us learn this important hadeeth:

Hadeeth Shareef

عن صهيب الرومي رضي الله عنه قال: قال رسول الله ﷺ:
"عَجَباً لِأَمْرِ المؤمنِ إنَّ أمْرَهُ كُلَّهُ خيرٌ وليسَ ذلكَ لأَحدٍ إلا للمؤمنِ، إنْ أصابَتْهُ سَرَّاءُ شَكَرَ فكان خيراً له، وإنْ أصابَتْهُ ضَرَّاءُ صَبَرَ فكان خيراً له." رواه مسلم

The Prophet Muhammad ﷺ said, "The attitude of the believer is amazing. All of his matters are righteous. This is only for the believer. If a joy is brought to him, he thanks (Allah for it). This is better for him. If a calamity befalls him, he is patient. This is also good for him."

[Reported by Imam Muslim]

3. The belief in Al-Qadar teaches contentment. Many times a person finds it difficult to miss what he likes, or to accept what he dislikes. We sometimes feel miserable for losing or not gaining what we like to have. Allah sometimes chooses for us what we dislike, because he knows that it is good for us in the future. Similarly, he may prevent us from getting what we like because it will be bad for us in the future. Therefore, when we believe in this, we put our full trust in Allah and accept the hardships or inconveniences we face in this life. In the beginning, we may feel disheartened and sad; however it is only a matter of time before we realize that what we considered bad was actually good for us in this life, or in the next. Allah says:

You may like something but it is actually bad for you, and you may dislike something else, but it is actually good for you.

4. The belief in Al-Qadar encourages generosity. A Muslim understands that financial status is decided by Allah. The believer knows that Allah loves charity and He gives back to the generous giver more than what he or she has given to the needy. Therefore, one cannot feel that giving in charity will reduce one's wealth.

5. The bbelief in Al-Qadar protects the believers from social diseases. Envy and jealousy are social diseases that will be in check. The believer knows that it is by Allah's will that people have or do not have wealth, possessions, children, and other. Surely, the one who is envious of others is indeed objecting to Allah's decree, or Al-Qadar.

6. The belief in Al-Qadar saves the person from dealing with magic, soothsayers, fortune-tellers. Believers realize that Allah alone is the true helper to mankind. They believe that no one other than Allah cannot benefit anyone without the will and permission of Allah. Therefore, maaicians, fortune-tellers, and all other people have no true effect on man's life.

7. The Belief in Al-Qadar teaches humility. When a believer succeeds in education, the workplace, or gains wealth, he humbles himself and becomes thankful to Allah for the favors He has bestowed upon him or her. All successes happen because of Allah's favor and help. Therefore, when people become proud and boastful when they succeed in achieving a high grade or good deed, it makes them forget to thank Allah. He permitted and helped them to successfully perform this achievement.

CHAPTER REVIEW

Projects and Activities

Read a story from the Qur'an on Al-Qadar.

Stretch Your Mind

Imagine someone approaches you claiming that man has no free will. "If God has already ordained what I will do, I have no free will," he claims. "God has already chosen my path." How would you respond? Write a convincing answer to this man's claim that man has no free will.

Study Questions

1. What is Al-Qadar?
2. What are the main aspects of Al-Qadar? Define each of them.
3. Does man have free will to choose good or evil actions? Support your answer with an ayah and logical evidence.
4. What actions do humans have free will to control? List three examples.
5. What actions do we not have free will to control? List three examples.
6. Outline at least five benefits of the belief in Al-Qadar.

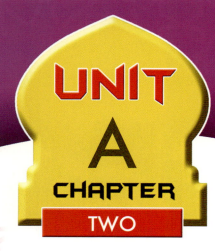

Only Allah Gives Life and Death

CHAPTER OBJECTIVES

1. Believe that only Allah gives life and death.
2. Understand how the belief in Al-Qadar treats people from the fear of death.
3. Learn when human life starts in the womb according to Islam and medicine.
4. Learn when human life ends according to Islam and medicine.
5. Memorize and understand the names of Allah that relate to giving and taking human life.
6. Memorize and understand the Hadeeth on the stages of human life in the womb.

VOCABULARY

Hayah حَيَاة

Mawt مَوْت

Ajal أَجَل

Life and death are two unavoidable and fascinating topics. They have continuously mystified and puzzled people throughout the ages. Scholars and philosophers have tried to find answers to age-old questions like: "What is life?"; "How did life come into being?"; and "When did life begin?" They also search for answers to questions such as "What is death?" and "How does it occur?"

People of all religions, and even those without faith, understand that death will come to everyone at some point in time. Allah has mentioned life and death many times in the Qur'an. To believe that Allah alone is the One who gives life and takes it away through death is an important element of the belief in Al-Qadar in Islam.

All the verses in the Qur'an confirm that

Allah is the only one who gives life and takes it away. Allah says in Surat Al-Waqi'ah:

﴿ نَحْنُ قَدَّرْنَا بَيْنَكُمُ الْمَوْتَ ۝ ﴾ الواقعة: ٦٠

"We have decreed death among you." [Surat-ul-Waqi'ah 56: 60]

Allah also says in Surat Ghafir,

﴿ هُوَ الَّذِى يُحْىِۦ وَيُمِيتُ فَإِذَا قَضَىٰٓ أَمْرًا فَإِنَّمَا يَقُولُ لَهُۥ كُن فَيَكُونُ ۝ ﴾ غافر: ٦٨

"He it is Who gives life and causes death. And when He decides upon a thing He only says to it: 'Be!' And it is." [Surat-ul-Ankabut 40:68]

In another verse, Allah (S.W.T.) says in Surat Qaaf,

﴿ إِنَّا نَحْنُ نُحْىِۦ وَنُمِيتُ وَإِلَيْنَا الْمَصِيرُ ۝ ﴾
ق: ٤٣

"Verily, We give life and cause death; and to Us is the final return." [50: 43]

Lessons on Life and Death

The Qur'an and Sunnah provide us with the following lessons about life and death:

1. Allah created life and death to test mankind. He wants us to prove whether we commit good or bad deeds. Allah says in Surat Al-Mulk,

﴿ الَّذِى خَلَقَ الْمَوْتَ وَالْحَيَوٰةَ لِيَبْلُوَكُمْ أَيُّكُمْ أَحْسَنُ عَمَلًا وَهُوَ الْعَزِيزُ الْغَفُورُ ۝ ﴾ تبارك: ٢

"He is the One Who created life and death to test which of you is best in deeds."[67: 2] Life is given to man kind only for the purpose of worshipping Allah, our Creator.

2. Death is a definite end to every created being; no one is immortal except Allah. Allah (S.W.T.) says in Surat-ur-Rahman,

﴿ كُلُّ مَنْ عَلَيْهَا فَانٍ ۝ وَيَبْقَىٰ وَجْهُ رَبِّكَ ذُو الْجَلَٰلِ وَالْإِكْرَامِ ۝ ﴾ الرحمن: ٢٦-٢٧

"Whatsoever is on it (the Earth) will perish. And the face of your Lord full of Majesty and Honor will abide forever." [55: 26-27]

He also says in surat-ul-Ankabout:

﴿ كُلُّ نَفْسٍ ذَآئِقَةُ الْمَوْتِ ثُمَّ إِلَيْنَا تُرْجَعُونَ ۝ ﴾ العنكبوت: ٥٧

Every soul will taste death , and you all will return to Us [29: 57]

In an authentic hadeeth, reported by Imam At-Tabarani and Al-Hakem the prophet ﷺ said: "Jibreel came to me and said: Oh Muhammad, live as much as you want, you will die, and love whomever you want, you will part with them"

3. Death occurs at a specific time and in a specific place. It does not change or happen before it is due or after it is due. Allah (S.W.T.) says in Surat-ul-A'raf,

﴿ وَلِكُلِّ أُمَّةٍ أَجَلٌ فَإِذَا جَآءَ أَجَلُهُمْ لَا يَسْتَأْخِرُونَ سَاعَةً وَلَا يَسْتَقْدِمُونَ ۝ ﴾ الأعراف: ٣٤

"When their term is reached, neither can they delay it nor can they advance it an hour (or a moment)." [7:34)]

Selected Story

Imam Muslim reported that Umu-Habeebah, the Prophet's wife said, "Oh Allah, make the lives of my husband (the Prophet), my father (Abu Sufyan), and my brother (Mu'awiah) long."

"You have asked Allah to change a previously dictated end and a defined number of days (things that are already dictated)," replied the Prophet Muhammad ﷺ. "Allah will not hasten anything before its time, and He will not put off anything after its time. If you had asked Allah to shelter you from Hell-Fire and protect you from the punishment of the grave, it would have been better," the Prophet concluded.

How Does the Belief in Al-Qadar, Influence the Fear of Death?

Islam addressed the fear of death. It teaches us to get ready for it and to prepare for the Day of Judgment. What is important is that people should think about what they want from this life. Do they want to abandon the duties of belief and to worry only about this worldly life? Or do they want to look and work for the Hereafter? Allah says in Surat Al-Imran:

"And whoever desires a reward in (this) world, We shall give him of it: And whoever desires a reward in the Hereafter, We shall give him of it. " [3:145]

How different is this life from the Hereafter, and how different is the interest in this life from the interest in the hereafter? Whoever wants to live for this life alone will live as an animal, and he will die at his dictated time without delay. And whoever longs and yearns for the Hereafter, he will live the life of a man honored by Allah, following Allah's rules. He too shall die at his dictated time.

Allah alone gives life and He alone brings it back at a specific time. This applies to the people who are sitting at home among their families or the people who are protecting themselves inside a castle and the people who are fighting in a battle. The time of death has nothing to do with war or peace, and it has nothing to do with how protected the place is. Death comes when it is time. Allah says in Surat-un-Nisaa':

"Where so ever you may be, death will overtake you even if you are in fortresses built up strong and high!" [4: 78]

He also says in Surat Al-Imran,

Say (O Muhammad): Even if you had remained in your homes, those for whom death was decreed would certainly have gone forth to the place of their death. " [3:154]

Since it is not known when death will come, if someone wants to die as a Muslim, he should be a Muslim from this moment without delay and every moment without exception. Allah says in Surat Al-Imran:

"O you who believe, obtain taqwa of Allah as should be, and do not die except in a state of Islam."[3:102]

The Prophet ﷺ said in a hadeeth reported by Imam Ibn-Hibban and Al-Bazzar: "Remember often the one that defeats all joys: death. Indeed whoever remembers it in time of hardship, it will alleviate it; and whoever remembers it in good times, it will make him less joyful."

Allah emphasizes in the Qur'an the importance of striving to lead noble and good lives. It has also been made clear to us the reward or punishment we would expect according to the lives we lead. Allah, the Merciful, has also provided us roles, responsibilities, and a way of life outlined in the Qur'an and the Sunnah. If we follow Allah's guidance, He will help us to live in a righteous way leading to the reward of Al-Jannah.

Death is dictated by Allah; you cannot escape it, you cannot resist it, and you cannot keep it away from you.

99 Names of Allah

| Al-Muhyee | المُحْيي | Al-Mumeet | المُميت |
| Al-Qabid | القابض | Al-Basit | الباسِط |

Science Corner
The Beginning of Life-Conception

The beginning of life is called conception. It takes place when the egg of the female is penetrated by the sperm of the male. This union between the sperm and the egg is known as fertilization. The entire process of conception in the human, as well as in other animals, is one of nature's great wonders. Let's start from the very beginning:

As mentioned elsewhere, the male sperm are deposited in the vagina near the entrance of the cervix of the uterus or womb. Nature seems to have sensed that it would be a difficult trip for the sperm to bring about conception. For this reason, 100-200 million sperm are provided, just for the purpose of fertilizing one female egg! The millions of tiny sperm, which can be seen only under a microscope, are so delicate that they live only a few minutes unless they are successful in passing through the cervix into the uterus.

The sperm have tails, called flagella, that push them forward. Actually, sperm look very much like miniature tadpoles, and they move forward like tadpoles by wiggling their tails from side to side. When they reach the cervix, the sperm must swim through a mucous barrier that covers the entrance to the inside of the uterus. Tens of millions of sperm are unable to do this, and are lost. Those sperm that pierce the cervix then swim up the three to four inches of the inside of the uterus. They find the two exits at the upper ends where the fallopian tubes begin. Tens of millions more sperm are lost before they get to the fallopian tubes. Those that do survive swim into the narrow passageway of the fallopian tube where they may finally meet an egg. But this meeting can take place only during two to three days of each month.

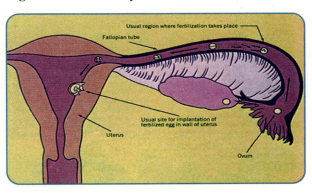

The egg leaves the ovary and enters the fallopian tube. There, it is fertilized by a single sperm. The fertilized egg begins to divide and to make many cells. When it reaches the uterus some 3 to 4 days later, the fertilized egg buries itself in the wall of the uterus.

Females normally have one egg, no larger than the point of a pin, that leaves an ovary each month. This is called ovulation. Ovulation usually occurs halfway between two menstrual periods.

When an egg leaves an ovary it finds its way to the funnel-shaped opening of the fallopian tube. Nobody knows how it manages to get from the ovary to the Fallopian tube, because an egg has no ability to move by itself. However, it gets there somehow. Once inside the Fallopian tube, the egg is very slowly swept down toward the uterus by tiny hairlike structures that line the tubes. These hairlike structures, called cilia, are so small they can be seen only under a microscope. It takes anywhere from three to five days for the egg to travel the three inches of the Fallopian tube, and during this time it may meet the sperm.

If an egg meets the sperm in the Fallopian tube, there is a good chance that one of the sperm will enter the egg and unite with it. This is called fertilization.

So, even if there are 100 million sperm that meet an egg in the Fallopian tube, only one will usually be able to pierce the outer coating of the egg and cause fertilization. When this happens, all the other millions of sperm die. Sometimes, however, two or more

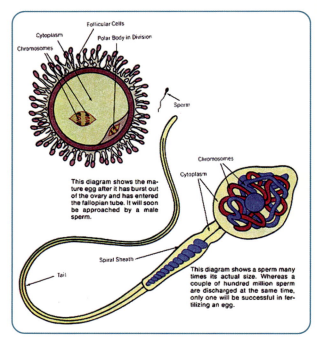

eggs emerge from the ovary. They, too, may be fertilized, each one by a different sperm, and the result will be twins, or triplets, or even more children. Also, twins can result by the splitting of a single fertilized egg into two.

Source: http://www.medical-health.info/2007/01/the-beginning-of-life-conception/

Hadeeth Shareef

عن أبي عبدالرحمن عبد الله بن مسعود رضي الله عنه ، قال : حدثنا رسول الله ﷺ وهو الصادق المصدوق قال :

(إنَّ أحدَكم يُجمَعُ خَلقُهُ في بَطنِ أمِّهِ أربَعينَ يَوماً نُطفةً ، ثمَّ يَكونُ عَلَقةً مِثلَ ذلِكَ ، ثمَّ يَكونُ مُضغةً مِثلَ ذلِكَ ، ثمَّ يُرسَلُ إليهِ المَلَكُ فيَنفُخُ فيهِ الرُّوحَ ، ويُؤمَرُ بأربَعِ كَلِماتٍ : بكَتبِ رِزقِهِ ، وأجَلِهِ ، وعَمَلِهِ ، وشَقيٌّ أم سَعيدٌ . فواللهِ الذي لا إلهَ غَيرُهُ ، إنَّ أحَدَكم لَيَعمَلُ بعَمَلِ أهلِ الجَنَّةِ ، حتى ما يَكونَ بَينَهُ وبَينَها إلا ذِراعٌ ، فيَسبِقُ عليهِ الكِتابُ فيَعمَلُ بعَمَلِ أهلِ النَّارِ ، وإنَّ أحَدَكم لَيَعمَلُ بعَمَلِ أهلِ النَّارِ حتى ما يَكونَ بَينَهُ وبَينَها إلا ذِراعٌ ، فيَسبِقُ عليهِ الكِتابُ ، فيَعمَلُ بعَمَلِ أهلِ الجَنَّةِ) رواه البخاري و مسلم .

Hadeeth Shareef

Abu Abdal-Rahman Abdullah bin Masud (may Allah be pleased with him) reported that Prophet Muhammad (peace be upon him) said:

"Verily, the creation of any one of you takes place when he is assembled in his mother's womb; for forty days he is as a drop of fluid. Then it becomes a clot. Thereafter it is a lump, looking like it has been chewed. Then an angel is sent to him, who breathes the soul into him. This angel is commanded to write four decrees: his provision, his life span, his deeds [based on what Allah knows the person will choose to do during his or her life], and whether he will be among the wretched or the blessed.

I swear by Allah - there is no God but He - one of you may perform the deeds of the people of Paradise until [it appears] there is naught but an arm's length between him and it, when that which has been written will outstrip him so that he performs the deeds of the people of the Hell-Fire; one of you may perform the deeds of the people of the Hell-fire, until [it appears] there is naught but an arm's length between him and it, when that which has been written will overtake him so that he performs the deeds of the people of Paradise and enters therein."

[Reported by Imams Al-Bukhari & Muslim]

When and How Does Human Life Start?

Based on the above hadeeth, human life begins in the womb. Muslim scholars and scientists have two opinions on when exactly the fetus becomes a human being. The first opinion is that life begins at the time of conception. The other opinion is that life does not begin until the soul is breathed into the fetus.

Muslim scholars also have two opinions on when the soul is breathed into the fetus. Some scholars argue forty days after conception, while others argue 120 days after conception.

Contemporary Muslim scholars increasingly support the opinion that the soul is breathed into the fetus only forty days after conception. This hadeeth, and another version of it narrated by Imam Muslim, supports this opinion. Also, scientific facts tell that in forty days, the fetus becomes like a chewed lump of flesh, as the hadeeth describes. At that point, the angel breathes the soul into it.

Commentary

At a conference in Cairo, Professor Keith Moore presented a research paper and stated: "It has been a great pleasure for me to help clarify statements in the Qur'an about human development. It is clear to me that these statements must have come to Muhammad from God, or Allah, because most of this knowledge was not discovered until many centuries later. This proves to me that Muhammad must have been a messenger of God, or Allah." [1]

"For the past three years, I have worked with the Embryology Committee of King Abdulaziz University in Jeddah, Saudi Arabia, helping, them to interpret the many statements in the Qur'an and Sunnah referring to human reproduction and prenatal development. At first, I was astonished by the accuracy of the Qur'an's statements that were recorded in the 7th Century AD, before the science of embryology was established.

Professor Moore also stated,
"...Because the staging of human embryos is complex, owing to the continuous process of change

during development, it is proposed that a new system of classification could be developed using the terms mentioned in the Qur'an and Sunnah. The proposed system is simple, comprehensive, and conforms with present embryological knowledge.

"The intensive studies of the Qur'an and hadeeth in the last four years have revealed a system of classifying human embryos that is amazing, since it was recorded in the Seventh Century A.D... the descriptions in the Qur'an cannot be based on scientific knowledge in the Seventh Century..."[1]

[1] Dr. Keith Moore is a former President of the Canadian Association of Anatomists, and of the American Association of Clinical Anatomists. He was honored by the Canadian Association of Anatomists with the prestigious J.C.B. Grant Award, and in 1994 he received the Honored Member Award of the American Association of Clinical Anatomists "for outstanding contributions to the field of clinical anatomy."

When and How Does Human Life Ends?

The Qur'an and the Sunnah are clear that human life ends when the angel of death takes away the person's soul, upon an order from Allah. The soul that was breathed into that person when he or she was a fetus in the womb (as you learned earlier) is now retaken. And the body of that deceased person will deteriorate and later vanish in the grave. The soul will be spared until it is united with another new body created for that same person in the Hereafter.

Let us now learn how human life medically ends. In 1985, the Islamic Organization of Medical Sciences organized a seminar on "The Islamic Concept on Human Life, Its Beginning and Its End." A group of major Muslim scholars and medical doctors, and experts met in Kuwait. They discussed matters concerning the beginning and end of human life, according to scientific facts and Islamic law.

The seminar concluded that in most cases where death occurs there is no real difficulty in recognizing it on the basis of commonly known indications through medical examination. These ascertain the absence of life signs in the deceased. It was determined that a death case is established only if the brain stem becomes void of life signs, as this part of the brain is responsible for basic biological functions. This is what is termed "death of the brain stem." A case can only be considered hopeless if the brain stem is established to be dead. In this case the life of the patient can be said to have ended, even if movement or function remains for a while in the other organs of the body. These will definitely come to a standstill after the death of the brain stem.

CHAPTER REVIEW

Projects and Activities

1. Write a one-page essay on the importance of believing that only Allah controls matters of life and death.

2. Go to a hospital lab and watch a human fetus at different stages of development.

Stretch Your Mind

1. Imagine that there is more than one god who controls life and death. How would our world look?

2. Suppose that someone came to you and said, "It is not only Allah who controls matters of life and death. Doctors, judges, governors, and criminals can cause people to die or remain alive!" How would you respond to them?

Study Questions

1. Who has the ultimate power of controlling matters of life and death? Support your answer with an ayah and a hadeeth.
2. Why did Allah create life and death? Support your answer with an ayah.
3. When does human life start?
4. When does human life end?

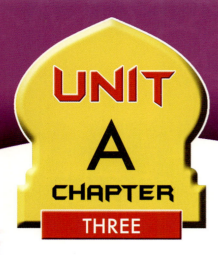

Allah Gives and Deprives Wealth

CHAPTER OBJECTIVES

1. Understand that Allah is the One who gives wealth and health.
2. Learn the attitudes that causes our wealth to be blessed and increased.
3. Learn and memorize the two ahadeeth in this chapter.

VOCABULARY

- Rizq — رزق
- Taqwa — تقوى
- Tawakkul — توكل

Allah is the one who provides for the human family and all other creations. His mercy is clear to His servants at all times and all situations, everywhere in the world. People usually think that the source of their rizq (sustenance) is their parents, bosses, or employers. The fact of the matter is that Allah is the ultimate provider of rizq to all of His creations. Ar-Razzaq, Ar-Raziq, Al-Mu'ti and Al-Wahhab are some of the names of Allah. If you ponder upon these names, they mean that He is the only owner of provision and He's the provider, forever. Allah says in Surat Hud,

﴿ وَمَا مِن دَابَّةٍ فِى ٱلْأَرْضِ إِلَّا عَلَى ٱللَّهِ رِزْقُهَا وَيَعْلَمُ مُسْتَقَرَّهَا وَمُسْتَوْدَعَهَا كُلٌّ فِى كِتَـٰبٍ مُّبِينٍ ﴾ هود: ٦

There is no moving creature on Earth but its sustenance depends on Allah: He knows the time and place of its definite abode and its temporary deposit: all is in a clear Record. (11:6)

In Surat-ur-Room, Allah challenges the idol worshipper by saying:

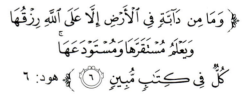

It is Allah Who has created you; further, He has provided for your sustenance; then He will cause you to die; and again He will give you life. (30:40)

Conditions for Obtaining Sustenance

The equation of natural resources and human effort to obtain sustenance has very eloquently been presented in Surat-ul-Waaqe'ah. Allah says:

"Consider your contribution against Our laws in agriculture. You plow a field and sow seeds. Who produces crops from seeds, you or We?

Who looks after crops? A calamity may fall and destroy a crop, leaving you shocked and sym-pathizing with your fellows and agonizing over the comprehensive loss of not only crops, but also of seeds and hard work!

Consider water, which is essential not only for crops, but also for your own existence. Do you bring it down from clouds or do We? Clouds are formed from salty sea-water which is unusable for either farming or your own consumption. What could you do if rain-water was as salty? Why can't you arrive at the right conclusion in such a clear and simple matter? Why can't you appreciate Allah's systems?

Consider fire which you use in so many ways. Who has caged heat (in firewood) in that manner? You or We?

We have created all this (you only provide work). We state these facts to remind you of that forgotten truth that We have put all this, in place so that the needy get sustenance." [56:63-73]

Laws and Guidance Concerning Rizq

1. Everyone should spend according to his capacity. A poor Muslim should spend as little as he or she can afford, while a wealthy person should spend more for the convenience of his family and himself. Allah says in Surat-ut-Talaaq,

﴿ لِيُنفِقْ ذُو سَعَةٍ مِّن سَعَتِهِۦ وَمَن قُدِرَ عَلَيْهِ رِزْقُهُۥ
فَلْيُنفِقْ مِمَّآ ءَاتَىٰهُ ٱللَّهُ لَا يُكَلِّفُ ٱللَّهُ نَفْسًا إِلَّا
مَآ ءَاتَىٰهَا سَيَجْعَلُ ٱللَّهُ بَعْدَ عُسْرٍ يُسْرًا ٧ ﴾ الطلاق: ٧

Let the man of means spend according to His means; and the man whose resources are restricted, let him spend according to what Allah has given him. Allah puts no burden on any person beyond what He has given him. After a difficulty, Allah will soon grant relief. [65: 7]

2. Allah likes moderate spending. Islam encourages Muslims to follow the middle way between two extremes regarding spend-ing: extravagance and miserliness. Allah says in Surat-ul-Furqan,

﴿ وَٱلَّذِينَ إِذَآ أَنفَقُوا۟ لَمْ يُسْرِفُوا۟ وَلَمْ يَقْتُرُوا۟
وَكَانَ بَيْنَ ذَٰلِكَ قَوَامًا ٦٧ ﴾ الفرقان: ٦٧

Those who, when they spend, are not extrava-gant and not miserly, but hold a just (balance) between those (extremes). [25:67]

3. Wealthy Muslims must avoid arro-gance and mischief. Wealth has the ten-dency to make people arrogant and even mis-chievous. Since money is power, wealthy people often get into the habit of using this power that Allah tested them with in a wrong manner. Rather than appreciating Allah's favors on them, they disobey Him and break His rules. They may cheat, involve haram deals and show off in front of less for-tunate people. Allah says in Surat-ul-Alaq,

كَلَّآ إِنَّ ٱلْإِنسَٰنَ لَيَطْغَىٰٓ ۝ أَن رَّءَاهُ ٱسْتَغْنَىٰٓ ۝

العلق: ٦-٧

Nay, but man does break the rules in that he looks upon himself as wealthy [and powerful]. [96:6-7]

Therefore, Allah may restrict wealth on his servant to protect them from falling in major transgression. Allah says in Surat Al-Shura,

وَلَوْ بَسَطَ ٱللَّهُ ٱلرِّزْقَ لِعِبَادِهِۦ لَبَغَوْا۟ فِى ٱلْأَرْضِ وَلَٰكِن يُنَزِّلُ بِقَدَرٍ مَّا يَشَآءُ إِنَّهُۥ بِعِبَادِهِۦ خَبِيرٌۢ بَصِيرٌ ۝

الشورى: ٢٧

If Allah were to enlarge the provision for His servants, they would indeed transgress beyond all bounds through the Earth; but He sends (it) down in due measure as He pleases. For He is with His servants Well-Acquainted, Watchful. [42:27]

4. Allah may favor some over others in wealth.
For a certain wisdom, Allah may bless some people more than others. Allah is our Lord and He knows best how much each should receive. Allah says in Surat Al-Nahl,

وَٱللَّهُ فَضَّلَ بَعْضَكُمْ عَلَىٰ بَعْضٍ فِى ۝

النحل: ٧١

"Allah has made some of you better than others in rizq." [Surat-ul-Baqarah (16:71)]

5. Do not envy others.
Allah instructed us not to envy others when they acquire more wealth or other blessings different from ours. Envy is haram in Islam, and it does not help us gain more wealth and blessings. It may harm people, and we will be harmed too! How?. Well, envy (known as hasad in Arabic) is a sin penalized by Allah. When we allow our hearts to do it, we are not thanking Allah for His blessings. When Allah blesses someone with one of His favors, a good Muslim should be happy for him/her. We are even encouraged to make dua for our brothers and sisters who have won Allah's favors. Allah says in Surat-Taha,

وَلَا تَمُدَّنَّ عَيْنَيْكَ إِلَىٰ مَا مَتَّعْنَا بِهِۦٓ أَزْوَٰجًا مِّنْهُمْ زَهْرَةَ ٱلْحَيَوٰةِ ٱلدُّنْيَا لِنَفْتِنَهُمْ فِيهِ وَرِزْقُ رَبِّكَ خَيْرٌ وَأَبْقَىٰ ۝ طه: ١٣١

Do not strain your eyes in longing for the things We have given for enjoyment to parties of them, the splendor of this lower life, through which We test them: but the sustenance of your Lord is better and more enduring. [20:131]

Things That Help us Gain and Increase Wealth

1. Having True Faith

Allah provides His sustenance to all people, whether they are believers or disbelievers. However, Allah blesses the sustenance He gives to His faithful and obedient believers. He makes wealth easy to obtain and useful. Allah says in Surat-ul-Baqarah,

وَإِذْ قَالَ إِبْرَٰهِـۧمُ رَبِّ ٱجْعَلْ هَٰذَا بَلَدًا ءَامِنًا وَٱرْزُقْ أَهْلَهُۥ مِنَ ٱلثَّمَرَٰتِ مَنْ ءَامَنَ مِنْهُم بِٱللَّهِ وَٱلْيَوْمِ ٱلْأَخِرِ قَالَ وَمَن كَفَرَ فَأُمَتِّعُهُۥ قَلِيلًا ثُمَّ أَضْطَرُّهُۥٓ إِلَىٰ عَذَابِ ٱلنَّارِ وَبِئْسَ ٱلْمَصِيرُ ۝ التوبة: ١٢٦

And remember Abraham said: "My Lord, make this [Makkah] a land of peace, and feed its People with fruits, - those among them who believe in Allah and the Last Day." He [Allah] said; "(Yes), and those who reject Faith, - I grant them their pleasure for a while, but will soon drive them to the torment of Fire, - an evil destination (indeed)! [2:126]

وَلَوْ أَنَّ أَهْلَ ٱلْقُرَىٰٓ ءَامَنُوا۟ وَٱتَّقَوْا۟ لَفَتَحْنَا عَلَيْهِم بَرَكَٰتٍ مِّنَ ٱلسَّمَآءِ وَٱلْأَرْضِ وَلَٰكِن كَذَّبُوا۟ فَأَخَذْنَٰهُم بِمَا كَانُوا۟ يَكْسِبُونَ ۝

الأعراف: ٩٦

If the people of the towns had but believed and feared Allah, We should indeed have opened out to them (All kinds of) blessings from Heaven and Earth; but they rejected (the truth), and We penalized them for their [evil] deeds. [7:96]

Companion Abdullah Ibn `Abbas , the great interpreter of the Qur'an said: "Meaning, We would enrich them with what is good, and facilitate it for them from every side." [Tafsir Abi Sa`ood 3/253]

2. Practicing Taqwa, or Righteousness.

As you learned earlier, Allah is the owner of this universe, and He is the ultimate One who distributes wealth. Therefore, the best way to obtain His good favors is by obeying Him. Indeed, obedience brings you Allah's favors. Allah says in Surat-ut-Talaaq,

﴿ وَمَن يَتَّقِ ٱللَّهَ يَجْعَل لَّهُۥ مَخْرَجًا ۝ وَيَرْزُقْهُ مِنْ حَيْثُ لَا يَحْتَسِبُ ۝ ﴾

الطلاق: ٢-٣

[2] And for those who fear Allah, He (ever) prepares a way out, [3] And He provides for him from (sources) he never could imagine [65:2-3]

Companion Abdullah Ibn Mas`ood said: "Taqwa is that Allah is obeyed and not disobeyed, that He is remembered and not forgotten, and that He is thanked and not shown ungratefulness." [Reported by At-Tabaraani in al-Kabeer]

3. Observing Tawakkul, or True Reliance on Allah.

Tawakkul means putting full trust in Allah and showing true reliance on Him. A true believer trusts Allah and relies on Him more than on anyone else. He firmly believes that even if he worked very hard and got the help of all people, nothing will happen except what Allah has permitted. On the other hand, if he didn't put forth much work, and had little or no help from people, he would get the sustenance he needed if Allah permitted. Allah said in Surat-ut-Talaaq:

﴿ وَمَن يَتَوَكَّلْ عَلَى ٱللَّهِ فَهُوَ حَسْبُهُۥ ۝ ﴾

الطلاق: ٣

And whoever relies upon Allah - then He is sufficient for him. [65: 3]

Also Prophet Muhammad once said,

عن عمر رضي الله عنه قال: قال رسول الله :
" لو انكم تتوكلون على الله حق توكله لرزقكم مثل ما يرزق الطير ، تغدو خماصا و تروح بطانا"
رواه الترمذي

"If you relied on Allah with a true reliance, He would provide for you the same as He provides birds: for they set off in the early morning with empty stomachs and return back at the end of the day with full stomachs." [Reported by At-Tirmithi and Ahmad]

4. Being Kind to Relatives.

Additional to the great rewards they will win in the Hereafter, Allah rewards those who are good to their relatives by increasing and blessing their wealth in this life. Look at this great hadeeth;

عن أبي هريرة -رضي الله عنه- قال: قال رسول الله :
"مَنْ أَحَبَّ أَنْ يُبْسَطَ عَلَيْهِ فِي رِزْقِهِ، وَأَنْ يُنْسَأَ لَهُ فِي أَثَرِهِ فَلْيَصِلْ رَحِمَهُ"
رواه البخاري ومسلم

Abu Hurayrah رضي الله عنه narrated that Rasoolullah ﷺ said: "Whoever likes to have his wealth expanded and his good deeds remembered for a long time, he should be kind and close to his relatives."

Does that mean that we are not instructed to work hard to obtain our sustenance?

No, Allah and His Prophet instructed us to trust Allah and rely on Him, but also to work hard and to try our best to achieve our goals. Indeed, relying on Allah doesn't mean that one stop striving in this world. Allah says in Surat-ul-Mulk:

﴿ هُوَ ٱلَّذِى جَعَلَ لَكُمُ ٱلْأَرْضَ ذَلُولًا فَٱمْشُوا۟ فِى مَنَاكِبِهَا وَكُلُوا۟ مِن رِّزْقِهِۦ ۖ وَإِلَيْهِ ٱلنُّشُورُ ﴾ الملك: ١٥

It is He Who has made the Earth manageable for you, so navigate through its tracts and enjoy of the Sustenance which He furnishes: but unto Him is the Resurrection. [67:15]

﴿ فَإِذَا قُضِيَتِ ٱلصَّلَوٰةُ فَٱنتَشِرُوا۟ فِى ٱلْأَرْضِ وَٱبْتَغُوا۟ مِن فَضْلِ ٱللَّهِ وَٱذْكُرُوا۟ ٱللَّهَ كَثِيرًا لَّعَلَّكُمْ تُفْلِحُونَ ﴾ الجمعة: ١٠

And when the prayer has concluded, disperse within the land and seek the bounty of Allah. [62:10]

Types of Rizq

When we think of rizq, or wealth, one immediately thinks of money. Wealth indeed is a blessing from Allah. Allah is Ar-Razzaq, (the Ever-Provider of livelihood and all bounties,) Indeed, Allah tells us in the Qur'an that He allocates wealth.

﴿ إِنَّ ٱللَّهَ هُوَ ٱلرَّزَّاقُ ذُو ٱلْقُوَّةِ ٱلْمَتِينُ ﴾ الذاريات: ٥٨

"Allah is He who is the provider of all "rizq", the lord of all power." [51:58]

The term 'rizq' in the Islamic context is used to mean wealth, but there is a wider meaning to it. It refers to all of the bounties of Allah which are needed for us to be successful in this life, and in the Hereafter. Rizq not only refers to money and income but also means iman, akhlaq, noble offspring, and other benefits. Therefore, there are two kinds of rizq (sustenance):

1. **Material Rizq:** Some call "the lower Rizq" which consists of money, food, spouses, children, and other benefits.

2. **Higher Rizq:** Some call it "elevated Rizq," which consists of guidance, iman (faith), taqwa, generosity, comprehension, wisdom, light, cleansing of the soul, elevation in Jannah (Paradise), forgiveness, and the ability to do numerous good deeds.

CHAPTER REVIEW

Projects and Activities

1. Write a 500-word essay on who controls the distribution of wealth and natural resources in our world.

2. Find or write a story which tells that Allah is the One who grants people their wealth.

Stretch Your Mind

1. A successful businessman comes to you and boasts about the fortune he collected over the years. He claims that his own hard work alone made it all possible! How would you respond to him?

2. Why do you think Allah increases the wealth of those who are good to their relatives?

Study Questions

1 Who has the ultimate power of distributing rizq, or wealth? Support your answer with an ayah and a hadeeth.

2 What will Allah do to us on the Day of Judgment concerning the wealth we collect in this life? Support your answer with an ayah or a hadeeth.

    a. Allah gives equal wealth to everyone.

    b. A Muslim must be balanced when he or she spends their money.

    c. If person a becomes rich, he should spend on his family in the same manner he used to do when he was poor.

    d. A Muslim should demonstrate true tawakkul on Allah in matters of rizq.

    e. True tawakkul means that you rely on Allah to bring you rizq, and that you do not exert much effort to make money.

    f. It is haram to envy others who are blessed with more wealth than you.

3 What are the practices that help us have our wealth increased and blessed?

4 What are the two major types of rizq? Which one is more important, in your opinion?

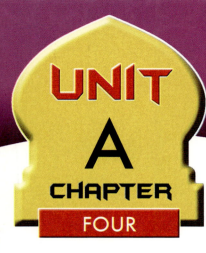

Ayyoub, The Prophet of Patience and Thankfulness

CHAPTER OBJECTIVES

1. Recognize who Ayyoob was.
2. Learn the life story of Prophet Ayyoob.
3. Explore the lessons that can be learned from Prophet Ayyoob's story.
4. Appreciate the value of patience.
5. Learn the different types of patience.
6. Learn what the Muslim should for to his or her sick fellow Muslim.

VOCABULARY

Sabr صبر

Ayyoob أيوب

Ayyoob, or Job, was a descendant of Prophet Ibraheem عليه السلام, as Allah Almighty said in Surat-ul-An'am',

﴿ وَمِن ذُرِّيَّتِهِ دَاوُدَ وَسُلَيْمَانَ وَأَيُّوبَ وَيُوسُفَ وَمُوسَىٰ وَهَارُونَ ۚ وَكَذَٰلِكَ نَجْزِي الْمُحْسِنِينَ ۝ ﴾

الأنعام: ٨٤

"And among his progeny, Dawood, Suleyman, Ayyoob, Yousuf, Musa, and Haroon." [Surat-ul-An'am 6: 84].

Ibn Is'haq, a great Muslim historian, said: "Ayyoob is son of Mus, son of Razih, son of Al-'Ays, son of Is'haq, son of Ibraheem." Ibn Asakir, another Muslim scholar, said: "Ayyoob's mother was the daughter of Lut."

Ayyoob Becomes a Messenger

Ayyoob was one of the prophets whom Allah Almighty sent as a messenger to Bilad-ush-Sham (the Levant), or present Syria.

Allah Almighty said in Surat-un-Nisaa'

﴿وَأَوْحَيْنَا إِلَىٰ إِبْرَاهِيمَ وَإِسْمَاعِيلَ وَإِسْحَاقَ وَيَعْقُوبَ وَالْأَسْبَاطِ وَعِيسَىٰ وَأَيُّوبَ وَيُونُسَ وَهَارُونَ وَسُلَيْمَانَ ۚ وَآتَيْنَا دَاوُودَ زَبُورًا ١٦٣﴾

النساء: ١٦٣

We sent inspiration to Nuh and Isma'eel, Is'haq, Ya'qoob and the Tribes, to Isa, Ayyoob." [Surat-un-Nisaa' 4: 163]

When Ayyoob (Job) عليه السلام was chosen to be a prophet, he started to teach people about God and His religion. He advised the people to do good and shun evil. As usual, with all the prophets, very few people believed in him in the beginning. Gradually the number of his followers began to increase.

Allah's Favors upon Ayyoub

Prophet Ayyoob عليه السلام was a prosperous man. God granted him all kinds of wealth and bliss. He had been blessed with a big family, a faithful and beautiful wife, seven boy,s and seven girls. He also had many friends who always gathered around him. He was also the owner of a gigantic business. He had money, numerous barley and wheat fields, hundreds of slaves, physical strength, horses, and livestock. All that lasted for fifty years. Yet, his finest bliss was his great faith in Allah Almighty.

Prophet Ayyoob Tested

In His infinite wisdom, Allah chose to try Ayyoob. He afficted him with a number of calamities. One day, his big farm was attacked by thieves. They killed many of his servants and carried away forcibly all his cattle. Prophet Ayyoob (peace be upon him) accepted what happened to him and praised Allah.

After some time the roof of his house fell in and many members of his family were crushed. Prophet Ayyoob عليه السلام was very shocked, but he held fast to his faith in Allah. He remarked that possessions and children were the gifts from Allah. If He had taken His things, it was useless to lament over their loss.

Prophet Ayyoob عليه السلام was an example of humility, faith in Allah and patience. He suffered a number of calamities, but he did not utter a single word of complaint.

As a further test from Allah, he became very ill and was covered with loathsome sores from head to foot. Some said his whole body was covered with sores, to the point that he became crippled. Even some went as far as saying his flesh started to fall off. His false friends attributed his afflictions to sin. But that was far from the truth, because Prophets are without major sins. Nobody truly sympathized with him as his wife did. But all these calamities made Ayyoob عليه السلام more patient and more thankful to Allah Almighty.

What should a Muslim do when another Muslim becomes sick?

1. It is a right of the Muslim to visit the other Muslim when he or she becomes ill.
2. Offer the sick the help he or she needs.
3. Make a sincere du'aa.

Exemplary Patience

It is narrated that Ayyoub's wife once asked him to implore Allah to cure him and have mercy on him. He asked her: "How many years have we lived in total happiness and bliss?"

She replied: "Eighty years." He said: "I feel ashamed to ask Allah before we spend an equal period in trial."

The historians gave several reports about the period of time which Ayyoob spent in his calamity: WahbIbn Munabbih said, three years, Anas Ibn Malik said: "seven years and few months. Others said,eighteen years. During these years, Ayyoob was silent. He never complained or voiced his distress.

Faithful Wife

As the time went by, only his wife remained with him. She took care of all his needs. She even was working as a servant to feed him. But then people refused to let her work for them because they were afraid that she might be afficted with the disease, too.

She spent all the money she had on Ayyoub, until it had run out. When all finances ran out, the faithful wife sold her braids to put food on the table. Ayyoob asked her about the source of that food. She did not answer. But he insisted, and she uncovered her head. She was bald. At this point, Ayyoob عليه السلام cried to his Lord,

﴿ وَأَيُّوبَ إِذْ نَادَىٰ رَبَّهُ أَنِّي مَسَّنِيَ ٱلضُّرُّ وَأَنتَ أَرْحَمُ ٱلرَّٰحِمِينَ ۝ ﴾ الأنبياء: ٨٣

"Truly distress has seized me, but You are the Most Merciful of those that are Merciful."

Allah said: *Commemorate our servant Ayyoob, behold, he cried to his Lord: "Satan has inflicted me with distress and suffering!"* He attributed his difficulty to Satan not to Allah.

Allah's Response

Allah answered Prophet Ayyoob's prayers immediately.

﴿ فَٱسْتَجَبْنَا لَهُۥ فَكَشَفْنَا مَا بِهِۦ مِن ضُرٍّ ۖ وَءَاتَيْنَٰهُ أَهْلَهُۥ وَمِثْلَهُم مَّعَهُمْ رَحْمَةً مِّنْ عِندِنَا وَذِكْرَىٰ لِلْعَٰبِدِينَ ۝ ﴾ ص: ٨٤

"So We answered his call," Allah Almighty told him, "*Strike with your foot: here is (water) wherein to wash, cool and refreshing, and (water) to drink.*" [Saad:42]. So, when he washed, the disease came out of his skin, and when he drank the water the disease purified his inside.

It was said that his wife was off for some chores, and when she returned she could not recognize her husband. She got used to seeing him for many years as a sick person, not at a healthy one.

Allah's Rewards and Compensation

After the long years of calamity, Allah Almighty compensated Prophet Ayyoob. Allah Almighty said: *"And We gave him [back] his people and doubled their number as a grace from Us, and a thing for commemoration, for all who have understanding."*

Abu Hurayrah narrated that Rasoolullah said: "While Ayyoob was naked, taking a bath, a swarm of gold era locusts fell on him, and he started collecting them in his garment. Allah then called him: "O Ayyoob! Have I not made you rich enough to need what you see? He said: "Yes, O Lord! But I cannot dispense with Your Blessing." [Reported in

Sahih Al-Bukhari]

Then Allah recalled to Ayyoob all His mercies on him. He was restored to prosperity, with twice as much as he had had before; his brethren and friends came back to him. He had a new family of more than twenty sons and daughters. He lived to a good old age, and he saw four generations of descendants.

Ibn Abbas said: "Allah was not only generous with Ayyoob, but with his wife." Allah transformed her into a young woman and gave Ayyoob twenty-six children.

The story of Ayyoob is the utmost example in holding fast to faith and being patient.

The Virtue of Patience

Prophet Ayyoob عليه السلام suffered because of sickness like no one had suffered before. But he demonstrated a great patience and never allowed himself to weaken his belief and trust in Allah Almighty. He was patient and perseverant. Therefore, Allah listened to Ayyoob and restored his health and wealth. He was commanded to strike the Earth with his foot. Ayyoub did, and a fountain gushed forth to give him a bath, clean his body, refresh his spirit, and to give him a drink and rest. Allah said:

"So We listened to him: We removed the distress that was on him, and We restored his people to him, and doubled their number,- as a grace from Ourselves, and a thing for commemoration, for all who serve Us." [Surat-ul-'Anbiya' 21: 83-84]

Du'aa' of One Who is Tested

BY LYNNE ALI

Oh Allah, you are testing me.
You've been testing me for years.
For most of this I was brave and strong.
My iman kept me from wrong.

I loved that You were testing me.
I felt Your love in my soul.
But somehow I slipped and now I am weak.
How I fell, I don't know

I felt close to the Prophets who were tested the most
Felt like Sumayyah, who was promised the garden
Like the Prophet Ayyoob, who never complained
Except of his own lack of sabr

Oh Allah I have lost my sabr.
I am failing your test, please help!
How easy it is to lose iman.
Only myself I have harmed.

The Day I will stand before you,
And no excuse will prevail,
I can point a finger at all else,
But four will be pointing at me.

Even Shaytan will run away,
Saying he only whispered to me.
Yet I followed him instead of praying to You,
Asking You for the help that would have kept me strong.

But its not too late yet, please help me return
Give me the strength to bear this test.
For hardship is upon those You love.
Help me to deserve Your love.

I feel like no one could love me,
But Your forgiveness exceeds your wrath.
So shower upon me Your mercy,
And turn all my sins to dust.

The Qur'an on Patience

In this chapter you learned about Prophet Ayyoub's patience on sickness and pain. Let's learn what the Qur'an says about the different types of patience:

1. Patience during calamities and difficult times

"O my son! Perform prayer regularly, enjoin (and support) what is good (and just), and stop (and prevent) what is wrong: And be patient and constant with whatever happens to you, verily, these are of the firm commandments."

2. Patience when facing dangerous enemies

Allah says in Surat-ul-Baqarah, "And when they advanced to meet Jaloot (Goliath) and his forces, they prayed: "Our Lord! Pour forth on us patience and make us victorious over the disbelieving people." [2:250].

3. Patience when facing the aggression of tyrants and hateful people

"And why should we not put our trust in Allah while He indeed has guided us our ways. And we shall certainly bear with patience all the hurt you may cause us, and in Allah, Almighty."

4. Patience when facing non-Muslims false accusations

And endure you patiently (O Muhammad), your patience is not but from Allah. And grieve not over them (polytheists and pagans, etc.), and be not distressed because of what they plot.

5. Patience when separated from parents, family and love ones

And We made their hearts firm and strong (with the light of Faith in Allah and bestowed upon them patience to bear the separation of their kith and kin and dwellings, etc.)

So bear with patience (O Muhammad SAW) all that they say, and glorify the Praises of your Lord, before the rising of the sun and before (its) setting.

6. Patience in accepting Allah's Qadar, or fait

"So wait with patience for the Decision of your Lord, and be not like the Companion of the Fish, when he cried out (to Us) while he was in deep sorrow.

7. Patience continuing to be good deeds

Except those who show patience and do righteous good deeds, those: theirs will be forgiveness and a great reward (Paradise). (Chapter #11, Verse #11)

"Except those who believe (in Islamic Monotheism) and do righteous good deeds, and recommend one another to the truth (i.e. order one another to perform all kinds of good deeds

8. Patience in learning and seeking knowledge

"[Al-Khidr] said: "This is the parting between me and you, I will tell you the interpretation of (those) things over which you were unable to hold patience.
This ayah hints to the story of Prophet Musa and the knowledgeable teacher Al-Khidr. The story shows that Al-Khidr left Musa because he was impatient in learning from Al-Khidr until the end of the learning journey as Allah wanted him to do.

CHAPTER REVIEW

Projects and Activities

1. Write a poem on sabr, or patience.

2. Write a 500-word essay on patience and perseverance for the sake of Allah.

Stretch Your Mind

1. Why do you think Allah tested Prophet Ayyoob with painful calamities?

2. Compare and contrast the way Allah tested Prophet Ayyoob and the way he tested Prophet Suleyman.

Study Questions

1. Write a brief profile on Prophet Ayyoob.
2. Describe the calamity that hit Prophet Ayyoob.
3. What did Prophet Ayyoob do when he lost his wealth and family?
4. What should the believer do when he or she is tested by a calamity, or blessed with a favor from Allah? Support your answer with a hadeeth.
5. Was Ayyoob's wife faithful to him during his severe sickness? List three actions she did that support your answer.
6. List five types of patience. Support your answer with the fitting ayaat.

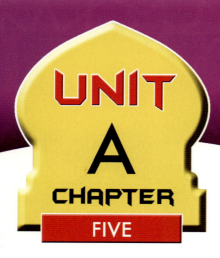

Patience and Perseverance: The Signs of Strong Faith

CHAPTER OBJECTIVES

1. Learn and understand the virtue of patience in Islam.
2. Internalize the importance of patience, and become inspired to practice patience in daily life.
3. Learn about the three main types of patience.
4. Become inspired with the patience and perseverance of Prophet Muhammad and his companions.
5. Internalize the ideal of patience and perseverance, and become encouraged to apply it as a virtue and attitude.
6. Learn and memorize the hadeeth of this chapter.

VOCABULARY

The true belief in Al-Qadar requires the Muslim to demonstrate two attitudes:

1. Patience toward life's trials and difficulties

2. Gratefulness to Allah for His favors

In this chapter and the following one, you will learn the two important attitudes a Muslim should demonstrate in his or her daily life: sabr, or patience, and shukr, or thankfulness to Allah. These two positive attitudes are signs of strong faith, and they show particularly clear understanding of the belief in Al-Qadar and proper application of it.

عَن صُهَيْبٍ الرُّومِيِّ رَضِيَ اللهُ عَنْهُ قال: قال رَسولُ الله ﷺ:
"عَجَبًا لِأَمْرِ المُؤْمِنِ ، إنَّ أمْرَهُ كُلَّهُ خَيْرٌ ، وَلَيْسَ ذلِكَ لِأَحَدٍ إلا لِلْمُؤْمِنِ ، إنْ أصابَتْهُ سَرّاءُ شَكَرَ فَكانَ خَيْرًا لهُ ، وَإنْ أصابَتْهُ ضَرّاءُ صَبَرَ فَكانَ خَيْرًا لهُ"   رواه مسلم

Suhayb ibn Sinan ar-Rumi narrated that Rasoolullah said, "Strange is the manner of the believer, for there is good in all of his manners. And only the believer has this manner. If he is blessed with a happy time, then he will thank [Allah]; thus there is a good for him in it, and if he gets into trouble, he endures it patiently, thus there is a good for him in it."

Related Wisdom

"You must first have a lot of patience to learn to have patience. "Stanislaw J. Lec (1909 - 1966), "Unkempt Thoughts"

"We could never learn to be brave and patient, if there were only joy in the world." Helen Keller (1880 - 1968)

What Is Patience?

"Sabr" is an Arabic word which means patience, perseverance, and stead-fasting. Scholars have defined "patience" as a good human trait or attitude. A patient person bravely faces pains and difficulties of life, and he/she refrains from doing evil actions in reaction to life's calamities.

In the spiritual sense, patience means to stop ourselves from despairing and panicking, to stop our tongues from complaining, and to stop our hands from striking our faces and tearing our clothes at times of grief and stress.

Abu Uthman said: "The one who has patience is the one who trained himself to handle difficulties." Amr ibn Uthman al-Makki said: "Patience means to keep close to Allah, and to accept calmly the trials He sends, without complaining or feeling sad." Al-Khawwas said: "Patience means to adhere to the rules of the Qur'an and Sunnah." Another scholar said: "Patience means to refrain from complaining." 'Ali ibn Abi Talib رضي الله عنه said: "Patience means to seek Allah's help."

Patience is when a person restrains himself from being fearful during hard times. Also, a person who is patient restrains himself from doing prohibited acts, and he does what is obligatory and righteous.

Faces of Patience

Imam Ibn-ul-Qayyim said, "There are three types of patience:

1. Patience in obeying Allah and doing righteous deeds.

Worshipping Allah and obeying Him requires patience, perseverance and discipline. Therefore, Allah commanded Prophet Muhammad to be patient as he was making act of worship and obedience. Allah says in Surat Maryam, "[Allah is the] Lord of the Heavens and the Earth, and all that is between them, so worship Him and be constant and patient in His worship."[19:65] Allah also ordered the Prophet and all parents, "And enjoin prayer on your family, and be patient in offering them." [Surat Taha: 20 132]

The messengers of Allah and all true believers needed great patience in order to fulfill their obligations of conveying the message, and of uplifting the conditions of individuals and society. Without this patience, they could not have succeeded in their tasks. Therefore, Allah (S.W.T.) commanded the Prophet Muhammad ﷺ, "Therefore be patient [O Muhammad] as did the messengers of strong will." [Surat Al-Ahqaf:35]

2. Patience on abstaining from evil, disobedience and prohibited acts.

Abstaining from haram, or prohibited acts, requires a great struggle and discipline against one's desires. It takes much patience to reject the evil influences of Shaytan. Therefore, Allah (S.W.T.) will generously reward those who patiently abstain from evil.

The Prophet Muhammad (S.A.W) told us about the people who will receive a special reward: "Seven are (the persons) whom Allah would give protection with His shade on the day when there would be no shade but His shade (i.e., on the Day of Judgment), and among them: a youth who grew up with the worship of Allah, …a man whom an extremely beautiful woman seduces (for illicit relations), but he rejects this offer by saying: I fear Allah…." {Imams Bukhari and Muslim}

Prophet Yousuf is another example of a person who abstained patiently from the evil lure of the wife of the King of Egypt. Prophet Yusuf chose incarceration for several years rather than committing an evil act.

3. Patience during times of hardship without complaints.

A true believer practices patience during times of hardship without voicing complaints. Facing calamities and hardship without complaining is the fruit of believing in Al-Qadar and accepting Allah's will. Prophet Muhammad (S.A.W.) said: "Never a believer is stricken with a discomfort, an illness, an anxiety, a grief, or mental worry, or even the picking of a thorn, that his sins are not removed for him." [Reported by Al-Bukhari and Muslim]

Benefits of Patience

Allah has guaranteed those who are patient that He will give them rewards and blessings without measure. Following are few important benefits of sabr, or patience:

1. Allah supports those who are patient.

He tells them that He is with them by guiding and supporting them and granting them a clear victory. Allah says in Surat-ul-Anfal:

﴿ وَٱصۡبِرُوٓاۡ إِنَّ ٱللَّهَ مَعَ ٱلصَّٰبِرِينَ ٤٦ ﴾

الأنفال: ٤٦

"Surely, Allah is with those who are patient." [8:46]

2. Allah loves those who are patient.
Allah says in Surat Al-Imran:

﴿ وَٱللَّهُ يُحِبُّ ٱلصَّٰبِرِينَ ﴾ آل عمران: ١٤٦

"And Allah loves the patient."[3:146]

3. Allah forgives and rewards those who are righteous and patient. Allah says in Surat Hud:

﴿ إِلَّا ٱلَّذِينَ صَبَرُوا۟ وَعَمِلُوا۟ ٱلصَّٰلِحَٰتِ أُو۟لَٰٓئِكَ لَهُم مَّغْفِرَةٌ وَأَجْرٌ كَبِيرٌ ﴾

"Except those who show patience and do righteous good deeds: those will be forgiven and win a great reward (Paradise)."[11:11]

4. Patience is a quality of leaders.
Allah has made leadership in terms of religion conditional upon patience and certain faith. Allah tells us that the patience and piety of his prophet Yousuf brought him to a position of power and leadership. Allah says in Surat As-Sajdah:

﴿ وَجَعَلْنَا مِنْهُمْ أَئِمَّةً يَهْدُونَ بِأَمْرِنَا لَمَّا صَبَرُوا۟ وَكَانُوا۟ بِـَٔايَٰتِنَا يُوقِنُونَ ﴾ السجدة: ٢٤

"And We made from among them (Children of Isra'eel), leaders, giving guidance under Our command, when they were patient and used to believe with certainty in Our ayaat." [32:34]

5. Patience enables believers to turn enemies into close friends.
Allah tells us that repelling evil with a kind attitude makes the evildoer become like a close friend. Allah says in Surat Fussilat:

﴿ وَلَا تَسْتَوِى ٱلْحَسَنَةُ وَلَا ٱلسَّيِّئَةُ ٱدْفَعْ بِٱلَّتِى هِىَ أَحْسَنُ فَإِذَا ٱلَّذِى بَيْنَكَ وَبَيْنَهُۥ عَدَٰوَةٌ كَأَنَّهُۥ وَلِىٌّ حَمِيمٌ ۞ وَمَا يُلَقَّىٰهَآ إِلَّا ٱلَّذِينَ صَبَرُوا۟ وَمَا يُلَقَّىٰهَآ إِلَّا ذُو حَظٍّ عَظِيمٍ ۞ ﴾

فصلت: ٣٤-٣٥

"The good deed and the evil deed cannot be equal. Repel (the evil) with one which is better (i.e. Allaah orders the faithful believers to be patient at the time of anger, and to excuse those who treat them badly) then verily he, between whom and you there was enmity, (will become) as though he was a close friend." [41:34]

6. Allah rewards the believers with Jannah for their patience.

﴿ وَجَزَىٰهُم بِمَا صَبَرُوا۟ جَنَّةً وَحَرِيرًا ﴾

الإنسان: ١٢

"And [Allah] rewarded them, because they were patient, with garden and silk." [76:12]

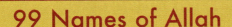
99 Names of Allah

| As-Saboor (The Patient) | الصبور |
| Al-Haleem (The Tolerant) | الحليم |

Foundations of Patience

To have true patience a Muslim must have the following foundations and ideals in his or her heart and mind. These foundations and virtues help the Muslim to develop patience and perseverance as long lasting traits and attitudes :

1. Following clear conscience.
2. Demonstrating high morals.
3. Shunning Shaytan's deceit
4. Fearing nothing but Allah

1. Following Clear Conscience

Allah created each person with a conscience to let him or her know what is right and wrong in all situations. This conscience calls upon people to think and behave in the manner that pleases Allah and earns His approval. Every person also has a lower self that urges him to follow his whims and desires. However, believers always display a sure determination to ignore their lower selves by listening only to their consciences. Even if their lower selves calls them to do something that appears attractive and appealing, they ignore and resist these urges.

Throughout their lives, faithful people make this judgment call and then select the most correct attitude. In daily life, this can mean ignoring the lower self's urges to behave selfishly, and instead follow the conscience's advice to be self-sacrificing. This behavior of the faithful people is the result of the extreme patience they display while following their consciences.

2. Living the Qur'an's Morality

Only those who possess the superior morality portrayed in the Qur'an can always display true patience. For example, one might have a very strong temper, but upon learning that Allah refers to believers as "those who control their rage and pardon other people" [3: 134], he or she exhibits forgiving behavior

even when faced with an event that normally makes him or her angry. Whatever may happen, believers continue to speak pleasantly, remain tolerant, control their anger, and show other fine moral characteristics taught by the Qur'an.

In short, what makes the believers' character superior is their consistent and high morality. The faithful try to display high morality, not only in pardoning other people, but also in displaying self-sacrifice, humility, compassion, kindheartedness, tolerance, justice, love, and respect. Allah tells the faithful to be consistent in their worship: "He is Lord of the Heavens and Earth and everything in between them, so worship Him and persevere in His worship." [Surat Maryam 19: 65]

3. Shunning Satan's Deceit

When Allah created Prophet Adam (as), He required all angels to prostrate to him. However, Iblees rebelled against Allah's order and refused to do so. Faced with Satan's rebellion, Allah cast him out of Paradise and declared him cursed until the end of time. But Satan demanded that Allah allow him to tempt people to lose themselves in the allures of this world until the Day of Judgment, when they would be resurrected. Allah granted this, but He also declared that Satan would have no power over His faithful servants:

"He [Satan] said: "My Lord, because You misled me, I will make things on Earth seem good to them, and I will mislead them all, every one of them, except those of Your servants among them who are sincere." He [Allah] said: "This is a Straight Path to Me. You have no authority over any of My servants, except for the misguided who follow you." [Surat al-Hijr, 15: 39-42]

Satan cannot influence those who display patience in maintaining their faith in our

Lord, because Allah has declared that Satan can deceive and divert only those who rebel against Allah, as he himself did. Allah calls on the faithful to take refuge in Him from Satan's deceptions. "If an evil impulse from Satan provokes you, seek refuge in Allah. He is All-Hearing, All-Seeing." [Al-An'am 6: 200]

Heeding Allah's advice, "O you who believe, seek help in steadfastness and prayer. Allah is with the steadfast." [Surat Al-Imran 3:153]. In order to guard themselves against Satan, they ask for our Lord's help and set their faces against Satan's deceptions.

4. Fearing Nothing but Allah

People who do not truly believe in Allah's power and greatness are subject to innumerable fears. Among these fears are the fears of other people, the dark, or certain numbers or colors, believing that they have an independent power of their own. True believers, however, know that only Allah has power, and that no one can harm or help anybody else without His permission and will. They are aware of the fact that no people or creatures can have power that is independent of Allah, and that everything owes its existence to Him. If they encounter some harm, they believe wholeheartedly that only our Lord can remove it. Allah tells the faithful to fear nothing but Him;

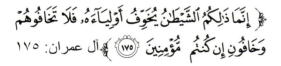

"It was only Satan frightening you through his friends. But do not fear them—fear Me, if you are believers." [3: 175]

Due to their firm belief and trust in Allah, the true believers experience no severe sadness or depression when confronted with frightening or intimidating events. Oppression or aggression do not cause them to swerve in their devotion to Allah and their striving to earn His approval and pleasure. The Qur'an explains this attribute as follows:

"Those to whom people said: "The people have gathered against you, so fear them." But that merely increased their faith, and they said: "Allah is enough for us, and [He is] the Best of Guardians." [3:173]

As this verse indicates, even if the faithful are faced with pressure, they fear only Allah and show their patience by not abandoning their faith. Allah has declared that He will test His servants with fear to separate the true believers from those who have weak—or no—faith.

Selected Story

A Glimpse of the Prophet's Patience and Perseverance

Ten years after receiving his mission from his Lord, the Prophet (peace be upon him) set out towards At-Ta'if, about 60 kilometers from Makkah. He was hoping that the people of Ta'if might believe in him after he was persecuted by the people of Makkah for years. In his company was Zaid bin Harithah. But contrary to his expectations, the general atmosphere was terribly hostile.

The Prophet approached three brothers from the chieftains of Thaqeef. 'Abd Yaleel, Mas'ud and Habeeb, the sons of 'Amr bin 'Umair Ath-Thaqafy, met the Prophet ﷺ. He invited them to embrace Islam and worship Allah, but they boldly jeered at him and refused his invitation. "Is it true that Allah has sent you as a Messenger?" said one of them. "Has not Allah found someone else to entrust him with His message?" said the second. "I swear by Allah that I will never have any contact with you," said the third.

For ten days Rasoolulah stayed there delivering his message to several people, one after another, but all to no purpose. Stirred up to hasten the departure of the unwelcome visitor, the people hooted him through the alley-ways, showered him with stones and he obliged him to flee from the city pursued by a relentless mob. Blood flowed down both his legs; and Zaid, endeavoring to shield him, was wounded in the head. The mob did not desist until they had chased him two or three miles across the sandy plains to the foot of the surrounding hills. There, wearied and exhausted, he took refuge in one of the numerous orchards, and rested against the wall of a vineyard. At a time when the whole world seemed to have turned against him, Muhammad (peace be upon him) turned to his Lord and betook himself to prayer. The following touching words are still preserved, as those through which his oppressed soul gave vent to its distress. He was weary and wounded, but confident in the help of his Lord:

O Allah! To You alone I make complaint of my helplessness, the scarcity of my resources and my insignificance before mankind. You are the most Merciful of the merciful. You are the Lord of the helpless and the weak, O Lord of mine! Into whose hands would You abandon me: into the hands of an unsympathetic relative who would sullenly frown at me, or to the enemy who has been given control over my affairs? But if Your wrath does not fall on me, there is nothing for me to worry about."
"I seek protection in the light of Your face, which illuminates the Heavens and dispels darkness, and which controls all affairs in this world as well as in the Hereafter. May it never be that I should incur Your wrath, or that You should be wrathful to me. And there is no power nor resource but Yours alone."

Seeing him in this helpless situation, Rabi'a's two sons, wealthy Makkans, were moved on grounds of kinship and compassion, and sent to him one of their Christian servants with a tray of grapes. The Prophet (peace be upon him) accepted the fruit with pious invocation: "In the Name of the Allah." The Christian servant 'Addas was greatly impressed by these words and said: "These are words which people in this land do not generally use." The Prophet (peace be upon him) inquired of him from where he came, and what religion he professed. 'Addas replied: "I am a Christian by faith and come from Nineveh." The Prophet (peace be upon him) then said: "You belong to the city of the righteous Younus (Jonah), son of Matta." 'Addas asked him anxiously if he knew anything about Jonah. The Prophet ﷺ significantly remarked: "He is my brother. He was a Prophet, and so am I." Thereupon 'Addas paid homage to Muhammad ﷺ and kissed his hands.

Heart-broken and depressed, Muhammad (peace be upon him) set out on the way back to Makkah. 'Aishah (R) said: "I asked the Prophet ﷺ if he had ever experienced a worse day than Uhud. He answered that he had suffered a lot from those people (Makkans), but the most painful was on the day he went to Ta'if. "I went seeking support from Ibn 'Abd Yalil bin 'Abd Kalal, but he rejected me. I set out wearied and grieved, heedless of anything around me until I suddenly realized I was in Qarn Ath-Tha'alib, called Qarn Al-Manazil. There, I looked up and saw a cloud casting its shade on me, and Gabriel addressing me: "Allah has heard your people's words and sent the angel of mountains to your aid." The latter called and gave me his greetings, and he asked for my permission to bury Makkah between the two mountains flanking Makkah. I said in reply that I would rather have someone from their offspring who would worship Allah, the All-Mighty, with no associate."

The Prophet's patience and perseverance paid off. Ten years later, the people of Makkah, Ta'if, and throughout Arabia rejected paganism and accepted Islam. They followed Prohet Muhammad and recognized him as their prophet and leader.

Source: Saifur Rahman al-Mubarakpuri, *The Sealed Nectar*.

How the Prophets Complained about Life's Calamities

Prophet Ya'qoob عليه السلام said:
"I only complain of my distraction and anguish to Allah." [Surat Yousuf 12:86]

Ya'qoob also said "patience is most fitting for me."

The Qur'an also tells us about Ayyoob عليه السلام:

"And (remember) Ayyoob (Job), when he cried to his Lord, "Truly distress has seized me..." [Surat-ul-Anbiyaa' 21:83]

Musa (AS) prayed to Allah saying: "O Allah, all praise is due to You, and complaint is made only to You, and You are the only One from Whom we seek help and in Whom we put our trust, and there is no power except by Your help."

Prophet Muhammad said, "O Allah, I complain to You of my weakness and helplessness."

Poem.. Mu'min and Sabr

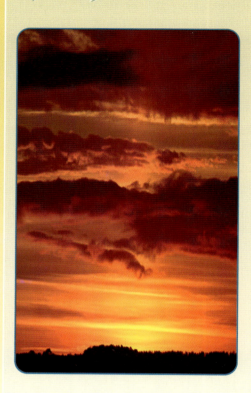

Tallal Alie Turfe

Patience is a virtue I'll try to explain
A blessing in disguise always to remain
From very deep inside the well of my heart
Peace of body and mind and the will to start
I'm summoned by a call at the dawn of the day
Just giving thanks to Him as I kneel to pray
Endurance is my counsel and faith my guide
The door is open to the struggle inside
With knowledge of certainty, I now can see
The reality of truth, plain as can be
It is charity that gives meaning to life
From the love of my caring in times of strife
Piety and wisdom help me through the day
But always I will return to kneel and pray
For it is patience, the essence of my goal
That enlightens and gives meaning to my soul.

CHAPTER REVIEW

Projects and Activities

1. Create a piece of artwork for Allah's name "As-Saboor."

2. Write a story about the virtue of patience.

3. Create a play about the sacrifice and patience of Bilal (R) with your classmates.

Stretch Your Mind

1. Do you think patience is a passive behavior? Support your answer with ayaat, hadeeth, and logical arguments.

2. The prophet is our role model in everything including patience and tolerance. Use what you know from the Seerah to support this statement.

3. How can fearing only Allah help you to be patient?

Study Questions

1. Explain the virtue of sabr in Islam.
2. What did Allah promise those who practice sabr?
3. Explain the three main types of patience.
4. What are the foundations that you need to develop the attitude to be patient and perseverant?
5. How did the prophets complain of the difficult situations they went through?

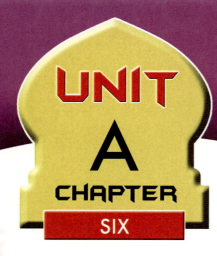

Patience and Perseverance in Daily Life

CHAPTER OBJECTIVES

1. Understand that patience and perseverance are required on a daily basis.
2. Learn the circumstances that require patience and understand how to apply patience and perseverance in each situation.
3. Become inspired by the story of Bilal's (R) sacrifice, patience and perseverance.

Patience is a way of life that Muslims should apply every day and in different situations. In this chapter you will learn about common life situations that require patience and how you should apply patience in these circumstances, whenever they happen.

1. Patience When Losing Loved Ones.

One of the most emotional and painful calamities is the loss of a loved one. The death or injury of parents, children, spouses, relatives, friends, and other special individuals is sometimes hard to comprehend. Once the Prophet was passing by a woman who had been weeping over the grave of her son. The Prophet advised her to calm down and accept Allah's will. The woman did not recognize the Prophet and said, "Leave me alone; you don't know how hard his death was on me!" The Prophet, withdrew politely, but he said to her, "True patience [works well and is best rewarded] when you observe it as the first shock hits."

Allah retains a great reward for the one who acts patiently when he or she loses a loved one. Rasoolullah once said that Allah promised, " If I test my servant with the loss of his [or her] loved one, and he or she demonstrates patience, I will grant him [or her] Jannah. "

Umm Salamah lost her dear husband and felt deeply sad. She said: "I heard Rasoolullah say: 'Whoever is put through a trial and says:

Du'aa'

إنا لله وإنا إليه راجعون

اللهم أجرني في مصيبتي واخلفني خيرا مِنها

"Inna lillah wa inna ilayhi raaji'oon (to Allah we belong, and to Him is our return)
Oh, Allah, help me through my ordeal and grant me better than it [what I lost] after."

Allah will help him through his ordeal and gave him better than it afterward. She said: "So when Abu Salamah (her husband) died, I said what I was told to say by the Messenger of Allah سبحانه وتعالى, and Allah, Almighty, granted me better than him, the Prophet of Allah himself!" [Reported by Al-Bukhari, Muslim, Al-Tirmidhi and Abu Da'ud].

One time, Prophet Muhammad lost his only son, Ibraheem, so when he buried him, he cried and said,

عن عمران بن حصين قال : "لما توفي ابن رسول الله صلى الله عليه وسلم دمعت عيناه فقالوا : يا رسول الله تبكي؟ فقال رسول الله صلى الله عليه وسلم : العين تدمع ، والقلب يحزن، ولا نقول إلا ما يرضى ربنا ، وإنا بك يا إبراهيم لمحزونون."

رواه أحمد وأبو داود

Imran Ibn-ul-Husayn said, "When the son of Rasoolullah died, the Prophet's eye shed some tears." The people then said, "Are you crying, O Rasoolullah?" The Prophet then said, "The eye sheds tears, the heart feels the sorrow, and we don't say anything except what pleases our Lord, but we are truly sad."
Reported by Ahmad and Abu Dawoud

We learn from this important hadeeth that it is natural to become sad and even cry when we lose a loved one. However, we should not say or do anything that displeases Allah, like objecting to what happened, or questioning God concerning the calamity that He chose to test us with. We can feel the sorrow, but at the same time, we should accept what happened, act patiently, and hope for Allah's reward and compensation.

2. Patience with Property Loss or Damage

Allah has decorated this life with many beautiful things to make mankind happy. People are required to use the blessings showered on them in the best possible way, without becoming passionately attached to them. They should realize that whatever people acquire here will remain here, and that they will have to account for their use of these blessings in the Day of Judgment. Those who understand that everything is a gift from Allah and show gratitude to Him will be rewarded, while those who forget the Day of Judgment, and so try to seize these blessings for themselves with greed, will suffer disappointment.

In the Qur'an, Allah lists some of the many blessings that He has granted to people, as follows:

﴿ زُيِّنَ لِلنَّاسِ حُبُّ الشَّهَوَاتِ مِنَ النِّسَآءِ وَالْبَنِينَ وَالْقَنَاطِيرِ الْمُقَنْطَرَةِ مِنَ الذَّهَبِ وَالْفِضَّةِ وَالْخَيْلِ الْمُسَوَّمَةِ وَالْأَنْعَامِ وَالْحَرْثِ ذَلِكَ مَتَاعُ الْحَيَوةِ الدُّنْيَا وَاللَّهُ عِنْدَهُ حُسْنُ الْمَآبِ ١٤ ﴾

آل عمران: ١٤

"To mankind, the love of worldly appetites is painted in glowing colors: women and children, heaped-up mounds of gold and silver, horses with fine markings, and livestock and fertile farmland. All that is merely the enjoyment of the life of this world. The best homecoming is in the presence of Allah [in Heaven]. [3: 14]

The faithful use these blessings in the best possible way, but at no time become addicted to them. They know that, as with everything else in the world, possessions and goods are part of the environment created to test them. Knowing that the blessings of this world are temporary, and that the home of the real blessings is the Afterlife, they have no selfish ambitions.

Since they feel neither ambition nor passion for worldly goods, they show patience whether times are good or bad. When they lose their property or it is damaged, they do not sink into sorrow or worry. If they obtain a large amount of property by working for years, and then lose it all in a day, they know that Allah is testing their faith and patience. Therefore, they do not become distraught if their houses, orchards, or gardens are destroyed, or if their businesses end up going bankrupt. Despite all of these trials, they live in the comfort provided by the knowledge that Allah will ease their burdens, clear their way, conclude matters to their benefit, and reward their patience with better things in the Afterlife.

People who are passionately attached to this life cannot stand it when their hard-earned property suffers any loss or damage, and so they display rebellious behavior. Forgetting that Allah is the true owner of all property, and that He can give more than He has taken away if He so wills, they cannot see any good in such an event and so they cannot show any patience.

Such tests reveal the difference between the faithful, who show patience for the sake of Allah, and those who pursue worldly pleasure only and forget about the Afterlife. The believers do not grieve or dispair when they lose their property, for their only intention is to use everything they possess, physically and spiritually, to worship Allah and earn His approval. In other words, they have already devoted these possessions to Allah. In return for their devotion, they receive the following reward:

﴿ وَلَنَبْلُوَنَّكُمْ بِشَيْءٍ مِنَ الْخَوْفِ وَالْجُوعِ وَنَقْصٍ مِنَ الْأَمْوَالِ وَالْأَنْفُسِ وَالثَّمَرَاتِ وَبَشِّرِ الصَّابِرِينَ ١٥٥ الَّذِينَ إِذَآ أَصَابَتْهُمْ مُصِيبَةٌ قَالُوٓا إِنَّا لِلَّهِ وَإِنَّآ إِلَيْهِ رَاجِعُونَ ١٥٦ أُولَئِكَ عَلَيْهِمْ صَلَوَاتٌ مِنْ رَبِّهِمْ وَرَحْمَةٌ وَأُولَئِكَ هُمُ الْمُهْتَدُونَ ١٥٧ ﴾

البقرة: ١٥٥-١٥٧

"We will test you with a certain amount of fear and hunger and the loss of wealth, life, and fruits. But give good news to the steadfast. Who say, when hit with calamity: "To Allah We belong, and to Him is our return" They are those on whom (Descend) blessings from Allah, and mercy, and they are the ones that receive guidance. "[Surat-ul-Baqarah 2:155-157]

3. Patience During Hunger or Poverty

In addition to testing people with a loss of property or their business, Allah may also test them with poverty and hunger.

However, it should be realized that Allah creates a different test for every person. For this reason, not everyone will face all of these tests in the same way and under the same conditions. In fact, Allah creates the secret of the test by sending the same test to people in a wide variety of forms and in unexpected ways. Those who have true faith and devotion are prepared to face these difficulties in all of their forms by relying on the power of their faith and by their submission to Allah.

Disbelievers forget that only Allah gives the countless favors that He blessed them with in this world, but they show Him no gratitude. In fact, if even one blessing is removed, they rebel against Allah and show ingratitude. In communities that are far from religion, one can find such examples on a regular basis. Rich people who become poor lose many blessings that Allah has bestowed upon them in the past. Ignoring the fact that their houses, cars, clothes, food, and drink were Allah's gifts to them, they believe that all such things belonged to them alone. Unable to learn the intended lesson and ask Allah to grant new blessings, they do not put their trust in Allah, and thus they turnthe test against themselves.

On the other hand, true believers remain pleased with their Lord when rich or poor, hungry or well fed, and they will be reward-ed with Allah's mercy. Allah says in Surat-ul-Baqarah,

﴿ أَمْ حَسِبْتُمْ أَن تَدْخُلُوا۟ ٱلْجَنَّةَ وَلَمَّا يَأْتِكُم مَّثَلُ ٱلَّذِينَ خَلَوْا۟ مِن قَبْلِكُم مَّسَّتْهُمُ ٱلْبَأْسَآءُ وَٱلضَّرَّآءُ وَزُلْزِلُوا۟ حَتَّىٰ يَقُولَ ٱلرَّسُولُ وَٱلَّذِينَ ءَامَنُوا۟ مَعَهُۥ مَتَىٰ نَصْرُ ٱللَّهِ أَلَآ إِنَّ نَصْرَ ٱللَّهِ قَرِيبٌ ۝ ﴾

التوبة: ٢١٤

Or did you suppose that you would enter Paradise without facing the same as those who came before you? Poverty and illness afflicted them, and they were shaken to the point that the Messenger and those who believed with him said: "When is Allah's help coming?" Be assured that Allah's help is very near." [Surat-ul-Baqarah 2:214]

Allah tells us that these people were afflicted with poverty and illness and sought refuge in His help. We must always remember that He gives the good news. For those who are patient and meet such a test with good behavior, whatever the circumstances, His help is very near. We know this because He promises that while testing the faithful, He will ease their burden. Allah also proclaimed in Surat-ul-Inshirah

﴿ إِنَّ مَعَ ٱلْعُسْرِ يُسْرًا ۝ ﴾ الشرح: ٦

"For truly with hardship comes ease." [Surat-ush-Sharh 94:6]

Although he could become a very rich man, the Prophet preferred to live as a poor man. A'ishah once said, "Two or more months used to pass without being able to cook food." Most of the Sahabah led a very modest and poor life, but they stood fast on their faith and devotion to Allah. In order to win Allah's approval, they remained patient on His path despite thirst, poverty, and intolerable hunger, and they continued to struggle along with our Prophet ﷺ.

Allah says about those patient believers in Surat-ut-Tawbah:

﴿ذَٰلِكَ بِأَنَّهُمْ لَا يُصِيبُهُمْ ظَمَأٌ وَلَا نَصَبٌ وَلَا مَخْمَصَةٌ فِي سَبِيلِ اللَّهِ وَلَا يَطَئُونَ مَوْطِئًا يَغِيظُ الْكُفَّارَ وَلَا يَنَالُونَ مِنْ عَدُوٍّ نَيْلًا إِلَّا كُتِبَ لَهُم بِهِ عَمَلٌ صَالِحٌ ۚ إِنَّ اللَّهَ لَا يُضِيعُ أَجْرَ الْمُحْسِنِينَ ۝﴾

التوبة: ١٢٠

"That is because no thirst or weariness or hunger will afflict them in the Way of Allah, nor will they take a single step to infuriate the unbelievers, nor to secure any gain from the enemy, without a right action being written down for them because of it. Allah does not let the wage of the good-doers go to waste." [Surat-ut-Tawbah 9:120]

As we can see, Allah announces that the patience displayed by the tested believers will be rewarded, and that none of their good acts will be overlooked on the Day of Judgment. He also proclaims His mercy toward the faithful by describing them as those "who [He] has preserved them from hunger and secured them from fear" [Surat Quraysh 106: 4].

Selected Story

Abu Hurayrah: Hungry Most of the Time

Abu Hurayrah narrated : "The people used to say, "Abu Hurayrah narrates too many narrations." In fact, I used to keep close to Allah's Apostle and was satisfied with what filled my stomach. I ate no leavened bread and I wore no decorated, striped clothes, and never did a man or a woman serve me. I often used to press my belly against stones because of hunger, and I used to ask a man to recite a Qur'anic verse to me, although I knew it, so that he would take me to his home and feed me..

And the most generous of all the people to the poor was Ja'far bin Abi Talib. He used to take us to his home and offer us what was available therein. He would even offer us an empty folded leather container (of butter), which we would split and lick whatever was in it.

[Reported by Al-Bukhari]

Hadeeth Shareef

عن ابن عباس رضي الله عنه قال: قال رسول الله ﷺ :

"احْفَظِ اللهَ تَجِدْهُ أَمَامَكَ، تَعَرَّفْ إِلَى اللهِ فِي الرَّخَاءِ يَعْرِفْكَ فِي الشِّدَّةِ، وَاعْلَمْ أَنَّ مَا أَخْطَأَكَ لَمْ يَكُنْ لِيُصِيبَكَ، وما أَصَابَكَ لَمْ يَكُنْ لِيُخْطِئَكَ، وَاعْلَمْ أَنَّ النَّصْرَ مَعَ الصَّبْرِ، وَأَنَّ الفَرَجَ مَعَ الكَرْبِ، وَأَنَّ مَعَ العُسْرِ يُسْرا"

رواه أحمد والترمذي

Ibn Abbas narrated that the Prophet Muhammad also says,
"Be mindful of Allah, [for] you will find Him before you. Get to know Allah in prosperity, and He will know you in adversity. Know that what has passed you by was not going to befall you, and that what has befallen you was not going to pass you by. And know that victory comes with patience, relief with affliction, and ease with hardship."
[Reported by Ahmad and At-Tirmithi]

4. Patience During illness

True believers are usually patient and steadfast in cases of illness, accident, and injury. When faced with such problems, the believers behave steadfastly and with patience because of their deep faith in Allah and the Hereafter. They hope that after they enter Paradise, Allah will re-create them in such a fine form that it cannot be compared with their worldly bodies. Their hope for a great reward causes them to become steadfast and patient when facing medical calamities. They always remember that whatever they have suffered in this short life will entitle them to a great reward in the eternal Afterlife.

Prophet Ibraheem (as) is quoted in the Surat-ush-Shu'araa' saying:

﴿ وَإِذَا مَرِضْتُ فَهُوَ يَشْفِينِ ﴾

الشعراء: ٨٠

"And when I am ill, He heals me." [Surat-ush-Shu'raa' 26: 80].

Like Prophet Ibraheem (as), believers also know that Allah creates both the illness and the cure, and so there is hope when they fall ill. They are grateful to Allah for those years in which He allowed them to live in health. Understanding that a healthy life is only one of Allah's many gifts to them, they continue to behave gratefully even when they are ill.

Disbelievers cannot show patience in events of serious illness, so they sink into great hopelessness, depression, and grief. For example, those with crippled limbs say that they would rather die than live with a handicap; some even try to commit suicide. Believing that this life is the only one that they have, they think that living with certain defects and deficiencies makes life meaningless. Even if they do not try to commit suicide, they develop a very unpleasant personality and try to create problems for those around them. Whether they accept their situation or not, there is no way that they can avert such an event. If they put their trust in Allah, however, they may hope that He will allow them to be reborn in Paradise with a brand new body that is flawless, imperishable, and cannot be damaged. But if they fail to trust in Allah, their present life and their future life in the Hereafter will be destroyed. Their ignorance will cause them to rebel against Allah and be "rewarded" with Hell.

The behavior of those who live the Qur'an's morality is completely different. When they are injured, lose an organ, or experience a similar disaster, their behavior does not change. Knowing that they are being tested, and that the end result will be positive, they remain patient and do their best to earn Allah's approval. Even if they can no longer make any physical effort to realize this goal, they try to develop ideas that can benefit people and remind them of the Hereafter.

Those who turn away from Allah when they become ill, or when they are injured, are not aware of their great error, for only Allah can heal them or rescue them from their illness. Doctors, medicines, and treatments can be provided only with Allah's permission. Understanding this, the faithful face their illness with patience and patiently ask Him for a cure. They also make the best possible use of doctors, medicines, and treatments, and always remember that these will be of benefit only if Allah wills it.

The Qur'an gives the example of Prophet Ayyoob (as), who always sought refuge in Allah when faced with illness. Allah praises his morality, as follows: "We found him steadfast. What an excellent servant! He truly turned to his Lord." [Surat Saad 38:44]. His patience and devotion to Allah are described, as follows:

"And Ayyoob, when he called out to his Lord, [said]: "Great harm has afflicted me, and You are the Most Merciful of the merciful." We responded to him and removed from him the harm that was afflicting him, restored his family to him and the same again with them, as a mercy direct from Us and a reminder to all worshippers." [Surat-ul-Anbiyaa' 21:83-84]

The superior morality shown by Prophet Ayyoob (as) when he was faced with this situation can be understood from his sincere prayer to Allah. When he was in trouble and sick, he turned to Allah, not away from Him. He showed steadfastness and patience, knowing that only Allah's mercy and compassion would help him.

As we can see in these and all other cases, Allah helps those who are patient. One verse expresses this assistance, as follows:

"And be steadfast. Allah is with the steadfast." [Surat-ul-Anfal 8:46]

5. Patience when Facing Injustice

Those who do not follow the Qur'an's morality cannot exercise true justice. They do not consider that they will have to account for all of their actions in the Afterlife, and so they feel no need to be careful in this matter. Since they follow their earthly desires rather than their consciences, they make impulsive, instead of rational, decisions. When they become angry, they immediately succumb to their anger and seek revenge. Such acts fill the newspapers and the television newscasts. We hear about it when someone attacks his boss when he is fired, slanders somebody who has interfered with her business, spreads malicious gossip about his fiancée who broke up with him, or responds to a person who threatens her with even worse threats. We meet such people all the time. They respond to a bad act or an injustice, in the same manner, and they violate the morality called for by the Qur'an. Indeed, sometimes people may even try to kill those who have interfered with their interests.

The faithful may be subjected to the unjust behavior of such people as part of their lifelong test. Unlike those given as examples above, they do not respond to injustice with injustice or to wrongdoing with more wrongdoing. But this does not mean that they stand by idly and do nothing to fight such injustice. However, rather than making rash decisions and jumping to conclusions, they act at all times in a well-balanced manner that comes from their trust in Allah.

Their patience and steadfastness in such cases springs from their awareness that Allah controls everything and possesses eternal justice. Allah tells us that on the Day of Judgment, everybody will have to account for what they did while in this world, and that no injustice will be done to them. Hence, those who committed injustice thoughtlessly, or behaved in an unfair manner, will receive their "reward" on that day. Allah's eternal justice is described as follows:

"We will set up the just balance on the Day of Rising, and no one will be wronged in any way. Even if it is no more than the weight of a grain of a mustard-seed, We will produce it. We are sufficient as a Reckoner." [Surat-ul-Anbiyaa' 21:47]

"There are only grounds against those who wrong people and act as tyrants in the land without any right to do so. Such people will have a painful punishment." (Surat-ush-Shu'raa' 42: 42]

Have fear of a Day when you will be returned to Allah. Then every self will be paid in full for what it earned. They will not be wronged. [Surat-ul-Baqarah 2:281]

The faithful who know this law of Allah are patient in the face of injustice, thanks to the serenity that they have inside themselves. In the following verse, Allah promises that in exchange for this patience, He will bring help:

"Allah will certainly help those who help Him—Allah is All-Strong, Almighty." [Surat al-Hajj, 40]

Selected Story
Prophet Yousuf Defeats Injustice with Faith and Patience

Prophet Yousuf (as) faced many injustices throughout his life, especially from his brothers. He faced such unfortunate injustice with remarkable devotion and patience; Allah helped him and gave him strength. All that happened to him from his childhood onward was designed to test his patience, and that of his father, Prophet Ya`qoob (as). First, Prophet Yousuf (as) was thrown into a well by his jealous brothers. After this, a passing caravan found him and took him to Egypt, were he was sold as a slave. The Qur'an speaks of Prophet Ya`qoob's (as) patience when confronted with this event, and of his request to Allah for help against this plot. Allah says in Surat Yousuf,

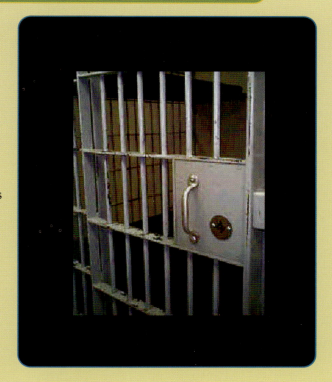

"They then produced his shirt with false blood on it. He [Ya`qoob] said: "It is merely that your lower selves have suggested something to you which you did, but beauty lies in showing steadfastness. Allah alone is my help in the face of the event you describe." [12: 18]

In addition to this, Prophet Yousuf (as) was slandered by the wife of his master, the Egyptian vizier. Even though his innocence was perfectly clear, Prophet Yousuf (as) was thrown into prison, where he remained for many years. However, he never forgot that Allah was testing him, and so he took refuge in Him, asked for His help, and exhibited outstanding patience. He did not forget that Allah would eventually confound the schemes of the unbelievers and that the faithful would be successful. In return for his steadfast devotion and patience, Allah gave him blessings that would please him both in this world and in the Afterlife.

"The king said: "Bring him to me straight away, so that I may draw him very close to me." When he had spoken with him, he [the king] declared: "Today you are trusted, established in our sight." He [Yousuf] said: "Entrust the treasures of the land to me, for in truth I am a knowing guardian." Thus We established Yousuf in the land so that he could live in any place he pleased. We grant Our grace to anyone We will, and do not allow to go to waste the wage of any people who do good. But the wages of the Hereafter are the best for people who believe and have done their duty." [Surat Yousuf 12: 54-57]

Years after these events, Allah brought Prophet Yousuf عليه السلام face-to-face with his treacherous brothers. He described his faith in Allah, despite the injustice that he had suffered, and the compassion that Allah had shown him, as follows:

"They asked: 'Are you Yousuf?' He said: 'I am indeed Yousuf, and this here is my brother. Allah has acted graciously to us. As for those who do their duty and are steadfast, Allah does not allow to go to waste the wage of any people who do good." [Surat Yousuf 12:90]

All of this material related in the Qur'an about Prophet Yousuf عليه السلام is an important example of the ultimate hidden causes that can be revealed by patience. The help that Allah gave to Yousuf is equally available for those who are faithful. Allah thwarts the plots devised against the believers, and He responds to the injustices committed against them.

6. Patience with Slander, Hurtful Words, and the Mistakes of Others

Allah says that among the tests believers may face are troubling statements made by the unbelievers, as follows:

"You will hear many abusive words from those given the Book before you, and from those who are unbelievers. But if you are steadfast and guard against evil, that is the most resolute course to take. [3:186]

All prophets throughout history have met with slander and accusations from the peoples to whom they were sent. In particular, the leaders of these people who deny faith take the lead in such behavior and try to incite the unbelievers against the believers.

The most important reason for this is that the true religion offers a moral code that may deprive them of some worldly advantages that they obtained by unjust means. Since the leaders hold a superior position in their communities in terms of wealth, rank, and status, they can easily exploit their people and convince them that injustice and wrongdoing are reasonable.

We can see one of the clearest examples of this in the behavior of Pharaoh, who enslaved and abused the Children of Isra'eel. Allah sent Prophet Musa عليه السلام as a savior to these people, who were exploited and forced to work in very arduous conditions. Pharaoh understood that the true religion instructed him to behave justly, mercifully, and with a good conscience toward the Children of Isra'eel. Instead of obeying Allah, he tried to discredit Prophet Musa (as) and his followers in the people's eyes. By doing this, he thought that nobody would respect the religion preached by Prophet Musa (as), and that a danger to his own interests would thereby be averted. He also hoped that such slander would destroy the believers' morale and that they might abandon their efforts to spread the faith. The Qur'an relates some of these slanders, as follows:

"We sent Musa with Our Signs and clear authority to Pharaoh, Haman, and Qarun. But they said: "A lying magician." [40:23-24]

"But he turned away with his forces, saying: "A magician or a madman!" [51:39]

What Pharaoh and his circle said to Prophet Musa (as) was not unique to them. All Allah's prophets and messengers who were sent to teach His religion faced the same accusations of lying and sorcery, being madmen or poets, or seeking profit for themselves. The fact that the faithful always have the same insulting words thrown at them, regardless of time or place, is not coincidental. On the contrary, these are tests that Allah created to observe their patience and steadfastness.

The Qur'an tells us of such situations, as follows:

"Equally, no messenger came to those before them without their saying: "A magician or a madman!" [Surat-uth-Thariyat 51:52]

Allah tells us that such insults were hurled at Prophet Muhammad ﷺ and his Companions:

"When they are told: "Believe in the way that the people believe," they exclaim: "What! Are we to believe in the way that fools believe?" No indeed! They are the fools, but they do not know it." [Surat-ul-Baqarah 2:13]

"When they were told, "There is no god but Allah," they were arrogant. They said, "Are we to forsake our gods for a mad poet?" [Surat-us-Saffat (37: 35-36)]

Faced with all of these slanderous remarks, Allah's Prophets and pious servants behaved with outstanding patience, took refuge in Him, and asked for His help. In the Qur'an, Allah responds to the behavior of the unbelievers who seek to abuse the prophets as follows:

"Do not obey the unbelievers and hypocrites, and disregard their abuse of you. Put your trust in Allah. Allah suffices as a Protector. [33:48]

As stated above, Allah points out that He expects the faithful to live by the Qur'an's morality regardless of what difficulties they may encounter. Thus, the faithful ignore all such behavior and move forward with devotion, patience, and true knowledge. In fact, without knowing it, the unbelievers' behavior only strengthens the believers' faith and increases the joy and excitement they feel about their religion and high moral code.

Keeping good friends usually requires patience and perseverance. Allah says in Surat-ul-Kahf:

"And keep yourself [O Muhammad] patiently with those [believers] who call on their Lord [your companions]." [18:28].

Hadeeth Shareef

عن ابن عباس رضي الله عنه: قال رسول الله ﷺ :
" المؤمن الذي يخالط الناس ويصبر على أذاهم خير من الذي لا يخالط الناس ولا يصبر على أذاهم."

رواه الترمذي وابن ماجه

The Prophet ﷺ said, "It is better for you to mix yourself around people who may harm you, and to be patient with them, than it is to isolate yourself from them, and to not practice patience from their harm."

Selected Story
Abu Bakr and the Slanderer

Once, a person was verbally abusing Abu Bakr رضي الله عنه while the Prophet ﷺ was curiously watching with a smile. After taking much abuse quietly, Abu Bakr responded to a few of the person's comments. At this, the Prophet exhibited his disapproval, got up, and left. Abu Bakr caught up with the Prophet and wondered, "O Messenger of Allah, he was abusing me and you remained sitting. When I responded to him, you disapproved and got up." The Messenger of Allah responded,
"There was an angel with you responding to him. When you responded to him, Satan took his place." He then said, "O Abu Bakr, there are three solid truths: if a person is wronged and he acts patiently (without seeking revenge) just for the sake of Allah Almighty, Allah will honor him and give him the upper hand with His help; if a person opens a door of giving gifts for cementing relationships with relatives, Allah will give him abundance; and, if a person opens a door of seeking charity for himself to increase his wealth, Allah will further reduce his wealth."

This story is reported by Musnad Ahmad, on the authority of Abu Hurayrah.

PROFILE

Bilal Ibn Rabah:

The Hero Who Taught the World Patience and Perseverance

Bilaal was an Abyssinian from Africa. His destiny made him a slave of some people of the tribe of Jum'ah in Makkah, where his mother was one of their slave girls. He led the life of a slave, whose bleak days were alike, and who had no right over his day and no hope for his tomorrow.

The Messenger of Allah (pbuh) and the holy religion of Islam made this weak Abyssinian slave a teacher to all humanity in the art of perseverance, faith, and defending it with whatever it takes.

When Bilal's owners found out he had embraced the religion of Islam, they would take him out in the mid-day sun heat when the desert sand created intense heat. They would throw him naked on its scorching rocks and bring a burning hot rock, which took several men to lift from its place, and throw it onto his body. This savage torture was repeated every day until the hearts of some of his tortures took pity on him. Finally, they agreed to set him free on condition that he would speak well of their gods, even with only one word. That would allow them to keep their pride so that the tribe of Quraysh would not say they had been defeated and humiliated by the resistance of their slave.

But even this one word, which he could simply say and with it buy his life and soul without losing his faith or abandoning his conviction, Bilal refused to say. Indeed, he refused to say it and began to repeat his lasting chant instead: "Ahad, Ahad, meaning the

One... the One!" (Allah is the One and Only God). His torturers shouted at him, imploring him, "Mention the name of Al-Laat and Al-'Uzzaa." But he answered, "The One. The One." They said to him, "Say as we say." But he answered them with remarkable mockery and sarcasm, "Indeed, my tongue is not good at that."

So Bilaal remained in the melting heat and under the weight of the heavy rock, and by sunset they raised him up and put a rope around his neck. Then they ordered their boys to take him around the hills and streets of Makkah. Bilaal did not mention anything other than his holy chant, "The One. The One."

When the night overtook them, they began bargaining with him, "Tomorrow, speak well of our gods. Say, `My lord is Al-Laat and Al `Uzzaa,' and we'll leave you alone. We are tired of torturing you as if we are the tortured ones." But he shook his head and said, "The One. The One." So, Umayah Ibn Khalaf, his master, kicked him and exploded with exasperating fury. He shouted, "What bad luck has thrown you upon us, O slave of evil? By Al-Laat and Al-'Uzzaa, I'll make you an example for slaves and masters." But Bilaal answered with the holy greatness and certainty of a believer, "The One. The One."

And he who was assigned to play the role of a sympathizer returned to talking and bargaining. He said "Take it easy, Umayah. By

A53

Al-Laat, he will not be tortured again. Bilaal is one of us and his mother is our slave girl. He will not be pleased to talk about and ridicule us because of his Islam." But Bilaal gazed at their lying cunning faces, and his mouth slackened like the light of dawn. He said with a calmness that shook them violently, "The One. The One."

It was the next day and midday approached. Bilaal was taken to the sun-baked ground. He was patient, brave, firm, and expecting the reward in the Hereafter.

Abu Bakr Al-Seddeeq went to them while they were torturing him and shouted at them, "Are you killing a man because he says, `Allah is my Lord?' Then he shouted at Umayah lbn khalaf, "Take more than his price and set him free." It was as if Umayah were drowning and had caught a lifeboat. It was to his liking and he was very much pleased when he heard Abu Bakr offering the price of Bilaal's freedom, since they had despaired of crushing him. And since they were merchants, they realized that selling him was more profitable to them than killing him.

They sold him to Abu Bakr, and he emancipated him immediately. Bilaal took his place among free men. When Al-Seddeeq put his arm round Bilaal, rushing with him to freedom, Umayah said to him, "Take him, for by Al-Laat and Al-' Uzzaa if you had refused to buy him except for one ounce of gold, I would have sold him to you." Abu Bakr realized the bitterness and disappointment hidden in these words. It was appropriate not to answer, but because they violated the dignity of this man who had become his brother and his equal, he answered Umayah saying, "By Allah, if you had refused to sell him except for a hundred ounces, I would have paid it." He departed with his companion to the Messenger of Allah, giving him news of his liberation, and there was a great celebration.

Source:"Men Around the Messenger(pbuh)." By Khalid Muhammad Khalid.

99 Names of Allah

As-Shakoor (The Thankfull and The Thanks-Deserving)

الشكور

CHAPTER REVIEW

Projects and Activities

Create an audio or video presentation explaining how a Muslim can observe patience in different various situations.

Stretch Your Mind

How does patience affect your behavior toward others.

Study Questions

1. Explain how a Muslim should react when losing a love one.
2. Explain how a Muslim should practice sabr in times of illness.
3. Explain how a Muslim should practice sabr losing property.
4. Explain how a Muslim should practice sabr in times of hunger.
5. Explain how a Muslim should practice sabr when hurt by slander.

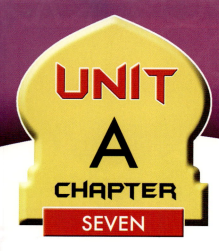

Shukr: Thankfulness to Allah

CHAPTER OBJECTIVES

1. Learn the concept of shukr in Islam.
2. Become inspired to demonstrate thankfulness to Allah in daily life.
3. Learn the three interrelated types of thankfulness.

VOCABULARY

Shukr — شُكْر

Ni'mah — نعمة

Shukr, or gratitude, is a very important principle in Islam. It is a quality of the believers and it is a source of all goodness. Shukr is used in the Qur'an sometimes as equivalent to faith. The faithful are thankful people to Allah and then to those who are kind to them. While the unfaithful are ungrateful to Allah and to the kind people around them.

The Qur'anic word for thanks and gratitude is shukr. It is mentioned in the Qur'an many times. It is the quality of human beings and it is also the quality of Allah. According to scholars, shukr means to recognize the favors of others. A faithful person thus is the one who acknowledges and recognize the endless favors of Allah.

Allah is the Source of All Favors and Blessings

Allah is the sole Creator of man and the whole universe. He made every single thing in the natural world and enabled us to utilize it for our own good. Allah says in Surat-ul-Mulk,

﴿ قُلْ هُوَ الَّذِي أَنشَأَكُمْ وَجَعَلَ لَكُمُ السَّمْعَ وَالْأَبْصَارَ وَالْأَفْئِدَةَ ۖ قَلِيلًا مَّا تَشْكُرُونَ ﴾

الملك: ٢٣

A56

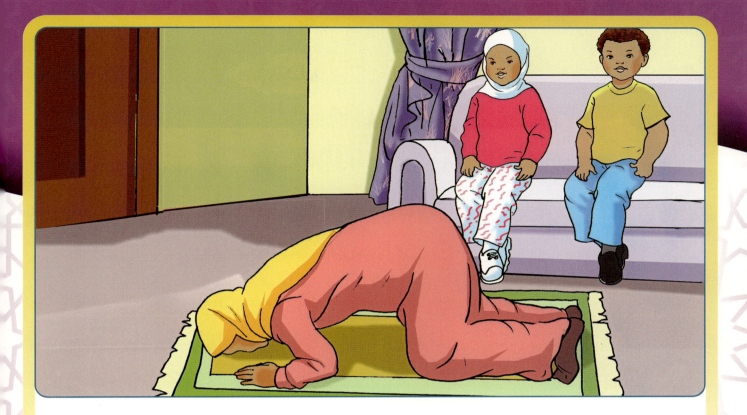

"Say: He is the One Who brought you into being and made for you the ears and the eyes and the hearts: little is it that you give thanks." [67:23]

﴿ هُوَ ٱلَّذِى جَعَلَ لَكُمُ ٱلۡأَرۡضَ ذَلُولٗا فَٱمۡشُواْ فِى مَنَاكِبِهَا وَكُلُواْ مِن رِّزۡقِهِۦۖ وَإِلَيۡهِ ٱلنُّشُورُ ۝ ﴾

الملك: ١٥

"He is the One Who made the earth smooth for you, therefore go about in the spacious sides thereof, and eat of His sustenance, and to Him is the return after death." [Surat Tabarak 67:15]

Every نِعْمَة ni'mah, or gift, we have in this world is from Allah. Allah says in Surat-un-Nahl,

﴿ وَمَا بِكُم مِّن نِّعۡمَةٖ فَمِنَ ٱللَّهِۖ ثُمَّ إِذَا مَسَّكُمُ ٱلضُّرُّ فَإِلَيۡهِ تَجۡـَٔرُونَ ۝ ﴾ النحل: ٥٣

"And whatever favor is (bestowed) on you it is from Allah; then whenever harm bothers you, you call upon Him and cry for aid." [16:53]

And the gifts of Allah cannot be counted, for he is giving us all things we need. Allah says in Surat-Ibraheem,

﴿ وَءَاتَىٰكُم مِّن كُلِّ مَا سَأَلۡتُمُوهُۚ وَإِن تَعُدُّواْ نِعۡمَتَ ٱللَّهِ لَا تُحۡصُوهَآۗ إِنَّ ٱلۡإِنسَٰنَ لَظَلُومٞ كَفَّارٞ ۝ ﴾

إبراهيم: ٣٤

"And He gives you of all that you ask Him; and if you count Allah's favors, you will not be able to number them; most surely man is very unjust, very ungrateful." [14:34]

Scholars call Surat-un-Nahl (The Bees) the surah of the favors of Allah. In this particular surah, Allah details many of his favors, blessings and gifts He granted to mankind and His other creations. Recite and reflect upon the following beautiful ayaat:

سورة النحل
Surat-un-Nahl 1-18

أَتَىٰ أَمْرُ ٱللَّهِ فَلَا تَسْتَعْجِلُوهُ ۚ سُبْحَٰنَهُۥ وَتَعَٰلَىٰ عَمَّا يُشْرِكُونَ ۝١ يُنَزِّلُ ٱلْمَلَٰٓئِكَةَ بِٱلرُّوحِ مِنْ أَمْرِهِۦ عَلَىٰ مَن يَشَآءُ مِنْ عِبَادِهِۦٓ أَنْ أَنذِرُوٓا۟ أَنَّهُۥ لَآ إِلَٰهَ إِلَّآ أَنَا۠ فَٱتَّقُونِ ۝٢ خَلَقَ ٱلسَّمَٰوَٰتِ وَٱلْأَرْضَ بِٱلْحَقِّ ۚ تَعَٰلَىٰ عَمَّا يُشْرِكُونَ ۝٣ خَلَقَ ٱلْإِنسَٰنَ مِن نُّطْفَةٍ فَإِذَا هُوَ خَصِيمٌ مُّبِينٌ ۝٤ وَٱلْأَنْعَٰمَ خَلَقَهَا ۗ لَكُمْ فِيهَا دِفْءٌ وَمَنَٰفِعُ وَمِنْهَا تَأْكُلُونَ ۝٥ وَلَكُمْ فِيهَا جَمَالٌ حِينَ تُرِيحُونَ وَحِينَ تَسْرَحُونَ ۝٦ وَتَحْمِلُ أَثْقَالَكُمْ إِلَىٰ بَلَدٍ لَّمْ تَكُونُوا۟ بَٰلِغِيهِ إِلَّا بِشِقِّ ٱلْأَنفُسِ ۚ إِنَّ رَبَّكُمْ لَرَءُوفٌ رَّحِيمٌ ۝٧ وَٱلْخَيْلَ وَٱلْبِغَالَ وَٱلْحَمِيرَ لِتَرْكَبُوهَا وَزِينَةً ۚ وَيَخْلُقُ مَا لَا تَعْلَمُونَ ۝٨ وَعَلَى ٱللَّهِ قَصْدُ ٱلسَّبِيلِ وَمِنْهَا جَآئِرٌ ۚ وَلَوْ شَآءَ لَهَدَىٰكُمْ أَجْمَعِينَ ۝٩ هُوَ ٱلَّذِىٓ أَنزَلَ مِنَ ٱلسَّمَآءِ مَآءً ۖ لَّكُم مِّنْهُ شَرَابٌ وَمِنْهُ شَجَرٌ فِيهِ تُسِيمُونَ ۝١٠ يُنۢبِتُ لَكُم بِهِ ٱلزَّرْعَ وَٱلزَّيْتُونَ وَٱلنَّخِيلَ وَٱلْأَعْنَٰبَ وَمِن كُلِّ ٱلثَّمَرَٰتِ ۗ إِنَّ فِى ذَٰلِكَ لَءَايَةً لِّقَوْمٍ يَتَفَكَّرُونَ ۝١١ وَسَخَّرَ لَكُمُ ٱلَّيْلَ وَٱلنَّهَارَ وَٱلشَّمْسَ وَٱلْقَمَرَ ۖ وَٱلنُّجُومُ مُسَخَّرَٰتٌۢ بِأَمْرِهِۦٓ ۗ إِنَّ فِى ذَٰلِكَ لَءَايَٰتٍ لِّقَوْمٍ يَعْقِلُونَ ۝١٢ وَمَا ذَرَأَ لَكُمْ فِى ٱلْأَرْضِ مُخْتَلِفًا أَلْوَٰنُهُۥٓ ۗ إِنَّ فِى ذَٰلِكَ لَءَايَةً لِّقَوْمٍ يَذَّكَّرُونَ ۝١٣ وَهُوَ ٱلَّذِى سَخَّرَ ٱلْبَحْرَ لِتَأْكُلُوا۟ مِنْهُ لَحْمًا طَرِيًّا وَتَسْتَخْرِجُوا۟ مِنْهُ حِلْيَةً تَلْبَسُونَهَا وَتَرَى ٱلْفُلْكَ مَوَاخِرَ فِيهِ وَلِتَبْتَغُوا۟ مِن فَضْلِهِۦ وَلَعَلَّكُمْ تَشْكُرُونَ ۝١٤ وَأَلْقَىٰ فِى ٱلْأَرْضِ رَوَٰسِىَ أَن تَمِيدَ بِكُمْ وَأَنْهَٰرًا وَسُبُلًا لَّعَلَّكُمْ تَهْتَدُونَ ۝١٥ وَعَلَٰمَٰتٍ ۚ وَبِٱلنَّجْمِ هُمْ يَهْتَدُونَ ۝١٦ أَفَمَن يَخْلُقُ كَمَن لَّا يَخْلُقُ ۗ أَفَلَا تَذَكَّرُونَ ۝١٧ وَإِن تَعُدُّوا۟ نِعْمَةَ ٱللَّهِ لَا تُحْصُوهَآ ۗ إِنَّ ٱللَّهَ لَغَفُورٌ رَّحِيمٌ ۝١٨

Understood Meaning

[1] Allah's commandment has come, therefore do not desire to hasten it; glory be to Him, and highly exalted be He above what they associate (with Him).

[2] He sends down the angels with the inspiration by His commandment on whom He pleases of His servants, saying: Give the warning that there is no god but Me, therefore be careful (of your duty) to Me.

[3] He created the Heavens and the Earth with the truth, highly exalted be He above what they associate (with Him).

[4] He created man from a small seed and lo! he is an open contender.

[5] And He created the cattle for you; you have in them warm clothing and (many) advantages, and of them do you eat.

[6] And there is beauty in them for you when you drive them back (to home), and when you send them forth (to pasture).

[7] And they carry your heavy loads to regions which you could not reach but with distress of the souls; most surely your Lord is Compassionate, Merciful.

[8] And (He made) horses and mules and asses that you might ride upon them and as an ornament; and He creates what you do not know.

[9] And upon Allah it rests to show the right way, and there are some deviating (ways); and if He please He would certainly guide you all aright.

[10] He it is Who sends down water from the cloud for you; it gives drink, and by it (grow) the trees upon which you pasture.

[11] He causes to grow for you thereby herbage, and the olives, and the palm trees, and the grapes, and of all the fruits; most surely there is a sign in this for a people who reflect.

[12] And He has made subservient for you the night and the day and the sun and the moon, and the stars are made subservient by His commandment; most surely there are signs in this for a people who ponder;

[13] And what He has created in the Earth of varied hues most surely there is a sign in this for a people who are mindful.

[14] And He it is Who has made the sea subservient that you may eat fresh flesh from it and bring forth from it ornaments which you wear, and you see the ships cleaving through it, and that you might seek of His bounty and that you may give thanks.

[15] And He has cast great mountains in the Earth lest it might be convulsed with you, and rivers and roads that you may go aright,

[16] And landmarks; and by the stars they find the right way.

[17] Is He then Who creates like him who does not create? Do you not then mind?

[18] And if you would count Allah's favors, you will not be able to number them; most surely Allah is Forgiving, Merciful.

Humans Must Grateful to Their Creator

The Qur'an teaches that human beings were created by God for the purpose of being grateful to him. ''It is he who brought you forth from the wombs of your mothers when you knew nothing, and he gave you hearing and sight and intelligence and affection so that you may give thanks (to God)'' [Surat-un-Nahl 16:78].

The Qur'an also explains that one of Satan's main aims is to keep people from being grateful. After God sent him out of the garden for his arrogance and disobedience, Satan vowed in response: ''I will lie in wait for them (human beings) on your straight way. Then I will assault them from in front of them and behind them, from their right and their left. Nor will you find, in most of them, gratitude (for your mercies).'' [Surat-ul-Araf 7:16-17]

Most faiths emphasize being grateful to God as a means of worship. At the essence of Islam is the teaching that those seeking inner peace must develop patience and trust in God such that they are thankful to him in every situation.

According to Islamic belief, one reason God allows people to undergo difficulty and trials during their lives is to test who will remain grateful to him. People who remain thankful, even in the face of great hardship, enter into a state of intimacy with their Lord. They attain an inner peace that protects them from the storms of the outside world.

Most of us can easily list many blessings for which we are thankful. We also tend to find it easy to list the difficulties in our lives. We often think that if God would just fix our problems for us, then we would be completely content. Our challenge is to learn to always be thankful for and content with God's bounties, even in adversity.

Gratitude to God does not arise from the removal of external stressors; rather, it is an internal state of the heart. This state is consciously achieved by continuous struggle and effort as we reflect on the blessings and mercy of God and strive to block out the whispers of negativism and discontent that keep our souls in a state of ingratitude.

The Prophets Were Thankful

Allah has described His prophets and messengers among those who were thankful people. Prophet Noah was a grateful servant of Allah (*Nuh; surely he was a grateful servant 17:3).* Prophet Abraham used to thank Allah for His many blessings (Surely Ibraheem was an exemplar, obedient to Allah, upright, and he was not of the polytheists. *Grateful for His*

favors; He chose him and guided him on the right path.16:121). Prophet David and his family were told to be grateful to Allah (*give thanks, O family of Dawood! and very few of My servants are grateful. 34:13).* Allah told His Prophet Muhammad: (*Nay, but worship Allah, and be of those who give thanks) [Surat-uz-Zumar 39:66].*

Prophet Muhammad Teaches Muslims the gratitude to Allah

Prophet Muhamad obeyed Allah and was a role model in showing his faithful gratitude to Allah. He used to thank Allah day and night. When he woke up, he would say, "Thanks be to Allah Who brought us to life after He made us to die, and to Him is the

resurrection." And when the Prophet ﷺ went to bed, he would say, "In Your name I die and I live." (Al-Bukhari).

When the Prophet ﷺ ate or drank, he would say, "Thanks be to Allah Who gave us food and drink and made us Muslims." (At-Tirmithi).

Whenever the Prophet ﷺ put on any new garment, he would say, "O Allah, thanks be to You; You gave me this to wear. I ask You to give me the good of this clothing and the good for which it is made, and I ask You to protect me from the evil of this clothing and from the evil of that for which it is made." (At-Tirmidhi).

When the Prophet (peace and blessings be upon him) mounted his camel to go on a journey, he would say "Allahu Akbar" (Allah is the Greatest) three times and then he would say, "Glory to Him Who has subjected these to our (use), for we could never have accomplished this (by ourselves). And to our Lord, surely, must we turn back! [43:13]. O Allah, we ask You on this journey righteousness and piety and the deeds that are pleasing to You. O Allah, make this journey easy for us and shorten its distance. O Allah, You are the Companion in journey and You are the Guardian for the family (left behind). O Allah, we ask You to protect us from the exhaustion of traveling, from bad scenes, and from a bad return to our property and family." When he returned he would say, "Returning, repenting, worshiping, and praising our Lord." (Muslim).

Islam does not only teach us to thank Allah, but we are also told to thank our parents, our spouses, our friends, our neighbors, and all those who do any good to us. The Prophet (peace and blessings be upon him) said, "Those who do not thank people, they do not thank Allah." (At-Tirmidhi).

Types of Thankfulness

To become a thankful servant to Allah, one should show his or her gratefulness to Allah through his or her (1) heart, (2) tongue and (3) all physical powers. Let us learn about these three interrelated types of thankfulness in some detail.

1. Shukr-ul-Qalb, or thankfulness felt in the heart . This is the most important type of thankfulness a Muslim should always experience. One time Prophet Musa spoke to Allah and said, "O Allah how can I thank you when I know that if I worship you all the time would not pay you back for only my eye sight!" Then Allah revealed to him "These thankful feelings in your heart are enough for me." Grateful inner feelings, then, are much appreciated by Allah.

2. Shukr-ul-Lisan, or thankfulness expressed by the tongue. A thankful person often expresses his or her gratefulness to his Creator for all His favors. Allah says in Surat-ud-Duha,

وَأَمَّا بِنِعْمَةِ رَبِّكَ فَحَدِّثْ ﴿١١﴾ الضحى: ١١

"And [acknowledge] and announce the favor of your Lord." [93:11]

A thankful Muslim always praises Allah and expresses his gratefulness to Allah during his prayers, du'aa', and verbal communications with others. It is important to remember the first ayah in the Qur'an, after the Basmalah,

الْحَمْدُ لِلَّهِ رَبِّ الْعَالَمِينَ ﴿٢﴾ الفاتحة: ٢

"All praise is due to Allah, the Lord of the Worlds." [Surat-ul-Fatihah 1:2]

Imam Ibn Katheer commented that denying the favors of Allah means hiding his gifts and/or relating them to others than Allah.

3. Shukr-ul-Jawarih, or Thankfulness expressed by the body and the limbs. This is the characteristic of the true believer. He or she always demonstrates his or her gratefulness through worship, loyalty, and readiness to serve Allah and His faith. Thankfulness to God can take many forms, including, but not limited to:

a. Prayer, fasting, charity, Hajj, Omrah, and other types of Ibadah, or worship. These rituals are physical expressions of offering gratitude to Allah. Rasoolullah ﷺ used to stand for long hours in Qiyam-ul-layl every night to the extent his feet swelled. A'ishah (ra) asked him, "Why do you do this when Allah has already forgiven you everything before and everything after? "He said:

أَفَلا أَكُونُ عَبْداً شَكُوراً

"Then shall I not be a grateful 'servant?"

b. Sujood-us-Shukr, or the Prostration of Thankfulness. This is a special Islamic ritual of showing gratitude to Allah. When the servant receives a blessing from Allah, or when Allah saves him from a disaster, he should simply fall in prostration thanking Allah for His favors. Rasoolullah used to prostrate to Allah whenever he received a pleasant thing or was told good news. This prostration, which is called Sujood-ush-Shukr, is conducted for the sole purpose of giving thanks to Allah, the Granter of favors and blessings, that the servant received.

Abdur-Rahman ibn 'Auf (R) narrated that Rasoolullah went out once and he followed him until he entered a grove of palm trees where he prostrated. His prostration was so long that 'Abdur-Rahman feared that Allah had taken his soul. 'Abdur-Rahman came to look at him and he raised his head and said: "What is wrong, Abdur-Rahman'?" The Prophet continued: "Gibreel came to me and said: 'Shall I not give you good news? Allah says to you, 'Whoever prays upon you, I pray upon him. Whoever salutes you, I salute him.' Therefore, I prostrated to Allah in thanks." [Reported by Ahmad and Al-Haakim]

How to pray Sujood-ush-Shukr

1. Say "Allahu Akbar" while standing, then make sujood on the floor.

2. During sujood, say "Subhana Rabiyal-A'la" three times and then praise Allah, and thank Him for His favor.

3. Say "Allahu Akbar," and raise your back to a sitting position.

Note: There is no need to make salam to the right and the left, like in regular prayer.

c. Helping other people. Helping those in need of our help is an important good deed and way to thank Allah for His favors. Allah likes the people who are helpful to His sevants, thus He will continue to shower them with His blessings. Prophet Muhammad ﷺ said,

"As the grants from Allah to a servant increase, so will the people's needs. If the servant ignores their needs, it will cause Allah's grants to him to be removed." [Reported by lbn Hibban].

The Prophet ﷺ also said, "If anyone strokes an orphan's head, doing so only for Allah's sake, he will have blessings for every hair over which his hand passes; and if anyone treats well an orphan girl or boy under his care, he and I shall be like these two in Paradise," putting two of his fingers together." [Reported by At-Tirmithi].

In conclusion, thanksgiving is not only a particular religious act or service; it is the whole life. The whole life should be lived in obedience to our Ultimate Benefactor, Allah. He created us and He has been good to us. Therefore, in our thankfulness we should always acknowledge His great favors, express our gratefulness to Him, and worship and serve Him.

Du'aa'

اللهم أَعِنّي عَلى ذِكْرِكَ وَشُكْرِكَ وَحُسْنِ عِبادَتِك

Mu'ath Ibn Jabal narrated that Rasoolullah once said to him "O Mu'ath, I love you. Let me teach you something: (the duah at the end of salah) Allahumma a'innee ala thikrika, wa shukruka, wa hussni ibadatik..

(O Allah help me to remember You, to show gratefulness to You, and to worship You well.) [Reported by Abu Dawood and An-Nasa'ee]

CHAPTER REVIEW

Projects and Activities

1. Create a poster showing the three types of thankfulness to God.

2. Create a Power Point a Flash presentation, or a video that shows how to perform Sujood-ush-Shukr.

Stretch Your Mind

1. How does gratefulness to Allah affect your behavior toward others.

2. From ayaat 1-18 of Surat-un-Nahl, infer the different favors and gifts that Allah grants mankind.

Study Questions

1. Explain the principle of shukr in Islam.
2. Define ni'mah, Shukr-ul-Qalb, shukr-ul-Lisan, Shukr-ul-Jawarih.
3. What are the three types of Shukr?
4. Explain how a Muslim should practice gratefulness to Allah in his or her heart.
5. Explain how a Muslim should practice gratefulness to Allah by his or her tongue.
6. Explain how a Muslim should practice gratefulness to Allah by his or her body.
7. Write a du'aa' you can say, in Arabic and English, praying to Allah to help you thank Him.
8. Describe how one can perform Sujood-ush-Shukr.

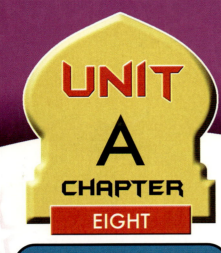

UNIT A CHAPTER EIGHT
LESSON ONE

سورة القيامة

Surat-ul-Qiyamah: Verses (1-15)
The Day of Judgment Is Inevitable

LESSON OBJECTIVES

1. Learn and memorize ayaat 1-15 of Surat-ul-Qiyamah.
2. What is Yawm-ul-Qiyamah?
3. Learn some of man's attitudes toward Allah.
4. Understand what the "blameful soul" is.

Introduction

This surah was revealed in Makkah. It includes forty ayaat that talk about death and the Day of Judgment. Towards the end of the surah, Allah tells us that the main reason for the kuffar not being affected by the Qur'an is that they are not afraid of the Day of Judgment. "No, they won't get it, and they are not afraid of the (punishment of the) Last Day." [Surat-ul-Muddathir 74:53] So in this surah, Allah starts by describing some of the terrors of that day.

Qur'anic Terms

يوم القيامة "Al-Qiyamah" means the standing, and here it means the standing in front of Allah during the Day of Judgment, which is also called in Arabic "Yawm-ul-Qiyamah." All people will stand then before Allah for questioning and judgment.

النفس اللوّامة "An-Nafs-ul-Lawwamah" means "the blameful soul." It is the person who often blames himself for committing sins. He or she feels awful when disobeying Allah.

Understood Meaning

(75:1) I swear by the day when people stand before their Lord
(75:2) And I swear by the blameful soul
(75:3) Does man think I will not gather his bones back together after they have turned to dust?
(75:4) Yes I can, and I can collect his fingers back together after they return to dust
(75:5) Actually humans want to commit sins now and delay becoming better people until later (when it will be too late)
(75:6) They ask, "When will the day of standing before our Lord come?"
(75:7) Then when the eyes are dazed (during Day of Judgment or death),
(75:8) When the moon is forever eclipsed,
(75:9) And the sun joins the moon in losing its light,
(75:10) On that day man will say, "Where can we escape to (from the terrors of that day)?"
(75:11) No, there is no hiding place of any kind to escape to.
(75:12) In front of your Lord is your final destination (for judgment).
(75:13) People will be told on that day exactly what good and bad deeds they have brought with them and what good deeds they missed back in their life.
(75:14) Actually, man knows what he did sin (and on the Day of Judgment their own bodies will testify against them about the sins they did),
(75:15) Even if he says his excuses to Allah

Lessons Learned

1. All People will Die and be Brought to Life Again for Yawm-ul-Qiyamah

People sometimes forget that they are going to die, and that Allah will bring them back to life during Yawm-ul-Qiyamah, the Day of Judgment. The kuffar, or the disbelievers, did not believe that they would live again after death. They argued with Prophet Muhammad and said that he was a liar. Rasoolullah told them that even after their bodies decompose and disappear, the bones and flesh will be put back together. Allah tells us here that we will surely live after death again. Then He will question us about our deeds in this life. We will also see the record of all our good and bad deeds.

2. The Blameful Soul

In this life, the believers are constantly regretful and blame themselves for not being better. They always see what they have done for Allah as small and insignificant. They always try to improve. These believers will be happy and content on the Day of Judgment. On the other hand, the disbelievers in this life are quite content with their behavior. But on the Day of Judgment they will be full of regret.

3. Disbelievers are Losers

It is said that this verse was revealed when some of the pagans of Makkah were making fun of the Day of Judgment. One of them said, "Even if I saw the bones come back together I wouldn't believe it." It is also reported that it was Abu Jahl who was ridiculing the Day of Judgment. Do you recall what happened to Abu Jahl and other idol worshipers? They all lost. By obeying Shaytan and disobeying Allah and His Prophet, they rejected the gift of faith and peace in this life, and the ultimate prize of Jannah in the next.

4. Look at Your Fingers and Fingerprints

After death, our bodies will change and then disappear. Even hard bones will disintegrate. When our fingers scatter around in the grave, no one can piece them back together in their perfect formation as before - no one, but Allah. This is how early Muslim scholars explained ayah 4.

Modern scholars, however, have suggested that this ayah also points to another lesson. They say that Allah attracts our attention to our fingerprints. Every human being has unique fingerprints, even identical twins who share the same DNA. No one can make the fingerprints of two people the same - no one, but Allah.

LESSON REVIEW

Stretch Your Mind

1. Choose an appropriate title of your own for this group of ayaat,

Study Questions

1. In what location was Surat-ul-Qiyamah revealed to Prophet Muhammad?
2. What does Yawm-ul-Qiyamah mean?
3. What is An-Nafs-ul-Lawwamah?
4. Can a person run away from Allah? Explain.

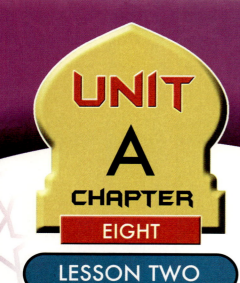

UNIT A
CHAPTER EIGHT
LESSON TWO

سورة القيامة

Surat-ul-Qiyamah: Verses (16-25)
Allah Teaches the Prophet

CHAPTER OUTLINE

1. Learn and memorize ayaat 16-25 of Surat-ul-Qiyamah.
2. Understand how the Prophet learned Al-Qur'an.
3. Understand the importance of good listening skills.
4. Learn about the destination of the believers in the Hereafter.
5. Learn what is the greatest joy a believer will experience in Jannah.

The Story of the Ayaat

When the Messenger of Allah was first receiving revelation, he was so in awe of the beautiful ayaat. He loved them so much that he became extremely worried that he would miss or forget something revealed to him. So he would hurriedly repeat the words he heard from Jibreel, even before Jibree had finished delivering them to him. Allah told him to listen to the full revelation, assuring him that He would enable him to learn the ayaat by heart once Jibreel left.

Understood Meaning

(75:16) O' Muhammad, do not move your tongue hurriedly to repeat the Qur'an while you are receiving it from Angel Jibreel.
(75:17) Do not worry, We will collect it in your heart (so that you can memorize it) and make it easy for you to recite it.
(75:18) So when Jibreel is finished revealing it to you, then recite it and follow what the Qur'an tells you to do.
(75:19) Then We will make the Qur'an clear for you so that you can explain it to others.
(75:20) No, you pagans, you love this life.
(75:21) And you neglect the next life (the Day of Judgment).
(75:22) Some faces on that day will be bright and happy,
(75:23) Looking at their Lord.
(75:24) And some faces on that day will be dark and gloomy,
(75:25) Knowing that the backbreaking punishment (being thrown into Hell) is going to hit them.

Lessons Learned

1. Listening Etiquettes: Allah teaches us an important lesson. When someone speaks to us, we should listen carefully. Most importantly, when someone reads Al-Qur'an or a hadeeth or teaches something about Islam, we should avoid interrupting. Instead we should listen carefully and understand what the person is trying to tell us. After we have listened to what he or she has said, we can then ask a question or write in our notebook.

2. How to Learn the Qur'an: These verses explain how we must learn the Qur'an. We should first read the Qur'an and follow what it tells us to do. As we do this, we will gain a better understanding of the message of the Qur'an. We will then see life through the Qur'an. Then we are ready to teach it to others. Abdullah ibn Mas'ood related that the companions used to learn ten verses at a time and they would not move on until they were putting into practice what those verses taught them. So they learned knowledge and practiced it at the same time.

From their noble example we can understand that the most important thing to do is to implement the things we learn in the Qur'an. Unfortunately, many people read the Qur'an but fail to practice it. A good Muslim applies Allah's guidance into his or her daily life immediately after he or she learns it.

3. Believers Will See Allah in the Hereafter. In these ayaat, Allah tells us great news. He said that we will see Him at some point during the next life. Rasoolullah also told us that the believers will be able to see Allah for the first time. Imams Al-Bukhari and Muslim reported that one night, Rasoolullah looked at the full moon and told a few Sahabah who were with him: "You will be able to see your Lord without any problem, as you can see this moon now." Then he advised his companions to be regular with their prayers, especially the Fajr and Asr prayers. In other ahadeeth, Rasoolullah said that the believers will enjoy looking at Allah more than anything else.

Related Literature
The Greatest Joy in Jannah

,In Jannah a caller will call: "O People of Paradise! Your Lord - Blessed and Exalted - requests you to visit Him, so come to visit Him!' So they will say: 'We hear and obey!' Until, when they finally reach the wide valley where they will all meet - and none of them will turn down the request of the caller - the Lord - Blessed and Exalted - will order His chair to be brought there. Then, pulpits of light will emerge, as well as pulpits of pearls, gemstones, gold, and silver. The lowest of them in rank will sit on sheets of musk, and will not see what those who are on the chairs above them are given. When they are comfortable where they are sitting, and are secure in their places, and the caller calls: 'O People of Paradise! You have an appointment with Allah in which He wishes to reward you!' So they will say: 'And what is that reward? Has He not already made our faces bright, made our scales heavy, entered us into Paradise, and pushed us away from the Fire?'

And when they are like that, all of a sudden a light will shine that encompasses all of Paradise. So, they raise their heads, and, behold: the Compeller - Exalted is He, and Holy are His Names - will come to them from above them and majestified them and say: 'O People of Paradise! Peace be upon you!' So, this greeting will not be responded to with anything better than: 'O Allah! You are Peace, and from You is Peace! Blessed are You, O Possessor of Majesty and Honor!' So the Lord - Blessed and Exalted - will laugh to them and say: 'O People of Paradise! Where are those who used to obey Me without having ever seen Me? This is the Day of Increase!'

So, they will all give the same response: 'We are pleased, so be pleased with us!' So, He will say: 'O People of Paradise! If I were not pleased with you, I would not have made you inhabitants of My Paradise! So, ask of Me!' So, they will all give the same response: 'Show us Your face so that we may look at it!' So, the Lord - Mighty and Majestic - will remove his covering and will majestify them

and will cover them with His Light, which, if Allah - the Exalted - had not willed not to burn them, would have burned them.

And there will not remain a single person in this gathering except that his Lord - the Exalted - will speak to him and say: 'Do you remember the day that you did this and that?' and He will remind him of some of his bad deeds in the Worldly life, so he will say: 'O Lord! Will you not forgive me?' So, He will say: 'Of course! You have not reached this position of yours (in Paradise) except by my forgiveness.'

So, how sweet is this speech to the ears, and how cooled are the righteous eyes by the glance at His Noble Face in the afterlife...

"Some faces that Day will be shining and radiant, looking at their Lord..."
   [Surat-ul-Qiyaamah 22-23)

Source: Haadil-Arwaah ila Bilad il-Afrah, pg. 193
By: Ibn-ul-Qayyim

LESSON REVIEW

Study Questions

1 Why did the Prophet repeat the ayaat as he was receiving them from Jibreel?

2 What did Allah instruct Prophet Muhammad to do while receiving the Qur'an?

3 Is Allah happy with the disbelievers' carelessness in terms of the next life? Explain why.

4 Describe how good people and bad people will look on the Day of Judgment.

5 What good news did Allah tell Prophet Muhammad in these ayaat?

6 What is the greatest joy in Jannah for the believers?

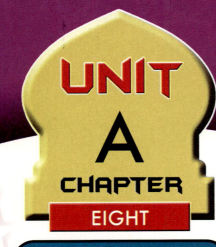

UNIT A
CHAPTER EIGHT
LESSON THREE

سورة القيامة

Surat-ul-Qiyamah: Verses (26-40)
Death and the Return Back to Allah

LESSON OBJECTIVES

1. Learn and memorize ayaat 26-40 of Surat-ul-Qiyamah.
2. How humans depart this life and return to their Lord.

The Story of the Ayaat

Concerning verses 34 and 35, it is said that the Messenger of Allah grabbed Abu Jahl (one of the enemies of Islam in Makkah) and said, "Terrible punishment is very close to you; it is so close! I say again, the terrible punishment is very close to you, it is so very close!" Then Abu Jahl said, "With what do you threaten me? Neither you nor your Lord can do anything to me. I am the best man in this valley. So Allah revealed verses 34 and 35.

(Reported in At-Tabari Book of Tafseer)

سورة القيامة
Surat-ul-Qiyamah 26-40

﴿ كَلَّا إِذَا بَلَغَتِ التَّرَاقِيَ ۝ وَقِيلَ مَنْ ۜ رَاقٍ ۝ وَظَنَّ أَنَّهُ الْفِرَاقُ ۝ وَالْتَفَّتِ السَّاقُ بِالسَّاقِ ۝ إِلَىٰ رَبِّكَ يَوْمَئِذٍ الْمَسَاقُ ۝ فَلَا صَدَّقَ وَلَا صَلَّىٰ ۝ وَلَٰكِن كَذَّبَ وَتَوَلَّىٰ ۝ ثُمَّ ذَهَبَ إِلَىٰ أَهْلِهِ يَتَمَطَّىٰ ۝ أَوْلَىٰ لَكَ فَأَوْلَىٰ ۝ ثُمَّ أَوْلَىٰ لَكَ فَأَوْلَىٰ ۝ أَيَحْسَبُ الْإِنسَانُ أَن يُتْرَكَ سُدًى ۝ أَلَمْ يَكُ نُطْفَةً مِّن مَّنِيٍّ يُمْنَىٰ ۝ ثُمَّ كَانَ عَلَقَةً فَخَلَقَ فَسَوَّىٰ ۝ فَجَعَلَ مِنْهُ الزَّوْجَيْنِ الذَّكَرَ وَالْأُنثَىٰ ۝ أَلَيْسَ ذَٰلِكَ بِقَادِرٍ عَلَىٰ أَن يُحْيِيَ الْمَوْتَىٰ ۝ ﴾

Understood Meaning

(75:26) No, when the soul almost reaches the throat at the time of death
(75:27) And the people around the dying person say, "Is there a healer that can heal him by reciting a prayer over him (this was a common practice for doctors back then)?"
(75:28) And the dying person realizes it is the end.
(75:29) And his two legs will stick together and get twisted because of the pain and difficulty of death.
(75:30) On that day you will be taken to your Lord.
(75:31) But he (the dying disbeliever) didn't believe in Allah's message or pray when he was alive.
(75:32) Instead he rejected the truth and turned away from it
(75:33) Then he walked to his family in an arrogant show-off way
(75:34) (How can you be so arrogant in rejecting your creator?) It had been better for you to believe because punishment is close to you, so close!
(75:35) I say it had been better for you to believe because punishment is close to you, so close!
(75:36) Does man think that I will just leave him to do whatever he likes and then just be left in the grave?
(75:37) Wasn't he once a small thing (in his mother's womb)?
(75:38) Then he became like a (hanging) blood clot, then he was molded and made a complete human being
(75:39) Then He made him either a male or a female
(75:40) Isn't the one who created people the first time capable of bringing the dead back to life?

Lessons Learned

1. The difficult time of death:

The time of death is a very serious time. Those who obeyed Allah throughout their lives will have a much easier death than those who disobeyed Allah or disbelieved in Him. The Angel of Death and the Angels of Mercy will be gentle with good servants of Allah when their soul is taken away. On the other hand, the Angel of Death and the Angels of Punishment will be firm with evil people as they die.

2. The journey back to Allah:

When a man dies he is wrapped with the kafan, or wrapping material. The people wrap his legs together, as Allah said in these ayaat, as well as the hands and the rest of the body. The dead person at that time will enter a different kind of life. It may be a wonderful life or a horrible one. It all depends on the person's behavior and how he spent his time on Earth. Good Muslims will gain Allah's mercy and go to Jannah. These are the people who believed in Allah, followed the Prophet's example, prayed and worshiped on time and in the proper manner and demonstrated great manners. On the other hand, disobedient Muslims and the disbelievers will suffer Allah's wrath and end up in Hell fire. They are the ones who disbelieved in Allah or disobeyed Him most of the time. They were lazy when it came to prayer and worship, and even if they did pray, they may not have performed it properly. They demonstrated insincerity and bad manners.

What should we say when we read or hear the last ayah?

Abu Hurayrah رضي الله عنه reported that Rasoolullah used to read verse (75:40) and say, " بلى bala, "or" Yes," or " سبْحانكَ بلى sub-hanaka bala, meaning praise be to you, yes." In another hadeeth, Rasoolullah said, "Yes, and to this I am a witness." This shows how we should interact with the Qur'an. If we truly feel the Qur'an when we read it, then we should naturally say, "O Allah, yes," when Allah asks a similar question to the one in this verse.

LESSON REVIEW

Study Questions

1. Why does Allah tell us about death in these verses?
2. How did the disbelievers behave when they heard what the Qur'an says about the Day of Judgment?
3. What will happen to the disbelievers at their time of death?
4. What will happen to the believers at their time of death?
5. Why did the disbelievers not believe that Allah is able to raise the dead on the Day of Judgment?
6. What should we say when we read or hear the last ayah of the surah?

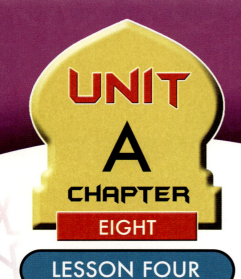

Tajweed: Types of Madd
Al-Madd: The Extension of the Vowels

UNIT A CHAPTER EIGHT — LESSON FOUR

Al-Madd (الـمَدْ) literally means "to lengthen, "or" to prolong. "In Tajweed, it means extending of the sound of a vowel letter." The Arabic vowels are:

ا	Alif
و	Waaw
ي	Yaa

The sign of madd is ~. Therefore, when you see an Arabic vowel with this sign on it, this means that the vowel should be pronounced in a prolonged manner.

In vowels to be extended, the letter preceding the و waaw should carry a dammah (madmoom); and the letter preceding ي yaa should carry a kasrah (maksoor). As for the ا alif, whatever precedes it must carry a fat-hah (maftooh).

سمآء	Alif	ا
سوء	Waaw	و
جيء	Yaa	ي

Types of Madd

There are many types of Madd:

1. Al-Madd-ut-Tabee'ee, or Normal
2. Al-Madd-ul-Lazim, or Mandatory
3. Al-Madd-ul-Muttasil, or Connected
4. Al-Madd-ul-Munfasil, or Disconnected
5. Madd-us-Silah, or Joining
6. Al-Madd-ul-Aarid Lissukoon, or Contingent upon Sukoon
7. Madd-ul-Badal
8. Madd-ul-Iwad

In this lesson, you will learn the most common Madd types in the Qur'an.

A78

In this lesson you will learn the first four types of Madd, leaving the rest of the Madd types until later.

1. Al-Madd-ut-Tabi'ee, or Normal Extension

In most cases, the vowels should not be extended beyond the normal level, which is called in Arabic "Madd Tabi'ee," or" Madd Asli. "The normal or original extension (المد الطبيعي), is when the vowel is not followed by a Hamzah (or a letter with a sukoon?). It is called normal because it follows the normal or natural sound (Tabi'ee) pronunciation without any decrease or increase in length. In this case, the vowel is held for two counts the same time you spend by counting "one, two," or simply for one second.

The examples of the Al-Madd-ut-Tabi'ee are highlighted in red below:

بِسْمِ اللهِ الرَّحْمانِ الرَّحِيمِ

﴿١﴾ الْحَمْدُ لِلّهِ رَبِّ الْعَالَمِينَ ﴿٢﴾ الرَّحْمانِ الرَّحِيمِ ﴿٣﴾ مَالِكِ يَوْمِ الدِّينِ ﴿٤﴾ إِيَّاكَ نَعْبُدُ وإِيَّاكَ نَسْتَعِينُ ﴿٥﴾

Notice that all of the highlighted vowels in the above ayaat from Surat-ul-Fatihah are not followed by a hamzah or sukoon. In these cases, you only pronounce these vowels for only one second of time, which is also called "Normal," or "Madd Tabi'ee."

You now learned about Al-Madd-ut-Tabi'ee, or the original madd. The rest of the Madd types are classified under what the scholars call, Al-Madd-ul-Fir'ee. These types include the following:

2. Al-Madd-ul-Lazim, or Mandatory Extension:

This type of Madd is called mandatory because the recitation must be necessarily and consistently lengthened to six counts, or three seconds, without exception. The mandatory lengthening (Al-Madd-ul-Lazim المد اللازم) takes place in two cases:

When the vowel is followed by a letter with shaddah.

Examples:

اهدِنَا الصِّرَاطَ الْمُسْتَقِيمَ ﴿٦﴾

صِرَاطَ الَّذِينَ أَنْعَمتَ عَلَيهِمْ غَيرِ الْمَغضُوبِ عَلَيهِمْ وَلاَ الضَّالِّينَ ﴿٧﴾

الْحَاقَّةُ ﴿١﴾ مَا الْحَاقَّةُ ﴿٢﴾ وَمَا أَدْرَاكَ مَا الْحَاقَّةُ ﴿٣﴾

When the vowel is followed by a sukoon in a particle way that comes in the beginning of some of the suwar.

Examples:

الم ﴿١﴾ ذلِكَ الْكِتَابُ لاَ رَيْبَ فِيهِ هُدًى لِّلْمُتَّقِينَ ﴿٢﴾

الر تِلْكَ آيَاتُ الْكِتَابِ الْمُبِينِ ﴿١﴾

ق وَالْقُرْآنِ الْمَجِيدِ ﴿١﴾

3. Al-Madd-ul-Muttasil (المد المتصل), Connected Extension:

Al-Madd-ul-Muttasil occurs when the vowel is followed by a Hamzah in the same word. It is called "connected lengthening" because the vowel is connected with an immediately following hamzah in one single word. Connected lengthening is compulsory, but the reciter has the choice to prolong it for four, five, or six counts (2, 2.5, or 3 seconds) at all of the recitation periods. That means that you cannot extend it for two seconds sometimes, and for three seconds at other times, during the same recitation setting.

Examples:

Examples:

سَأَلَ سَائِلٌ بِعَذَابٍ وَاقِعٍ ﴿١﴾

كُلُوا وَاشْرَبُوا هَنِيئًا بِمَا أَسْلَفْتُمْ فِي الْأَيَّامِ الْخَالِيَةِ ﴿٢٤﴾

4. Al-Madd-ul-Munfasil (المد المنفصل), Disconnected Lengthening:

Disconnected lengthening (Madd Munfasil) (المد المنفصل) occurs when the vowel is the last letter of a word, and it is followed by a hamzah that is on the first letter in the following word. It is called disconnected or separated lengthening because the vowel is separated from the hamzah which comes in the word immediately following. The Madd, or lengthening, here is optional, not compulsory. Therefore, you have two main choices in this case:

1. Prolong the vowel for four, five or six counts (2, 2.5, or 3 seconds).
2. Treat it as Madd Tabi'ee and extend the vowel for only two counts (1 second).

However, you have to prolong the vowels in this case for four, five or six counts in all your recitation period, or you shorten it to only two counts throughout.

Examples:

﴿ لَا أُقْسِمُ بِيَوْمِ الْقِيَامَةِ ۝١ وَلَا أُقْسِمُ بِالنَّفْسِ اللَّوَّامَةِ ۝٢ أَيَحْسَبُ الْإِنسَانُ أَلَّن نَّجْمَعَ عِظَامَهُ ۝٣ بَلَىٰ قَادِرِينَ عَلَىٰ أَن نُّسَوِّيَ بَنَانَهُ ۝٤ ﴾

بِسْمِ اللَّهِ الرَّحْمَٰنِ الرَّحِيمِ
﴿ قُلْ يَا أَيُّهَا الْكَافِرُونَ ۝١ لَا أَعْبُدُ مَا تَعْبُدُونَ ۝٢ وَلَا أَنتُمْ عَابِدُونَ مَا أَعْبُدُ ۝٣ وَلَا أَنَا عَابِدٌ مَّا عَبَدتُّمْ ۝٤ وَلَا أَنتُمْ عَابِدُونَ مَا أَعْبُدُ ۝٥ لَكُمْ دِينُكُمْ وَلِيَ دِينِ ۝٦ ﴾

CHAPTER REVIEW

Tajweed Exercises

1. Listen to your teacher or a professional reciter and observe how they recite all the examples in the lessons. Use Reciter.org or any other tool available to you.

2. Recite the ayaat in Surat-ul-Haqqah that have the types of Madd you have learned in this lesson.

3. Observe the Madd you learned in this lesson during your daily Qur'an recitation and during salah.

أَفَلَا يَعْلَمُ إِذَا بُعْثِرَ مَا فِي الْقُبُورِ ﴿٩﴾

وَحُصِّلَ مَا فِي الصُّدُورِ ﴿١٠﴾

إِنَّ رَبَّهُم بِهِمْ يَوْمَئِذٍ لَّخَبِيرٌ ﴿١١﴾

Study Questions

1. What is Madd?
2. List four types of Madd.
3. What are the letters of Madd?
4. In what situations must the Madd be observed?
5. In what situation do you have the choice to observe the Madd or not observe it?
6. Define the following types of Madd, and indicate for how long they should be observed:
   a. Al-Madd-ul-Lazim
   b. Al-Madd-ut-Tabi'ee
   c. Al-Madd-ul-Muttasil
   d. Al-Madd-ul-Munfasil

Portraits of Faith

Chapter One	Two Martyrs: The Stories of Prophets Zakariyya and Yahya	B4
Chapter Two	Purity of Faith: The Story of Maryam	B14
Chapter Three	The Miracle of Miracles: The Story of Prophet Isa	B24

Portraits of Faith

Introduction

The people who practice Judaism are traditionally known by several terms, such as Jews or the Children of Israel. Prophet Ya'qoob, whose father was Is'haaq, and whose grandfather was Ibraheem, was also called by the name Israel. His offspring, or descendants, are therefore the 'Children of Israel,' which is how the Qur'an refers to them.

Allah blessed the Children of Israel with many prophets and messengers in the Holy Land and surrounding areas. During their early history, they were devout to God and generally obedient to their prophets. When they began to drift away from Tawheed and worship, Allah blessed them with great prophets like Yousuf (Joseph), Musa (Moses), , Harun (Aaron), Dawood (David), Suleyman (Solomon), and many other prophets and messengers.

One major messenger of the Children of Israel was Prophet Musa, or Moses, whom Allah gave a divine revelation called At-Tawrah, or Torah. Historically, the Children of Israel encountered many difficulties and problems. They also fell into different forms of disobedience, disbelief and collective sin. Among these disobediences were their disobedience of their prophets, and sometimes the rejection and even killing of them.

Nations around the Holy Land were tempted to control this important region. Jeusalem, the hub of many prophets and messengers, was destroyed a few times by Roman and Persian forces. Among the losses were the Temple built by Suleyman, or Solomon, and religious manuscripts, including the Torah. Israelite priests, including Ezra, in around 400 B.C, tried to reconstruct the lost parts of the Torah on their own and from their collective memory. This caused many inaccuracies, corruption and loss to take place in the man-made manuscripts of the Torah.

Many of the Israelite priests also drifted away from their religious teachings and spiritual ideals. They became keen for worldly desires and temptations. Israelite prophets and sincere priests could not stop the spiritual deterioration in their nation. Among the last of the Israelite religious leaders were Zakariyya (Zachariah), Yahya (John), 'Imran, Maryam (Merriam, or Mary) and 'Isa (Jesus Christ) who was the last of all Israelite messengers. God made him as an extraordinary miracle to inspire the Israelites and other nations to return to the straight path.

In this unit you will learn about the latest Israelite prophets and religious personalities, including the magnificent stories of the Virgin Mary and her miraculous son, Prophet 'Isa, (Jesus Christ).

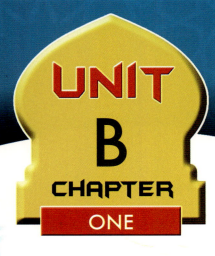

Two Martyrs: The Stories of Prophets Zakariyya and Yahya

CHAPTER OBJECTIVES

1. Learn about Prophets Zakariyya and Yahya.
2. Appreciate the faithfulness and piety of both of the prophets.
3. Briefly learn the relationship between Prophets Zakariyya, Yahya and 'Isa عليه السلام.
4. Appreciate the sacrifices prophets offer for the sake of Allah.
5. Learn and memorize ayaat 1-15 of Surat Maryam.

PEOPLE TO REMMEMBER

Zakariyya   زكريا

Yahya   يحيى

Zakariyya عليه السلام and Yahya عليه السلام were great prophets sent to the Children of Israel. Zakariyya was a righteous servant of Allah وتعالى سبحانه in a time and place where most of His people had forgotten the teachings of God, and they were interested in pursuing worldly pleasures. Zakariyya prayed for a righteous son who would continue to spread the message of Allah سبحانه وتعالى amongst the Children of Israel. His son, Yahya عليه السلام, and 'Isa عليه السلام, who were cousins, faced harsh treatment from their people. However, they held fast to the rope of Allah سبحانه وتعالى and continued working to spread the Truth, despite trials and tribulations.

To Zakariyya, in his old age, was born a so,n Yahya. Yahya was the herald of Jesus and was known as John the Baptist.

Who Was Zakariyya?

Zakariyya عليه السلام was one of the many great prophets who came to the Children of Israel. He worked to earn his living, and he also served as a priest to Allah in the temple at Jerusalem. He was among many other members of his family who worshipped and worked as a priest in the temple as well.

Zakariyya was saddened that many priests of his time served in the temple for power and praise. They no longer held the true spirit of sincerity to serve God and the people. Zakariyya was determined to remain faithful to Allah and sincerely serve his message. His fellow priests found his values and principles to be rigid, as they thought that his way gave no worldly benefit.

Zakariyya and Maryam

Zakariyya, as you will learn with more detais in the next chapter, used to watch over Maryam عليه السلام, the future mother of Jesus Christ, or Prophet 'Isa. Maryam was a relative of Zakariyya's wife and she grew up under Allah's سبحانه وتعالى special protection. A daughter of pious parents, she عليه السلام used to spend much time worshipping alone at the temple under Zakariyya's spiritual supervision. Her sustenance and food were given to her from Allah (SWT) and indeed her growth was a "goodly growth."

When Zakariyya entered her chamber, he would find her with sufficient food and fruit that were out of season. Allah says in Surat Al-Imran,

" He said: "O Maryam! Whence (comes) this to you?"
She said: "From Allah; for Allah provides sustenance to whom He pleases without measure." [3:37]

Although Zakariyya was very old, he wished that he would be blessed with a righteous offspring, just like Maryam.

A Father's Prayer

Zakariyya عليه السلام and his wife Elizabeth were devout, grateful, patient, and keen in serving their Lord and the people. Zakariyya عليه السلام was very old, and his wife was elderly as well, and barren. Now that he had reached old age, he was worried that there would be no one to continue spreading Allah's religion and practicing it. Thus, he desired to have a child of his own for spiritual reasons. He wanted to have a devout offspring who would be a sincere and faithful servant of Allah and a pious community leader. Since he was the prophet to the Children of Israel at that time, he thought that such a faithful personality would not develop within his community unless he raised and trained him.

Zakariyya was encouraged that if Allah سبحانه وتعالى could provide Maryam with special sustenance, then He might also bless them with a child, even in old age. His Tawakkul, or sincere reliance on Allah, and his faith were extremely strong. Therefore, Prophet Zakariyya عليه السلام turned to his Lord, praying for righteous offspring:

Understood Meaning

{1} Kaf Ha Ya Ain Suad.
{2} A mention of the mercy of your Lord to His servant Zakariyya.
{3} When he called upon his Lord in a low voice,
{4} "O my Lord! My bones became frail, and t my head is covered with grey hair: but I never failed as long as I pray to you!*
{5} Now I fear what my relatives [and colleagues will do] after me: but my wife is barren: so give me an heir,
{6} [One that] will [truly] represent me, and represent the family of Jacob; and make him, my Lord, please You.

A Prayer Answered

Allah knows what is in the hearts of men and women. While Zakariyya was standing in prayer, the angels called unto him:

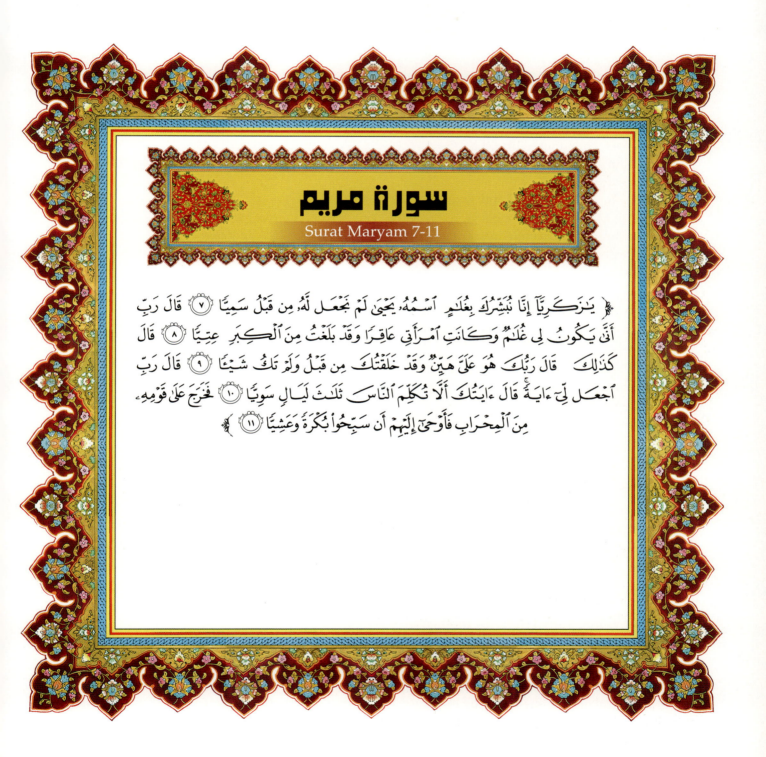

Understood Meaning

{7} O Zakariyya! surely We give you good news of a boy whose name shall be Yahya: We have not made before anyone his equal.
Zakariyya's du'aa' had been answered, but he was still in awe and surprise.
{8} He said: O my Lord! when shall I have a son, and my wife is barren, and I myself have reached indeed the extreme degree of old age?
{9} [God] said: So shall it be, your Lord says: It is easy to Me, and indeed I created you before, when you were nothing.
Zakariyya عليه السلام was elated and wanted to be sure:
{10} He said: My Lord! give me a sign. He said: Your sign is that you will not be able to speak to the people three nights while in sound health.
{11} So he went forth to his people from his place of worship, then he made known to them that they should glorify (Allah) morning and evening.

Zakariyya عليه السلام came out to his people from his chamber, and told them by signs to celebrate Allah's praises in the morning and in the evening. Zakariyya عليه السلام was a very grateful servant, as Allah سبحانه وتعالى had shown him mercy through accepting his Du'aa'. Allah bestowed on him a righteous son and blessed their family.

Yahya, the Righteous Son

God answered Zakariyya's عليه السلام prayers and bestowed him with a son, Yahya عليه السلام, or John who was wise, kind, obedient, and not rebellious.

We know that Yahya's عليه السلام mother was related to Maryam (P). Because Maryam was 'Isa's mother, Yahya عليه السلام and 'Isa عليه السلام were cousins by blood and spiritual brothers in task. Zakariyya, his wife Elizabeth, Maryam and her parents were all descendents of a priestly family. Their lineage goes back to Aaron, the brother of Musa and son of Imran.

> Men of God show their qualities in their private relationships, as much as in their public ministry. Zakariyya was anxious, in a world of unrighteousness,
> to find a successor to continue his godly errand. He was given a son, Yahya, who heralded Jesus and lived a life of wisdom, gentle love, and purity.

Allah's Grace

Allah سبحانه وتعالى chose Yahya as another messenger to the Children of Israel, like his father Prophet Zakariyya. Upon blessing him with prophethood, Allah ordered Yahya to hold to his message with all his power. This means that Allah wanted him to learn His guidance in a profound manner, and to practice it very thoroughly. Allah says in Surat Maryam:

Understood Meaning

{12} O Yahya! Take hold of the Book with strength, and We granted him wisdom while he was yet a child.
{13} And [he got] tenderness from Us and purity, and he was pious,
{14} And dutiful to his parents, and he was not rude, disobedient.
{15} And peace on him on the day he was born, and on the day he dies, and on the day he is raised to life

Yahya's Mission and Teachings

Imam Ahmad, on the authority of Al-Harith Al-Ash'ari, narrated that the Messenger of Allah سبحانه وتعالى said:"Allah ordered Yahya عليه السلام, the son of Zakariyya, عليه السلام with five commands, and to proclaim and establish these commands amongst the Children of Israel without delay. Therefore, Yahya عليه السلام gathered the Children of Israel in the Temple of Bayt Al-Maqdis, and he sat down on a high place. After praising God and thanking Him for His Grace, he said: "Allah Almighty ordered me to observe five commands, and to proclaim and establish these commands amongst you: (1) Worship Allah and worship none along with Him. (2) Offer prayers. (3) Observe fasting. (4) Give charity. (5) Continue your remembrance of Allah Almighty in your daily life.

God created you, and provided for you and sustained you. So, worship Him and do not associate partners with Him. And I order you to worship Allah سبحانه وتعالى, because the worshiper becomes closer to Allah سبحانه وتعالى when he prays to Him. I forbid you from turning away from Him. Fasting has been ordained for you; indeed the fasting person is like a jar of musk from which all the people passing by can benefit from the beautiful aroma.

Give charity, for indeed it is like the prisoner who has been captured and is ready to be executed, then asks his captor, "May I ransom myself?" Then he spends his own money to save his own neck. You must always remember Allah سبحانه وتعالى in your daily affairs, for the one who is in constant remembrance of Allah سبحانه وتعالى is like the man who is being chased by an enemy; after a tiring journey the man finds a fortress and seeks protection and security within it. Indeed Thikr, or remembrance of Allah وتعالى سبحانه, is one's fortress from Satan."

Incredible Piety

Even in his young life, Prophet Yahya was granted the following gifts:

(1) Wisdom and knowledge

(2) Empathy and love for all God's creatures

(3) Humility in his manners, his clothing and his possessions, as he despised luxury.

(4) Piety.

In addition to the above qualities, Prophet Yahya was very active in serving Allah وتعالى سبحانه, particularly during his youth. These characteristics in his personality were demonstrated through his conduct, as he loved God and loved God's creatures. He never used violence, nor did he ever mistreat any other human being or creature. He was particularly kind and merciful with his parents, always obedient to them.

"So peace on him the day he was born, the day that he dies, and the day that he will be raised up to life (again)! [19:15]

This ayah refers to the life of Yahya السلام عليه. Peace and blessings from Allah سبحانه وتعالى were bestowed upon his birth, during his life, at his unjust death at the hands of a tyrant, and most importantly on the Day of Judgment.

Prophet Yahya عليه السلام used to stay away from people because he loved to worship his Creator in solitude. He renounced the world and lived in the wilderness, until his family finally came looking for him because they missed his presence. They found him near the Jordan River, worshipping Allah وتعالى سبحانه. His parents cried tears of joy out of happiness that their son was a righteous and obedient young man who loved and feared Allah سبحانه وتعالى.

Bethlehem: Church of the Nativity: built over the cave where Jesus was born. One of the oldest churches in Christendom, from the 4th century.

Spiritual Brothers

Yahya عليه السلام was the forerunner of 'Isa عليه السلام. Just as his father had hoped, both Yahya and 'Isa served as Prophets of Allah سبحانه وتعالى, and they renewed the belief and message of Allah سبحانه وتعالى amongst the Children of Israel.

Yahya عليه السلام and 'Isa عليه السلام were sent to the same group of people, and they had a lot in common. They were brothers in spirit, and they were given complementary tasks as prophets of Allah سبحانه وتعالى. Yahya عليه السلام held fast to the teachings of Allah سبحانه وتعالى in a world which had not only forgotten these teachings, but people had also turned to evil and corruption in order to reap benefit. The greatness of Yahya عليه السلام was that he kept hold of God's teachings with all his might, not allowing any worldly affairs to distract him.

Yahya عليه السلام prepared the way for 'Isa عليه السلام, who came to renew and re-interpret the Torah. From the outset, 'Isa عليه السلام declared that he was the servant of God, thus negating the false notion that he was God or the son of God. Both 'Isa عليه السلام and Yahya عليه السلام shared the same devotion to the five commands that Allah سبحانه وتعالى ordered them

Yahya's Untimely Death

Yahya عليه السلام did not live long. He was imprisoned by Herod the Tetrarch, the provincial ruler under the Roman Empire. One time, Yahya scolded Herod for his sins and corruption. Eventually, Yahya عليه السلام was beheaded when Herod's mistress instigated him to kill the great Prophet.

It is said that Herod wanted once to marry his own niece, Herodias because she was very pretty. He then wanted to get the approval of Prophet Yahya because marrying a niece was prohibited in Judaism. The Prophet refused to approve a marriage that Allah has prohibited. He also gave a speech to the people in which he declared that it was a great sin and a crime of incest for anyone to marry his niece who was also before the wife of his half brother Philip and this marriage was prohibited in Hebrew law.

Herod's niece was an evil woman. She convinced the king to kill Prophet Yahya to clear the way to marry her uncle. The arrogant king sent his soldiers to kill Prophet Yahya, who was worshipping in the temple. Unfortunately, the evil soldiers viciously killed the Prophet while in prayer.

Shortly after the killing of Prophet Yahya, the same evil group killed Prophet Zakariyya too. Prophet Muhammad described the two martyred prophets as "the Martyr, and the son of the Martyr."

Yahya Tomb in the Ummayyad Mosque in Damascus

FAITH IN ACTION

★ Yahya عليه السلام was someone who did not 'go with the flow'. He decided to obey Allah سبحانه وتعالى even though the people treated him harshly because of it. As young people in today's world, many times we must choose to ignore 'the flow' in order to make the right choices. Next time you find it difficult to make the right decision, remember Yahya!

★ You can also make this du'aa' in times of hardship:

حسبي الله لا إله إلا هو . عليه توكلت وهو رب العرش العظيم.

Hasbiyal-laho-la-ilaha-illaho. Alayhi tawakalto wa howa Rabbol arshil adheem.

God suffices me. There is no God but He. On Him is my trust; He is the Lord of the Throne, Supreme!

CHAPTER REVIEW

Projects and Activities

1. Did you notice that many of the Prophets mentioned in this lesson were related to each other through kin? Make a family tree outlining how the prophets we have learned about were related through ancestry or kin.

2. You read that Zakariyya عليه السلام was a prophet and priest in the temple, and that many of the other priests no longer served Allah سبحانه وتعالى alone. Try doing some research on the Internet to find out more about the beliefs and practices of the people during the time of Zakariyya عليه السلام, Yahya عليه السلام, and 'Isa عليه السلام. Which other civilizations were present at that time?

Stretch Your Mind

1. We read in the story of Zakariyya عليه السلام that though he was a priest along with other priests in the temple, Zakariyya عليه السلام served for the sake of Allah سبحانه وتعالى, and the others did not. Even though many of their actions might have looked the same, their intentions were very different. Zakariyya عليه السلام had faith that Allah سبحانه وتعالى could make the humanly impossible possible. How does a sincere intention change the outcome of one's actions in this life and the next?

2. Prophet Zakariyya took care of his wife's niece, Maryam, while Herod the Tetrarch had a certain relationship with his niece. Draw lessons on the differences between the two stories.

Study Questions

1. What did Zakariyya عليه السلام pray for in his old age and why?

2. Describe Maryam عليه السلام and the miracles she experienced. How was she an encouragement for Zakariyya عليه السلام?

3. Why was Zakariyya عليه السلام given a sign to show the people the miracle he had experienced?

Purity of Faith: The Story of Maryam

CHAPTER OBJECTIVES

1. Learn the story of Maryam and admire her great personality.
2. Understand why Maryam was the greatest woman of all times.
3. Learn the events that led to the birth of Prophet 'Isa.
4. Appreciate the great miracle of the birth of 'Isa for a mother without a husband.
5. Appreciate the value and the benefits of purity, devotion and worship that were demonstrated by Maryam and her mother.
6. Learn and memorize ayaat 16-22 of Surat Maryam.
7. Learn and memorize the Hadeeth about the best women of all times.

PEOPLE TO REMMEMBER

Maryam	مَرْيَم
Imran	عِمْران
Hannah	حَنَّة
Zakariyya	زَكَرِيَّا
Yahya	يَحْيى

Next comes the story of Jesus and his mother Mary. She gave birth, as a virgin, to Jesus. But her people slandered and abused her. As a disgrace to her lineage. Her son. Was a servant of God, a true Prophet. Blessed in the gifts of Prayer and Charity. But no more than a man: to call him "The son of God" is to derogate from God's Majesty, for God is High above all His Creatures, the Judge of the Last Day.

Introduction

Imran عليه السلام was a righteous man who served of Allah سبحانه وتعالى among the Children of Israel. His people were disobedient to Allah سبحانه وتعالى, thus he and his wife Hannah desired to have a child that would continue to do Allah's سبحانه وتعالى work. They were blessed with a pious daughter Maryam عليها السلام, who was destined to be the mother of the holy Prophet 'Isa عليه السلام. Muslims believe that 'Isa عليه السلام was not crucified, but that he was taken up to the Heavens, and will return before the end of time.

The Chosen Ones

Allah say in Surat Al-Imran,

﴿ إِنَّ ٱللَّهَ ٱصْطَفَىٰٓ ءَادَمَ وَنُوحًا وَءَالَ إِبْرَٰهِيمَ وَءَالَ عِمْرَٰنَ عَلَى ٱلْعَٰلَمِينَ ۝ ذُرِّيَّةًۢ بَعْضُهَا مِنۢ بَعْضٍۗ وَٱللَّهُ سَمِيعٌ عَلِيمٌ ۝ ﴾ آل عمران: ٣٣-٣٤

"Allah did choose Adam and Noah, the family of Abraham, and the family of 'Imran above all people * Offspring, one of the other: and Allah hears and knows all things." Surat Al-Imran [33-34]

All prophets and messengers come from the same family tree of Adam, Nuh, Ibraheem and Imran that are mentioned in the ayah above. However, all women and men who love and obey Allah سبحانه وتعالى and His Messengers are all part of the same spiritual family.

The Birth of Maryam

Maryam, the daughter of 'Imran, came from a priestly family from the lineage of Prophet Dawood عليه السلام. We know that Maryam, the mother of Prophet 'Isa عليه السلام, was a relative of Prophet Yahya's عليه السلام mother. Therefore, Yahya عليه السلام and 'Isa عليه السلام were cousins by blood. They were also spiritual brothers as prophets and, in their efforts to obey Allah سبحانه وتعالى and spread the truth.

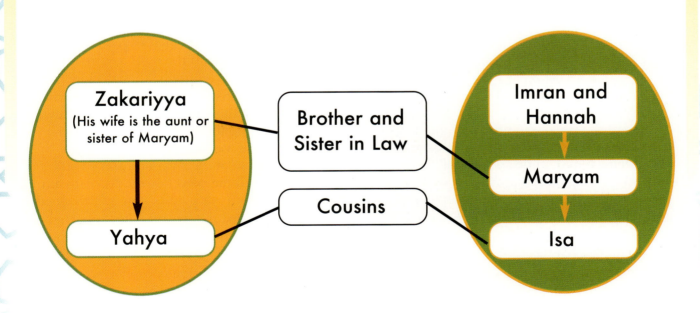

> In the Aramaic language, the name Maryam means "Servant of God."

Blessed Seed

'Imran, Maryam's father, was an Imam (Priest) for the Children of Israel in Bayt-ul-Maqdis. His wife, Hannah, was a very dedicated worshipper of God. She dedicated her unborn child to serve as an imam, or a priest, to serve God in Bayt-ul-Maqdis. Though she was in old age, she prayed to Allah سبحانه وتعالى for a child who would also devote his efforts to worshipping Allah سبحانه وتعالى and serving His house, as her husband Imran used to do.

Allah سبحانه وتعالى in His infinite wisdom gave her a blessed and miraculous daughter instead, and He portrayed how a daughter could be His pious and conscientious servant of Him سبحانه وتعالى as well.

Maryam عليها السلام is Born

Hannah was surprised to give birth to a daughter because all the priests of that time were male. Was she disappointed that she was given a female child? Not at all, because she had a strong faith that Allah سبحانه وتعالى is the best of planners. Her daughter Maryam عليها السلام was not an ordinary girl; she was chosen amongst all women to not only be the mother of Prophet 'Isa عليه السلام, but to be a devout worshipper herself. As a young woman she used to spend long periods of time in the temple praying to Allah سبحانه وتعالى and experiencing miracles.

Under Musa's law, the female child could not be devoted to temple service as Maryam's mother intended. However, Hannah asked for God's protection for her against all evil, and she was determined that her daughter would be a servant of Allah سبحانه وتعالى.

Maryam's Guardian

Hannah took Maryam to the Temple of Bayt-ul-Maqdis, where she hoped that Maryam عليها السلام would grow and be trained to serve God. The priests disputed amongst themselves as to which one of them would be her guardian. They all considered it a privilege to take care of Imran's daughter.

Zakariyya عليه السلام, was a Prophet sent to the Children of Israel, and he was Maryam's عليها السلام relative. Yet, other men challenged his authority in both religion and the right to care for Maryam عليها السلام. Eventually, they decided to cast lots with pens in order to determine who would take up this responsibility. They drew lots by throwing their pens into the Jordan River. The rule was that the pen that went against the flow of the river and stayed still should win. All the pens flowed downstream except for Zakariyya's عليه السلام pen, which stood stationary against the stream. They repeated the draw three times and ended up with the same result. Allah سبحانه وتعالى had planned that Zakariyya عليه السلام, a pious prophet, would be the guardian of Maryam عليها السلام.

B16

Bayt-ul-Maqdis - The city of Jerusalem.

Allah سبحانه وتعالى says in Surat Al-Imran:

﴿ إِذْ قَالَتِ ٱمْرَأَتُ عِمْرَٰنَ رَبِّ إِنِّى نَذَرْتُ لَكَ مَا فِى بَطْنِى مُحَرَّرًا فَتَقَبَّلْ مِنِّىٓ إِنَّكَ أَنتَ ٱلسَّمِيعُ ٱلْعَلِيمُ ۝ فَلَمَّا وَضَعَتْهَا قَالَتْ رَبِّ إِنِّى وَضَعْتُهَآ أُنثَىٰ وَٱللَّهُ أَعْلَمُ بِمَا وَضَعَتْ وَلَيْسَ ٱلذَّكَرُ كَٱلْأُنثَىٰ وَإِنِّى سَمَّيْتُهَا مَرْيَمَ وَإِنِّىٓ أُعِيذُهَا بِكَ وَذُرِّيَّتَهَا مِنَ ٱلشَّيْطَٰنِ ٱلرَّجِيمِ ۝ فَتَقَبَّلَهَا رَبُّهَا بِقَبُولٍ حَسَنٍ وَأَنۢبَتَهَا نَبَاتًا حَسَنًا وَكَفَّلَهَا زَكَرِيَّا كُلَّمَا دَخَلَ عَلَيْهَا زَكَرِيَّا ٱلْمِحْرَابَ وَجَدَ عِندَهَا رِزْقًا قَالَ يَٰمَرْيَمُ أَنَّىٰ لَكِ هَٰذَا قَالَتْ هُوَ مِنْ عِندِ ٱللَّهِ إِنَّ ٱللَّهَ يَرْزُقُ مَن يَشَآءُ بِغَيْرِ حِسَابٍ ۝ ﴾ آل عمران: ٣٥-٣٧

Behold! The wife of 'Imran said: "O my Lord! I do dedicate to you what is in my womb for your special service: So accept this of me: For you are the All-Hearing and All-Knowing all things."
When she was delivered, she said: "O my Lord! Behold! I am delivered of a female child!"- and Allah knew best what she brought forth- "And the male is not like the female. I have named her Maryam, and I commend her and her offspring to your protection from Satan, the Rejected."
Right graciously did her Lord accept her: He made her grow in purity and beauty: To the care of Zakariyya was she assigned. Every time that he entered (Her) chamber to see her, He found her supplied with sustenance. He said: "O Mary! Whence (comes) this to you?" She said: "From Allah. for Allah provides sustenance to whom He pleases without measure." Surat Al-Imran [3:35-37]

Maryam grew up under God's special protection. Her sustenance, including both her spiritual and physical needs came from God, and her growth was indeed a "blessed growth." She sought the support and protection of God alone, and no one else.

Historians state that Zakariyya assigned a special private chamber for her on the eastern side of the temple. He screened her chamber from people so that no one could enter it except for him, in order to give her safety and privacy. She used to worship Allah سبحانه وتعالى night and day, and serve in the temple as well.

Common knowledge says that Prophet Zakariyya became very old, so he asked Maryam's cousin, Joseph the carpenter, to take care of her. Joseph was a very pious man and accepted this blessed responsibility.

Chosen Woman and Son

Over the years, Maryam became a rare example of devotion and worship unparalleled among the Children of Israel. There was not a single other person equal to her in her 'ibadah, worship, and prolonged prayers. She was constantly in a state of 'itikaf, or ritual seclusion, in Bayt Al-Maqdis, not leaving the temple except for urgent necessities. She used to stand in prayer for long period until her feet were swollen.

Allah was very pleased with Maryam's worship and devotion. Upon orders from Allah, the angels came down to deliver a special message to Maryam.

﴿ وَإِذْ قَالَتِ ٱلْمَلَٰٓئِكَةُ يَٰمَرْيَمُ إِنَّ ٱللَّهَ ٱصْطَفَىٰكِ وَطَهَّرَكِ وَٱصْطَفَىٰكِ عَلَىٰ نِسَآءِ ٱلْعَٰلَمِينَ ۝ يَٰمَرْيَمُ ٱقْنُتِي لِرَبِّكِ وَٱسْجُدِي وَٱرْكَعِي مَعَ ٱلرَّٰكِعِينَ ۝ ﴾ آل عمران: ٤٢-٤٣

(42) Behold! the angels said: "O Mary! Allah has chosen you and purified you- chosen you above the women of all nations. (43) O Mary! worship Your Lord devoutly: Prostrate yourself, and bow down (in prayer) with those who bow down." Surat Al-Imran [3:42-43]

In these verses Allah mentions that the angels gave glad tidings to Maryam عليها السلام that Allah had chosen her from among all women of all nations. He would bestow upon her a unique miracle! She would have a son with no father, and indeed he would be an honorable prophet. He would speak from his cradle in his childhood and call the people to Allah سبحانه وتعالى in his youth.

﴿ إِذْ قَالَتِ ٱلْمَلَٰٓئِكَةُ يَٰمَرْيَمُ إِنَّ ٱللَّهَ يُبَشِّرُكِ بِكَلِمَةٍ مِّنْهُ ٱسْمُهُ ٱلْمَسِيحُ عِيسَى ٱبْنُ مَرْيَمَ وَجِيهًا فِي ٱلدُّنْيَا وَٱلْءَاخِرَةِ وَمِنَ ٱلْمُقَرَّبِينَ ۝ وَيُكَلِّمُ ٱلنَّاسَ فِي ٱلْمَهْدِ وَكَهْلًا وَمِنَ ٱلصَّٰلِحِينَ ۝ ﴾ آل عمران: ٤٥-٤٦

Behold! the angels said: "O Mary! Allah gives you glad tidings of a Word from Him: his name will be Christ Jesus, the son of Maryam, held in honor in this world and the Hereafter and of (the company of) those nearest to Allah. He shall speak to the people in cradle and in maturity. And he shall be (of the company) of the righteous." Surat Al-Imran[3:45-46]

The Holy Spirit Jibreel Meets Maryam عليها السلام

The Angel Jibreel عليه السلام is described in Al-Qur'an as Ar-Rooh-ul-Qudus, or the Holy Spirit. He appeared to Maryam عليها السلام one day in her chamber in the shape of a man. No man ever entered her chamber except for Zakariyya عليه السلام, so she became very frightened. Extremely worried, she sought refuge and protection from Allah سبحانه وتعالى, and she told the man not to come near her.

Indeed it was an angel, not a man, who had come to convey to her a message from Allah سبحانه وتعالى:

Understood Meaning

{16} Relate in the Book (the story of) Mary, when she withdrew from her family to a place in the East. {17} She placed a screen (to screen herself) from them; then We sent her our angel, and he appeared before her as a man in all respects. {18} She said: "I seek refuge from you to (Allah) Most Gracious: (come not near) if you dost fear Allah."
{19} "He [Jibreel] said: "Nay, I am only a messenger from your Lord, (to announce) to you the gift of a holy son."
Surprised, Maryam عليها السلام replied:
{20} She said: "How shall I have a son, seeing that no man has touched me, and I am not unchaste?
{21} He said: "So (it will be): Your Lord says, 'that is easy for Me: and (We wish) to appoint him as a sign unto men and a mercy from us':It is a matter (so) decreed." [Surat Maryam 19:20-21]

The Story in the Bible

26. And in the sixth month, the Angel Gabriel was sent from God unto a city of Galilee, named Nazareth. 27. To a virgin … and the virgin's name was Mary. 28. And the angel came in unto her, and said, Hail, you that art highly favored, the Lord is with you: blessed art you among women. 29. And when she saw him, she was troubled at his saying, and cast in her mind what manner of salutation this should be. 30. And the angel said unto her, Fear not, Mary: for you hast found favor with God. 31. And, behold, you shalt conceive in your womb, and bring forth a son, and shall call his name JESUS. 34. Then said Mary unto the angel, How shall this be, seeing I know not a man? 35. And the angel answered and said unto her, The Holy Ghost shall come upon you, and the power of the Highest shall overshadow you … 36. And, behold, your cousin Elisabeth, she hath also conceived a son in her old age: and this is the sixth month with her, who was called barren.

37. For with God nothing shall be impossible. 38. And Mary said, Behold the handmaid of the Lord; be it unto me according to your word. And the angel departed from her.

Source: Luke 1 (King James Version)

The Immaculate Conception

By Allah's power, Maryam conceived her son 'Isa miraculously, without a husband. Despite all challenges, she submitted to the will of Allah. When she felt the pains of birth increasing, she retired to a remote place.

"And (remember) her, who guarded her chastity: We breathed into her of Our spirit, and We made her and her son a sign for all peoples. " [21:91]

Historians say that Angel Jibreel breathed onto Maryam. That miraculous breath caused her to become pregnant and conceive her blessed baby. Maryam عليها السلام was but a human. Therefore, she suffered the pangs of an expectant mother with no one to help her. She could not ask anyone to help her as no one would believe that she was bearing a child without a father! She was in great pain, both physically and emotionally. The pangs of childbirth were hard on her, as well as the gossip of the people in her area. They started to accuse her of committing the great of fornication.

This is just part of the story of one of the most righteous woman of all time; Maryam. Her life was devoted to serving Allah. Allah protected her from the people and helped her through many hardships. He performed a great miracle by giving Maryam a son without a husband, and that blessed son became a great prophet. May peace and blessings be showered upon Maryam for all her righteous deeds.

The city of Nazareth (Galilee).

Hadeeth Shareef

عن ابن عباس قال رسول الله صلى الله عليه السلام:
(أفضل نساء أهل الجنة خديجة بنت خويلد وفاطمة بنت محمد ومريم بنت عمران وآسية بنت مزاحم امرأة فرعون)
رواه النسائي وابن حبان

Ibn Abbas narrated that Rasoolullah said, "The best four women in Jannah are Khadeejah bint Khuwaylid, Fatimah bint Muhammad, Maryam bint Imran, and Asia bint Muzahim, the wife of Pharoah."

Reported by An-Nasa'ee and Ibn Hibban.

Bethlehem: Entrance to the Church of the Nativity.

FAITH IN ACTION

★ Always have strong faith, and firm trust in Allah's help and support during difficult situations.

★ Worship Allah as much as you can, as Maryam used to do.

CHAPTER REVIEW

Projects and Activities

1. Recite ayaat of Surat Al-Imran and ayaat of Surat Maryam.

2. Write a poem about Maryam عليها السلام.

Stretch Your Mind

1. What would you do if you were accused of a heinous act that you never did?

2. Why do you think Allah blessed Maryam, and He selected her from among all women to experience a one-of-a-kind miracle and to become the mother of Isa عليها السلام?

Study Questions

1. Who was: a. Imran   b. Hannah   c. Maryam
2. What were the names of Maryam's mother and father?
3. What did Maryam's mother promise to Allah while she was pregnant? And how did Allah respond?
4. Who took care of Maryam while she was growing up? And how did he take this responsibility?
5. Where did Maryam go when she received the news that Allah was blessing her with a son?
6. What was her reaction at first when Angel Jibreel appeared to her?
7. What were the five commands that Yahya عليه السلام was ordered to propagate?
8. What are the qualities that Yahya عليه السلام is best known for?
9. Describe how Yahya عليه السلام was killed. What does the Qur'an say about Yahya's death?

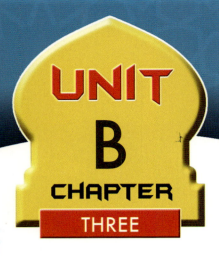

The Miracle of Miracles: The Story of Prophet 'Isa

CHAPTER OBJECTIVES

1. Learn the story of Prophet 'Isa, and admire his great personality.
2. Understand why Maryam was the greatest woman of all times.
3. Learn the events that led to the birth of Prophet 'Isa.
4. Appreciate the great miracles of Prophet 'Isa, and understand why Allah blessed him with these miracles
5. Appreciate the values and the benefits of purity, devotion, and worship that were demonstrated by Maryam and her mother.
6. Learn and memorize ayaat 23-33 of Surat Maryam.
7. Learn and memorize the hadeeth about the closeness between Prophets 'Isa and Muhammad.

VOCABULARY

- 'Isa — عيسى
- Al-Maseeh — المسيح
- Al-Hawariyyoon — الْحَوَارِيُّون

Prophet 'Isa, or Jesus Christ, was one of the greatest prophets Allah ever sent to mankind. He is one of the five messengers who are described in the Qur'an as the messengers of power and determination. These messengers are Ibraheem, Nuh, Musa, 'Isa and, Muhammad. In the previous chapter, you have learned about the Virgin Mary, Prophet 'Isa's mother. In this chapter, you will learn about Prophet 'Isa, peace be upon him.

The Birth of 'Isa

Maryam عليها السلام gave birth to 'Isa عليه السلام in Bethlehem, six miles south of Jerusalem, in a remote place, away from people. Some historians say that Maryam was then fifteen years old. She prayed to Allah سبحانه وتعالى for ease from her pain, and the angel immediately told her to shake the palm tree beside her. Dates dropped on her miraculously, as palm trees do not normally drop dates by the shaking of one person alone. Allah also made a stream of fresh water run by her. Allah says in Surat Maryam,

{23} And the pains of childbirth drove her to the trunk of a palm-tree: " Ah! Would that I had died before this! Would that I had been a thing forgotten and out of sight!" {24} But (a voice) cried to her from beneath the (palm-tree): "Grieve not! for your Lord has provided a stream beneath you;
{25} "And shake towards yourself the trunk of the palm-tree: It will let fall fresh ripe dates upon you.
{26} "So eat and drink and relax. And if you see anyone, say, 'I have vowed to the Most Gracious to refrain from speaking this day with any human being'"[19: 23-26]

Maryam عليها السلام took comfort in these signs, and she was pleased and content that Allah was taking good care of her and her newborn. She was under a vow to Allah سبحانه وتعالى that she would not speak to anyone, in order to demonstrate the miracle of Allah سبحانه وتعالى.

Jesus was of virgin birth, and performed many miracles. But those to whom he came as a prophet rejected him, and plotted for his death. Their plots failed, for God's Plan is above man's plots. So will it be with Islam, the Truth of all eternity.

THE DATE AND ITS USES AS DESCRIBED IN THE QUR'AN

There is considerable wisdom in Allah's recommendion of dates for Maryam. The date is an excellent choice of food for the pregnant women and for those who have just given birth. As scientists now know Maryam was inspired to understand this point, in order to make her own labour easier. The date has one of the highest sugar levels, 60-65%, of all fruits. Doctors recommend that pregnant women be given foods containing fruit sugar on the day they give birth. The aim behind this is to energize the mother's weakened body. and at the same time to stimulate milk hormones and increase the levels of mother's milk essential to the new-born baby.

In addition, loss of blood during birth leads to a fall in body sugar levels. Dates are important because they enable sugar to enter the body, and they prevent blood pressure from dropping. Their high caloric value strengthens people weakened by illness, or suffering from extreme fatigue.

Dates also contain a form of sugar that gives the body high levels of mobility and heat energy, and which can be easily broken down in the body. Furthermore, this sugar is not glucose, which rapidly raises the level of blood sugar, but rather fruit sugar fructose. A rapid rise in blood sugar levels in diabetics in particular has a damaging effect on a great many organs and systems, especially the eyes, kidneys, heart, circulatory system and nervous system. High blood sugar is one of the main causes of disorders as serious as loss of sight, heart attack, and kidney failure.

These facts reveal the wisdom in the way that Allah's recommendation for Maryam to eat dates. Allah designed dates to energize and invigorate woman and ensure the emergence of milk, the only food for a baby. For example, besides fruit sugar, the date contains more than ten elements of vital importance if the body is to remain healthy and energetic. Modern-day scientists state that human beings can actually live for years on nothing more than dates and water. Dowson, a recognized expert in this field, says that one piece of date and a glass of milk are enough to meet all of a person's daily nutritional requirements. ("Dates and Health," www.sgp-dates.com/ date.htm.)

The substance oxytocin, which is present in the date, is used in modern medicine to facilitate birth. In fact, oxytocin means "rapid birth." It is also known to increase levels of mother's milk after birth. (http://eilat.sci.brooklyn.cuny.edu/newnyc/DRUGS/OXYTOCIN.HTM)

Oxytocin is actually a hormone released by the pituitary gland which stimulates contractions of the womb during childbirth. All the pre-birth preparations in the body take place thanks to this hormone. The effects of the hormone can be seen in the muscles that form the mother's womb, and in cells in the muscular structure that enables the secretion of mother's milk. The effective contraction of

Fresh Dates.

the womb is essential if birth is to take place. Oxytocin enables the muscles that comprise the womb to contract in a very powerful manner. Moreover, oxytocin also initiates the secretion of mother's milk. This feature of the date alone, the way it contains oxytocin, is important evidence that the Qur'an is the revelation of Allah. The medical identification of the benefits of the date only became possible in recent times. Yet it was set out fourteen centuries ago in the Qur'an when Allah revealed to Maryam that she should eat dates.

Dates also contain a great many vitamins and minerals. They are very rich in fiber, fat, and proteins.

Source: http://www.miraclesofthequran.com/scientific_69.html

Maryam's Return to Jerusalem

After some time, Maryam عليها السلام returned to Jerusalem carrying her newborn baby in her arms. The town's people were shocked; Allah describes what happened in Surat Maryam.

سورة مريم

Surat Maryam 27-33

فَأَتَتْ بِهِ قَوْمَهَا تَحْمِلُهُ ۖ قَالُوا يَٰمَرْيَمُ لَقَدْ جِئْتِ شَيْئًا فَرِيًّا ۝ يَٰٓأُخْتَ هَٰرُونَ مَا كَانَ أَبُوكِ ٱمْرَأَ سَوْءٍ وَمَا كَانَتْ أُمُّكِ بَغِيًّا ۝ فَأَشَارَتْ إِلَيْهِ ۖ قَالُوا كَيْفَ نُكَلِّمُ مَن كَانَ فِى ٱلْمَهْدِ صَبِيًّا ۝ قَالَ إِنِّى عَبْدُ ٱللَّهِ ءَاتَىٰنِىَ ٱلْكِتَٰبَ وَجَعَلَنِى نَبِيًّا ۝ وَجَعَلَنِى مُبَارَكًا أَيْنَ مَا كُنتُ وَأَوْصَٰنِى بِٱلصَّلَوٰةِ وَٱلزَّكَوٰةِ مَا دُمْتُ حَيًّا ۝ وَبَرًّۢا بِوَٰلِدَتِى وَلَمْ يَجْعَلْنِى جَبَّارًا شَقِيًّا ۝ وَٱلسَّلَٰمُ عَلَىَّ يَوْمَ وُلِدتُّ وَيَوْمَ أَمُوتُ وَيَوْمَ أُبْعَثُ حَيًّا ۝

Understood Meaning

{27} At length she brought the (baby) to her people, carrying him (in her arms). They said: "O Mary! Truly an amazing thing hast thou brought! {28} Oh sister of Aaron! Your father was not an evil man nor was your mother an unchaste woman! {29} But she pointed to the baby. They said: "How can we talk to one who is a child in the cradle?"

The blessed baby 'Isa عليه السلام responded:
{30} "I am indeed a servant of God. He has given me Revelation and made me a prophet. {31} And He had made me blessed wheresoever I be, and has enjoined on me prayer and charity as long as I live; {32} (He) has made me kind to my mother, and not overbearing or miserable. {33} So peace is on me the day I was born, the day that I die, and the day that I shall be raised up to life (again)!"

According to a previous vow she had taken people, Maryam عليها السلام did not speak, but instead she pointed to the baby. They looked at her in complete disbelief; how did she think that pointing to her baby could help her now? But miraculously the child began to speak. He was inspired by Allah سبحانه وتعالى, and spoke in defense of his blessed mother, and he preached the truth to the unbelievers.

Only in the Qur'an
The incident of 'Isa speaking when he was an infant in the cradle was mentioned only the Qur'an. The story is not mentioned in the Bible or in any Christian gospel.

Maryam and 'Isa Move to Egypt

Some historical reports claim that Maryam felt that 'Isa was in danger in Jerusalem. King Herod the Great and other wicked people were a threat to her and her miraculous baby. Therefore, she journeyed to Egypt and stayed there for a number of years. When 'Isa was about thirteen years old, the danger for 'Isa was over. Thus, Maryam returned to the Holy Land and stayed in Nazareth. Therefore, 'Isa spent his adolescent years mainly in that city, where Allah taught him His guidance and prepared him as a great messenger.

Prophet 'Isa's Mission and Teachings

'Isa was brought to the world as a prophet with a beautiful personality and great miracles. When he was thirty years old Allah sent him to inspire his people, the Children of Israel, to return to God. The Children of Israel had fallen astray over time. Isaiah (AS), a major prophet of the Israelites, warned that they had started worshipping other idols, rebelled against Allah, and partook in corruption, treachery, oppression, hypocrisy, and murder. They no longer held a respect for life, truth, and justice, and instead cared only for their own worldly benefit. They oppressed others and neglected their own souls!

Prophet 'Isa was then sent mainly as a messenger to the Children of Israel. Allah describes Prophet 'Isa's mission in Surat Al-Imran:

﴿ وَرَسُولًا إِلَىٰ بَنِي إِسْرَائِيلَ ﴾ آل عمران: ٤٩

And [appointed Jesus] a messenger to the Children of Israel, [3:49]

Also, Allah quotes 'Isa's speech to the Children of Israel in Surat-us-Saff:

﴿ وَرَسُولًا إِلَىٰ بَنِي إِسْرَائِيلَ ﴾ آل عمران: ٤٩

And remember, Jesus, the son of Mary, said: "O Children of Israel! I am the apostle of Allah (sent) to you." [61:6].

In his teachings, Prophet 'Isa (AS) called his people to Tawheed (the oneness of God), brotherhood, love, and morality. He taught his people not to kill, steal, lie, commit adultery, cheat, or disrespect their parents.

Prophets come at times when the level of morality and spirituality are at their lowest within mankind. They come to remind the people of their beliefs and responsibility to Allah. When people are lost within the dark wilderness of a forest, the prophets are like guides with bright torches lighting the way out of the woods.

Jesus Christ was also brought to assure the repentant people of salvation and this is the case with all apostles of God.

The Miracles of Prophet 'Isa

Prophet 'Isa عليه السلام was himself a miracle, being born without a father. However, Allah blessed him with many other miracles to help him convince the Children of Israel of his true message. First, he could speak when he was an infant. Such a great miracle was only mentioned in the Qur'an and cannot be found in the Bible.

Prophet 'Isa عليه السلام could also cure people with serious handicaps and diseases. Allah enabled him to cure the sick by simply wiping their diseased spots. For that reason he was called Al-Maseeh, or the Messiah, which means in Arabic, among other things, the one who cures people by wiping on them.

In the Hebrew language, however, the "Mashiah" means "the anointed."

Prophet 'Isa عليه السلام even raised the dead in certain situations. Allah says in Surat Al-Imran:

﴿ إِذْ قَالَ ٱللَّهُ يَـٰعِيسَى ٱبْنَ مَرْيَمَ ٱذْكُرْ نِعْمَتِى عَلَيْكَ وَعَلَىٰ وَٰلِدَتِكَ إِذْ أَيَّدتُّكَ بِرُوحِ ٱلْقُدُسِ تُكَلِّمُ ٱلنَّاسَ فِى ٱلْمَهْدِ وَكَهْلًا وَإِذْ عَلَّمْتُكَ ٱلْكِتَـٰبَ وَٱلْحِكْمَةَ وَٱلتَّوْرَىٰةَ وَٱلْإِنجِيلَ وَإِذْ تَخْلُقُ مِنَ ٱلطِّينِ كَهَيْـَٔةِ ٱلطَّيْرِ بِإِذْنِى فَتَنفُخُ فِيهَا فَتَكُونُ طَيْرًا بِإِذْنِى وَتُبْرِئُ ٱلْأَكْمَهَ وَٱلْأَبْرَصَ بِإِذْنِى وَإِذْ تُخْرِجُ ٱلْمَوْتَىٰ بِإِذْنِى وَإِذْ كَفَفْتُ بَنِىٓ إِسْرَٰٓءِيلَ عَنكَ إِذْ جِئْتَهُم بِٱلْبَيِّنَـٰتِ فَقَالَ ٱلَّذِينَ كَفَرُوا۟ مِنْهُمْ إِنْ هَـٰذَآ إِلَّا سِحْرٌ مُّبِينٌ ﴾ المائدة: ١١٠ ﴿١١٠﴾

{110} Allah did say: "O Jesus the son of Mary! Remember My favor to you and to your mother. I strengthened you with the Holy Spirit, so that you did speak to the people in cradle and in maturity. Behold! I taught you the Book and Wisdom, the Law and the Gospel and behold! you make out of clay, as it were, the figure of a bird, by My leave, and you breath into it and it becomes a bird by My leave, and you heal those born blind, and the lepers, by My leave. And behold! you bring forth the dead by My leave. And behold! I did restrain the Children of Israel from (violence to) you when you didst show them the clear Signs, and the unbelievers among them said: 'This is nothing but evident magic.' [Surat-ul-Maidah 5:110]*

Prophet 'Isa عليه السلام then was a mortal human being who ate, drank, and slept just like all other humans. The miracles he practiced were possible only because Allah وتعالى سبحانه, the source of all miracles, blessed him with these abilities. It was only with God's permission and ability that 'Isa عليه السلام healed the sick and wounded.

The Hawariyyoon: The Disciples of Jesus Christ

Prophet 'Isa exerted great efforts to guide his people to the straight path. Instead of accepting his message, many disbelieved in him and conspired to kill him. At that point Prophet 'Isa wanted to see who was faithful to him. Twelve people declared their loyalty to his message and their willingness to travel with him. These twelve devout people are known as the Disciples, or ٱلْحَوَارِيُّونَ Al-Hawariyyoon as they are called in Al-Qur'an.

﴿ فَلَمَّآ أَحَسَّ عِيسَىٰ مِنْهُمُ ٱلْكُفْرَ قَالَ مَنْ أَنصَارِىٓ إِلَى ٱللَّهِ قَالَ ٱلْحَوَارِيُّونَ نَحْنُ أَنصَارُ ٱللَّهِ ءَامَنَّا بِٱللَّهِ وَٱشْهَدْ بِأَنَّا مُسْلِمُونَ ﴿٥٢﴾ رَبَّنَآ ءَامَنَّا بِمَآ أَنزَلْتَ وَٱتَّبَعْنَا ٱلرَّسُولَ فَٱكْتُبْنَا مَعَ ٱلشَّـٰهِدِينَ ﴿٥٣﴾ ﴾ المائدة: ٥٢-٥٣

"When Jesus found Unbelief on their part He said: "Who will be My helpers to (the work of) Allah?" The disciples said: "We are Allah's helpers: We believe in Allah and you bear witness that we are Muslims." [Surat-ul-Maidah 5:52-53]

One day, the Hawariyyoon, or the Disciples of Prophet 'Isa, wanted to confirm their belief in him with yet more miracles. Thus, they requested that Allah would send a banquet from Heaven down for them. This incident was documented in Surat-ul-Ma'idah, or the Banquet.

"Behold! The Disciples said: "O Jesus the son

﴿ إِذْ قَالَ ٱلْحَوَارِيُّونَ يَٰعِيسَى ٱبْنَ مَرْيَمَ هَلْ يَسْتَطِيعُ رَبُّكَ أَن يُنَزِّلَ عَلَيْنَا مَآئِدَةً مِّنَ ٱلسَّمَآءِ قَالَ ٱتَّقُوا۟ ٱللَّهَ إِن كُنتُم مُّؤْمِنِينَ ۝ قَالُوا۟ نُرِيدُ أَن نَّأْكُلَ مِنْهَا وَتَطْمَئِنَّ قُلُوبُنَا وَنَعْلَمَ أَن قَدْ صَدَقْتَنَا وَنَكُونَ عَلَيْهَا مِنَ ٱلشَّٰهِدِينَ ۝ قَالَ عِيسَى ٱبْنُ مَرْيَمَ ٱللَّهُمَّ رَبَّنَآ أَنزِلْ عَلَيْنَا مَآئِدَةً مِّنَ ٱلسَّمَآءِ تَكُونُ لَنَا عِيدًا لِّأَوَّلِنَا وَءَاخِرِنَا وَءَايَةً مِّنكَ وَٱرْزُقْنَا وَأَنتَ خَيْرُ ٱلرَّٰزِقِينَ ۝ قَالَ ٱللَّهُ إِنِّي مُنَزِّلُهَا عَلَيْكُمْ فَمَن يَكْفُرْ بَعْدُ مِنكُمْ فَإِنِّي أُعَذِّبُهُ عَذَابًا لَّآ أُعَذِّبُهُ أَحَدًا مِّنَ ٱلْعَٰلَمِينَ ۝ ﴾ المائدة: ١١٢-١١٥

of Mary, can your Lord send down to us a table set (with food) from Heaven?" Said Jesus: * "Fear God, if ye have faith." Therefore, They said: "We only wish to eat thereof and satisfy our hearts, and to know that thou hast indeed told us the truth; and that we ourselves may be witnesses to the miracle." 'Isa (AS) implored God: "O our Lord! Send us from Heaven a table set (with viands), that there may be for us-- for the first and the last of us a solemn festival and a sign from You; and provide for our sustenance, for You art

the best sustainer (of our needs)." [Surat-ul-Maidah 5:112-114]

God promised him that banquet on condition that:

"…If any of you after that resisted faith, I will punish him with a penalty such as I have not inflicted on anyone among all people." [Surat-ul-Maidah 5:112-115]

All the disciples stood fast on their faith and loyalty except, one as you will learn later.

Jesus did feed his disciples by miracle.
But he claimed no divinity: he was
a true servant of God, to Whom doth belong
The dominion of the Heavens and Earth:
Glory and power are His, and His alone.

Jesus Christ Foretells the Coming of Prophet Muhammad

Prophet 'Isa not only confirmed the message of Prophet Musa who came before him, but he foretold his people and the world about the coming of Prophet Muhammad (SAW). The Qur'an confirmed this fact in Surat-us-Saff:

﴿ وَإِذْ قَالَ عِيسَى ٱبْنُ مَرْيَمَ يَٰبَنِىٓ إِسْرَٰٓءِيلَ إِنِّي رَسُولُ ٱللَّهِ إِلَيْكُم مُّصَدِّقًا لِّمَا بَيْنَ يَدَيَّ مِنَ ٱلتَّوْرَىٰةِ وَمُبَشِّرًا بِرَسُولٍ يَأْتِي مِنۢ بَعْدِي ٱسْمُهُۥٓ أَحْمَدُ فَلَمَّا جَآءَهُم بِٱلْبَيِّنَٰتِ قَالُوا۟ هَٰذَا سِحْرٌ مُّبِينٌ ۝ ﴾ الصف: ٦

"And remember, Jesus, the son of Mary, said: "O Children of Israel! I am the apostle of Allah (sent) to you, confirming the law (which came) before me, and giving glad tidings of an Messenger to come after me, whose name shall be Ahmad." But when he came to them with clear signs, they said, "this is evident sorcery!" [61:6]

Since the Injeel was changed or lost after Prophet 'Isa, the name of Muhammad does not appear explicitly in the current gospels. However, there are parts of the gospels that hint at the coming of a messenger after Prophet 'Isa. Some Christian religious leaders are fast to contend that such verses do not talk about Prophet Muhammad, but refer to a Holy spirit. Here are examples of such verses:

John 16 (King James Version)
7 Nevertheless I tell you the truth; It is expedient for you that I go away: for if I go not away, the Comforter will not come unto you; but if I depart, I will send him unto you.

8 And when he is come, he will reprove the world of sin, and of righteousness, and of judgment:

13 Howbeit when he, the Spirit of truth, is come, he will guide you into all truth: for he shall not speak of himself; but whatsoever he shall hear, that shall he speak: and he will shew you things to come.

The Israelite Priests Reject Prophet Isa and Plot to Kill Him

As you learned earlier, some of the Children of Israel truly accepted the truth and followed the guidance of Prophet 'Isa عليه السلام. However, the Israelites' priests and many of their people disbelieved in him, rejected his message, and accused him of sorcery. They also accused him of trying to change the teachings of Prophet Musa and other Israelite prophets.

The Bible documents the bitterness Prophet 'Isa felt toward his rejecters. In the Gospel of Mathew 23:37, Prophet 'Isa is quoted a saying:

37. O Jerusalem, Jerusalem, you who kill the prophets and stone those sent to you, how often I have longed to gather your children together, as a hen gathers her chicks under her wings, but you were not willing. 38. Look, your house is left to you desolate.

Mathew 5:17 "Do not think that I have come to abolish the Law or the Prophets; I have not come to abolish them but to fulfill them.

Historians say that some Israelite leaders conspired with the Roman ruler in Jerusalem to kill Prophet 'Isa. They made him believe that Jesus Christ was planning to become the king of the Jews and topple his Roman authority in the Holy Land. The governor ordered that Jesus must come to his court. This meeting is recorded in the Gospel of Mathew as follows:

11 And Jesus stood before the governor: and the governor asked him, saying, Art thou the King of the Jews? And Jesus said unto him, Thou sayest. 12 And when he was accused of the chief priests and elders, he answered nothing. 13 Then said Pilate unto him, Hearest thou not how many things they witness against thee? 14 And he answered him to never a word; insomuch that the governor marveled greatly. 15 Now at that feast the governor was wont to release unto the people a prisoner, whom they would. 16 And they had then a notable prisoner, called Barabbas. 17 Therefore when they were gathered together, Pilate said unto them, Whom will ye that I release unto you? Barabbas, or Jesus which is called Christ? 18 For he knew that for envy they had delivered him. 19

When he was set down on the judgment seat, his wife sent unto him, saying, "Have thou nothing to do with that just man: for I have suffered many things this day in a dream because of him. 20 But the chief priests and elders persuaded the multitude that they should ask Barabbas, and destroy Jesus. 21 The governor answered and said unto them, Whether of the twain will ye that I release unto you? They said, Barabbas. 22 Pilate saith unto them, What shall I do then with Jesus which is called Christ? They all say unto him, Let him be crucified. 23 And the governor said, Why, what evil hath he done? But they cried out the more, saying, Let him be crucified." [Mathew 11-23]

According to Mathew, then, the Israelite priests rejected 'Isa عليه السلام completely and called for his death. They demanded that the Romans release the robber Barabbas from prison, rather than 'Isa عليه السلام, in order that 'Isa عليه السلام be killed. The Qur'an briefly document the conspiracy described above. Allah says in Surat Al-Imran,

وَمَكَرُوا وَمَكَرَ ٱللَّهُ وَٱللَّهُ خَيْرُ ٱلْمَٰكِرِينَ ﴿٥٤﴾ إِذْ قَالَ ٱللَّهُ يَٰعِيسَىٰٓ إِنِّى مُتَوَفِّيكَ وَرَافِعُكَ إِلَىَّ وَمُطَهِّرُكَ مِنَ ٱلَّذِينَ كَفَرُوا۟ وَجَاعِلُ ٱلَّذِينَ ٱتَّبَعُوكَ فَوْقَ ٱلَّذِينَ كَفَرُوٓا۟ إِلَىٰ يَوْمِ ٱلْقِيَٰمَةِ ۖ ثُمَّ إِلَىَّ مَرْجِعُكُمْ فَأَحْكُمُ بَيْنَكُمْ فِيمَا كُنتُمْ فِيهِ تَخْتَلِفُونَ ﴿٥٥﴾ آل عمران: ٥٤-٥٥

{54} And (the unbelievers) plotted and planned, and Allah too planned, and the best of planners is Allah. {55} Behold! Allah said: "O Jesus! I will take you and raise you to Myself and clear you (of the falsehoods) of those who blaspheme; I will make those who follow you superior to those who reject faith, to the Day of Resurrection: Then shall ye all return unto me, and I will judge between you of the matters wherein ye dispute. [Surat Al Imran 3:52-55]

Some of the priests plotted with the Roman governer to kill Jesus. They turned them against 'Isa عليه السلام by falsely accusing him of being a traitor.

FAITH IN ACTION

★ Always have patience with those who vilify you and make false accusations against you.

★ Always refute others' maligning by using short but convincing defense, just like Maryam did. Avoid getting involved in long arguments.

They Tried but Failed: The Story of Crucifixion

The belief in the crucifixion is very prominent among Christians. They believe that Jesus Christ was captured by the Romans and was crucified, or nailed to a cross, and left to die. All Christian culture promotes the crucifixion through speeches, books, movies, and other means.

Al-Qur'an is clear and firm that Prophet 'Isa was neither crucified nor killed عليه السلام. Instead, Allah سبحانه وتعالى raised Him up to the heavens. Some commentators explain that Judas Iscariot was made to look like Jesus, and he was the one who got crucified. The man was one of the twelve disciples of Prophet 'Isa, but he later betrayed him for money, according to the Gospels. The Gospel of Mark documents the incident in the following manner:

And Judas Iscariot, one of the twelve, went to the chief priests, to betray him to them. Who hearing it were glad; and they promised him they would give him money. (Mark 14:10-1)

Alternative historical interpretations claim that Jesus of Yeshua, Simon of Gyrene was the one on the cross.

Muslims do not believe in the crucifixion; the truth is that 'Isa عليه السلام ascended to Heaven alive, by the will of Allah سبحانه وتعالى and he will return again before the Day of Judgment.

" That they said (in boast) we killed Christ Jesus the son of Mary, the Apostle of God; * But they killed him not. * Nor crucified him, but so it was made to appear to them, and those who differ therein are full of doubts, with no (certain) knowledge, but only assumption to follow, for of surely they killed him not:* Nay, God raised him up unto Himself; and God is Exalted in Power, Wise and there is none of the People of the Book but must believe in him before his death; And on the Day of Judgment he will be witness against them." [4:157-159]

What Does the Qur'an Say about Jesus Christ?

1	Messenger of Allah 4:171
2	Word of Allah 4:171
3	Spirit of Allah 4:171
4	He is not God 5:119
5	He is a sign of the greatness of God 23:50
6	Servant of Allah 19:30
7	Blessed Prophet 4:171
8	Peace will be on him during his life, death, and resurrection 19:33
9	He came to confirm the Torah
10	He foretold the coming of Prophet Muhammad 61:6
11	Allah taught him the book, wisdom, Torah, and Injeel 3:48
12	He was kind to his mother 19:32
13	He is a sign of the hour 43:61
14	He was ordered to pray to God 19:31
15	He was ordered to give charity 19:31

CHAPTER REVIEW

Projects and Activities

1. Recite ayaat of Surat Al-Imran and ayaat of Surat Maryam.

2. Write a poem about Prophet 'Isa عليه السلام .

3. Write a 300 word essay proving that Jesus Christ was a great prophet and a human being, not a god.

Stretch Your Mind

1. What are the similarities and differences between the creation of Prophets Adam and 'Isa?

2. List three similarities and three differences between the Islamic and Christian views of Jesus?

Study Questions

1. Where was Prophet 'Isa born?
2. Describe the events that Maryam experienced before delivering her blessed baby?
3. How did Maryam answer the people's questions about her baby?
4. What are the main miracles Prophet 'Isa came with?
5. Why was Prophet 'Isa sent to the Children of Israel?
6. What were the most important teachings of Prophet 'Isa?
7. Did Prophet 'Isa die? Explain your answer, and support it with the appropriate ayaat.
8. What is crucifixion? What does the Qur'an say about it?
9. Who is Judas Iscariot? Support your answer with a text from the Bible.
10. In addition to Christianity, what is the only other major religion that believes in Jesus Christ as a great religious figure.
11. What did the people do when they knew about Maryam's birth? And how did she respond?

UNIT C

Beautiful Worship: The Rules of Siyam and Hajj

Chapter One	Ramadan: A Month of Blessings	C2
Chapter Two	Ahkam-us-Siyam: The Rules of Fasting	C10
Chapter Three	Mubtilaat-us-Siyam: The Nullifiers of Fasting	C20
Chapter Four	Hajjat-ul-Wadaa' (Part I)	C28
Chapter Five	Hajjat-ul-Wadaa' (PartI II)	C36

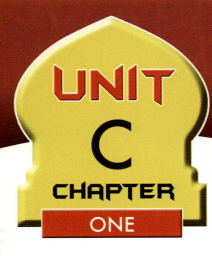

Ramadan: A Month of Blessings

CHAPTER OUTLINE

1. What is Ramadan?
2. Understand the special virtues of the month of Ramadan.
3. Learn and appreciate the spiritual, medical, psychological, and social benefits of fasting.
4. Learn and memorize the hadeeth about Ramadan and fasting in this chapter.

VOCABULARY

Ramadan	رمضان
Siyam	صيام
Taqwa	تقوى
Laylat-ul-Qadr	ليلة القدر

Sawm (صوم), or siyam (صيام), which mean fasting, is one of the five pillars of Islam. Fasting during the month of Ramadan is obligatory upon every Muslim, male and female, who is sane and mature. Allah Almighty has promised a great reward for those of us who fast, while punishing those that deliberately don't. Sawm has many spiritual, physical, moral, and social benefits. However, the most important lesson of fasting is the attainment of piety and consciousness of Allah سبحانه وتعالى.

Ramadan is the month of fasting in Islam. It is the 9th month of the Islamic lunar year, and it is either 29 or 30 days. Ramadan is an Arabic word that means heat and thirst.

Ramadan: The Special Month

The month of Ramadan has a special place in Islam. Here are some of the virtues of this unique month:

1. The Month of Qur'an

Allah chose to start revealing the Qur'an to Prophet Muhammad during the month of Ramadan. Allah says in Surat-ul-Baqarah,

﴿ شَهْرُ رَمَضَانَ ٱلَّذِىٓ أُنزِلَ فِيهِ ٱلْقُرْءَانُ هُدًى لِّلنَّاسِ وَبَيِّنَـٰتٍ مِّنَ ٱلْهُدَىٰ ﴾ البقرة: ١٨٥

The month of Ramadan is that in which the Qur'an was revealed, a guidance to men and clear proofs of the guidance and the distinction;

2. The night of Laylat-ul-Qadr

This month has a unique night of Laylat-ul-Qadr, in which the Qur'an was first revealed. To pray the night of Laylat-ul-Qadr, you will be rewarded similarly to a servant who worshipped God for one thousand months.

Allah says in Surat-ul Qadr:

﴿ إِنَّآ أَنزَلْنَـٰهُ فِى لَيْلَةِ ٱلْقَدْرِ ۝١ وَمَآ أَدْرَىٰكَ مَا لَيْلَةُ ٱلْقَدْرِ ۝٢ لَيْلَةُ ٱلْقَدْرِ خَيْرٌ مِّنْ أَلْفِ شَهْرٍ ۝٣ تَنَزَّلُ ٱلْمَلَـٰٓئِكَةُ وَٱلرُّوحُ فِيهَا بِإِذْنِ رَبِّهِم مِّن كُلِّ أَمْرٍ ۝٤ سَلَـٰمٌ هِىَ حَتَّىٰ مَطْلَعِ ٱلْفَجْرِ ۝٥ ﴾ القدر: ١-٥

{1} Surely We revealed it on the grand night. {2} And what will make you comprehend what the grand night is? {3} The grand night is better than a thousand months. {4} The angels and Jibreel descend in it by the permission of their Lord for every affair, {5} Peace! it is till the break of the morning. [Surat-ul-Qadr 97:1-5]

3. The Month of Fasting

Allah also decided to make the observance of fasting during Ramadan. Allah says:

﴿ فَمَن شَهِدَ مِنكُمُ ٱلشَّهْرَ فَلْيَصُمْهُ ﴾ البقرة: ١٨٥

"Whoever of you is present in the month, he shall fast therein." [Surat-ul-Baqarah 2:185]

4. The Month of Obedience

During Ramadan Allah inspires people to do the good deeds that lead to Jannah, and to avoid the sins that lead to Hellfire. He also locks up the devils and prevents them from working on people to make them sin and disobey Allah. This helps the believers to become more obedient to Allah during Ramadan, and to carry the habit of obedience after Ramadan. Imams Bukhari and Muslim that the Prophet has said,

عن أبي هريرة رضي الله قال: قال النبي صلى الله عليه وسلم أنه قال:

"إذا دخل رمضان فتحت أبواب الجنة، وغلّقت أبواب النار، وسلسلت الشياطين"

رواه البخاري ومسلم

Abu Hurayrah narrated that Rasoolullah said, "When Ramadan comes the gates of Jannah are opened, the gates of Hellfire are closed, and Satans will be locked up."

Reported by Al-Bukhari and Muslim

The Importance of Fasting

Siyam, or fasting, is the fourth pillar of Islam. It is a very important form of worship for many reasons. Let's take a look at what was mentioned about the virtues of fasting by Allah's Messenger  and his companions (R).

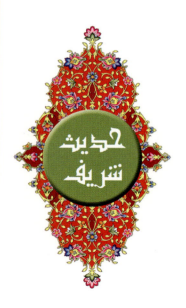

Hadeeth Shareef

Abu Umamah reported: "I came to the Messenger of Allah and said: 'Order me to do a deed that will allow me to enter Paradise.' He said: 'Stick to fasting, as there is no equivalent to it.' Then I came to him again and he said: 'Stick to fasting.'" Reported by Ahmad, an-Nasa'i, and al-Hakim.

Abu Hurayrah (RA) reported, that the Messenger of Allah said: "When Ramadan comes, the doors of Heaven are opened and the doors of Hell are closed, and the devils are put in chains, and the doors of mercy are opened."

Hadeeth Shareef

The Prophet Muhammad ﷺ said: "The fragrance of the mouth of a fasting person is more peasant to Allah than the smell of musk."

Anas reported that the Messenger of Allah ﷺ said: "Whoever fasts during the month of Ramadan with faith and is hopeful of reward, all his past sins will be forgiven, and whoever stands up in prayer with faith and is hopeful of reward, all his past sins will be forgiven, and whoever stands up in prayer during the blessed night with faith and is hopeful of reward, all his past sins will be forgiven."

From the previously mentioned ahadeeth, we see that fasting has many virtues designed to build a Muslim into a God-fearing individual. Siyam was an often performed practice of Allah's Messenger ﷺ and we are encouraged to fast during the month of Ramadan, as well as outside of Ramadan.

The Benefits of Fasting

Fasting has many virtues that benefit not only individuals, but societies as well. Fasting has spiritual, physical, psychological, as well as social benefits. We will take a look at those individually:

I. Spiritual Benefits of Siyam

1. Siyam Leads to Taqwa, or Piety.

Taqwa تقوى, or piety, is a state of love and closeness to Allah, as well as obedience to Him. A Muslim who observes taqwa always loves Allah, obeys Him, wishes to win His pleasure and Jannah, and fears His wrath and Hellfire. This causes the believer to become always mindful of Allah and aware of Him.

Siyam is an important pillar of Islam and great 'Ibadah, or worship. It clears the heart of the believer and inspires him to become pious.

Allah سبحانه وتعالى says in Surat-ul-Baqarah:

O you who believe! Observing the fasting is prescribed for you as it was prescribed for those before you, that you may become pious. [2:183]

The main purpose for prescribing fasting was to bring a sense of piety and God-consciousness to the individual that fasts. Fasting strengthens one's faith in the sovereignty and oneness of Allah سبحانه وتعالى. Up to dawn, one is free to eat lawful food as he/she likes, but as soon as the white line appears on the horizon, one begins, the abstinence from eating, drinking, and sexual relations. Other pleasures of life can continue till sunset and with it the fast will come to an end. This entire process of eating during the permitted time, and abstaining during the prohibited period, is a unique method of training the individual in compliance and obedience. This is the essence of taqwa, or piety, as you learned earlier. Piety, in general, is to willingly obey God's orders and avoid His prohibitions.

2. Siyam Helps the Believer to Win Great Rewards.

Allah promised the fasting Muslims gracious rewards. Imam Al-Bukhari reported that Rasoolullah said,

"Every action of the son of Adam is given manifold reward, each good deed receiving ten times its like, up to seven hundred times. Allah the Most High said, 'Except for fasting, for it is for Me and I will give recompense for it. He leaves off his desires and his food for Me.' For the fasting person there are two times of joy; a time when he breaks his fast and a time of joy when he meets his Lord. And the smell coming from the mouth of the fasting person is better with Allah than the smell of musk."

3. Siyam Brings Allah's Forgiveness.

Observing the fast in Ramadan with sincere intention causes the believer to be forgiven of all past sins. Scholars note however, that this forgiveness does not apply to major sins which require the Muslim to offer to Allah a sincere repentance before they are completely forgiven.

عن أبي هريرة رضي الله عنه أن رسول الله صلى الله عليه وسلم قال :
(مَن صَامَ رَمَضَانَ إِيمَاناً وَاحْتِسَاباً غُفِرَ لَهُ ما تَقَدَّمَ مِنْ ذَنْبِهِ) متفق عليه

4. Sawm Helps the Believer to Win Jannah.

The Prophet explained that the fasting Muslim will enter Jannah from a special gate called Ar-Rayyan.

عن سهل بن سعد رضي الله عنه عن النبي صلى الله عليه وسلم، قال:
(إن في الجنة بابا يقال له: الريان، يدخل منه الصائمون يوم القيامة، لا يدخل منه أحد غيرهم، يقال: أين الصائمون؟ فيقومون لا يدخل منه أحد غيرهم، فإذا دخلوا أُغلق، فلم يدخل منه أحد)
متفق عليه

Sahl ibn Sa' said that the Prophet said: "Indeed there is a gate of Paradise called ar-Rayyaan. On the Day of Resurrection those who fast will enter through it; no one enters it except for them. And when they have entered, it is closed so that no one enters it. So when the last of them enters it, it is closed. And whoever enters it drinks, and whoever drinks never becomes thirsty." [Reported by Ibn Khuzaimah and others].

5. Sawm Shields the Muslim from the Punishment in Jahannam.

Abdullah ibn 'Amr reported that Rasoolullah ﷺ said: "The fast and the Qur'an are two intercessors for the servant of Allah on the Day of Resurrection. The fast will say: 'O Lord, I prevented him from his food and desires during the day. Let me intercede for him.' The Qur'an will say: 'I prevented him from sleeping at night. Let me intercede for him.' And their intercession will be accepted." (Reported by Ahmad).

Abu Sa'eed al-Khudri reported that the Messenger of Allah said: "No servant fasts on a day in the path of Allah except that Allah removes the Hellfire seventy years further away from his face." (Reported by Al-Baukhari, Muslim and others).

II. Physical and Medical Benefits

Fasting is an ancient practice that wise people used to observe for spiritual, psychological, and medical improvement. Pythagoras, Socrates, Plato, and Aristotle practiced and prescribed prolonged fasting.

Plato said he fasted "for greater physical and mental efficiency." Philippus Paracelsus, famed Swiss physician, and one of three Fathers of Western Medicine, along with Greece's Hippocrates and Galen, once said,

"Fasting is the greatest remedy--the physician within!"--

Not only does fasting have spiritual benefits, but it also has physical and medical benefits. Abstaining from food periodically will aid the body in cleansing itself from impurities. Fasting allows the body to rid itself of poisonous substances that can lead to serious illness and disease.

Obesity is one of the many problems that plague our modern society. Around 61% of U.S. adults were already overweight or obese by 1999. The Los Angeles Times reported at the beginning of 2006 that vast numbers of Americans have outgrown the weightiest medical description: morbid obesity. About 725,000 to a million fit this 'super-obese' category. The economic cost of this epidemic was nearly $120 billion annually by 2006, not to mention the 300,000 American deaths it's causes each year.

The U.S. Surgeon General noticed that "obesity is reaching epidemic proportions in America, and could soon cause as much preventable disease and death as cigarette smoking." Being overweight or obese increases one's risk for heart disease, cancer, diabetes, stroke, arthritis, breathing problems (asthma and sleep apnea), reproductive complications, gall bladder disease, incontinence, increased surgical risk, and psychological disorders such as depression.

In his book *Staying Healthy with Nutrition: The Complete Guide to Diet and Nutritional Medicine*, Dr. Elson Haas recommends fasting as a remedy to obesity and many other diseases. He contended,

Fasting is the single greatest natural healing therapy. It is nature's ancient, universal "remedy" for many problems. Animals instinctively fast when ill. When I first discovered fasting, 15 years ago, I felt as if it had saved my life and trans-

formed my illnesses into health. My stagnant energies began flowing, and I became more creative and vitally alive. I still find fasting both a useful personal tool and an important therapy for many medical and life problems.

Fasting in Ramadan and voluntary fasting throughout the year can help reduce the effects of obesity and help guard the body from picking up excess weight. Ridding the body of these harmful impurities will even help people to look younger and stay full of energy, since wrinkles are often caused by a build up of acid forming waste matter. Fasting in fact, allows the body to undergo a thorough cleansing process that will not progress if it has to continue processing and digesting the food that we eat.

In short, our Islamic fasting programs is extraordinarily successful for losing unnecessary weight, detoxification, regeneration, cleansing, and more skillful orientation toward optimum physical and psychological health.

III. Psychological Benefits.

Closeness to Allah and purity of heart is the true way to attain happiness in life. Allah is the One who grants people happiness and positive psychological status, or deprives them from this. Attaining Taqwa and higher level of iman and spirituality through fasting is a natural way to become psychologically healthy.

By ridding the body of waste materials, it also allows the brain to think more clearly. A clean and clear mind helps us to think rationally, and to analyze problems and situations more appropriately. Illnesses such as depression, anxiety, and related issues can be eliminated or minimized by good health and sound thought, all of which can be gained with the help of fasting. Fasting won't cure these ills, however it allows the body to purge all of the wastes and impurities that aid in inducing these types of sickness.

Fasting teaches us high discipline and self- control. A Muslim learns how to control his or her desires and psychological urges. Many Muslims quit smoking and other harmful addictions during the month of fasting. It is difficult for people to see or smell delicious food but not eat; fasting teaches us to do so. This disciplinary practice helps individuals and groups to become strong and determined in front of temptations of life.

VI. Social Benefits

Fasting also promotes wellness within the society. Those who are wealthy and well-to-do can sympathize with those who are poor and unfortunate by sharing in their pain and hunger. Unfortunately, we live in a society that no longer urges us to feel any compassion for our fellow man; however Muslims have been encouraged to help their brothers and sisters under any circumstances. Through fasting, a newfound respect for those who are suffering can inspire those fortunate people to help the poor and needy, and to take actions in doing so.

Fasting also creates a sense of sympathy and fellow feeling in the hearts and minds of Muslims. By fasting, one feels the pains of poverty, hardships of starvation, and hunger that unfortunate people suffer. It is these pains that condition a Muslim to help others and sacrifice for the sake of Allah سبحانه وتعالى.

Observing fasts also creates and strengthens the sense of equality between Muslims. During the month of Ramadan all the Muslims, both rich and poor, the learned and the ignorant, are subjected to the same level of obedience. They also experience the same pains of hunger and thirst.

The month of Ramadan is the month of giving. Millions of Muslims give out most of their zakah and charity while they are fasting during the month of Ramadan. This brings the wealthy and the needy closer together, and this develop a more united and harmonious Islamic society.

CHAPTER REVIEW

Projects and Activities

1. Write a poem about the month of Ramadan.

2. Write a play about Ramadan and fasting. Perform it in front of your class, or in the masjid.

3. Research the medical benefits of Islamic fasting.

Stretch Your Mind

1. What are the similarities and differences between Christian and Islamic fasting?

2. How can Islamic fasting benefit American or Western societies?

Study Questions

1. Define: a. Ramadan   b. Siyam
2. What makes Ramadan a special month? Support your answer with related ayaat and hadeeth.
3. What are the main benefits of siyam?
4. What are the spiritual benefits of fasting? Support your answer with related religious texts.
5. How does siyam benefit society medically? Use available facts and figures to support your answer.
6. How could a Muslim attain positive psychlogical health through fasting?
7. How does Ramadan make society stronger?

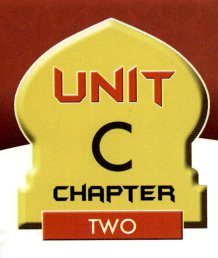

Ahkam-us-Siyam: The Rules of Fasting

CHAPTER OUTLINE

1. Learn and memorize the twelve months of the Islamic lunar year.
2. Understand how the month of Ramadan starts and ends.
3. Learn the main rules of fasting in Islam.
4. Learn about the obligatory actions of fasting.
5. Learn the recommended Sunan of fasting.
6. Learn and memorize the ayaat and hadeeth of the chapter.

VOCABULARY

Hijri calendar	السَنَة الهِجْرِيَّة
Lunar	قَمَرِي
Solar	شمسي
Imsaak	إمْسَاك
Suhoor	سحور
Iftaar	إفطار

Muslims use the Islamic calendar, also known as the Hijri calendar السَنَّة الهِجْرِيَّة. The Islamic calendar also consists of twelve months, from the month of Muharram to Thul-Hijjah. The Islamic calendar is based on the moon. This makes it a lunar قَمَرِي calendar. A lunar month happens when the moon travels around the Earth one full time. Therefore, the lunar year is completed when the moon travels around Earth twelve times.

The Beginning of the Islamic Calendar

The Islamic calendar begins the count of years with Al-Hijrah, or the journey of the Prophet from Makkah to Madinah. . This is why the calendar is often called the Hijri calendar. The year of the Hijrah is thus dated at

1 A.H. (after Hijrah). In the Gregorian calendar, this was the year 622. Omar ibn Al-Khattab رضي الله عنه was the first Khalifah, or Muslim ruler, to introduce the Hijri calendar.

The Islamic Calendar Is Lunar

The Islamic calendar is then lunar. This means that the calendar follows the patterns of the moon. The lunar month starts when the moon appears in crescent shape. This is called the "new moon." Slowly, the crescent shape becomes thicker and thicker. A full moon occurs in the middle of the month. Then, the full moon starts to go back to its crescent shape and gets thinner and thinner, until it disappears. That is the end of the lunar month.

The moon revolves around Earth. This is what causes the changes in the moon's shape. One lunar month is either 29 or 30 days. This means that it takes as many days for the moon to go through all its phases and to complete a revolution. In contrast the Gregorian calendar follows the patterns of the sun, Gregorian months usually have 30 or 31 days. Therefore, the lunar year is usually 354 days, while the solar year is usually 365 days long.

﴿ هُوَ ٱلَّذِى جَعَلَ ٱلشَّمْسَ ضِيَآءً وَٱلْقَمَرَ نُورًا وَقَدَّرَهُۥ مَنَازِلَ لِتَعْلَمُوا۟ عَدَدَ ٱلسِّنِينَ وَٱلْحِسَابَ ۚ مَا خَلَقَ ٱللَّهُ ذَٰلِكَ إِلَّا بِٱلْحَقِّ ۚ يُفَصِّلُ ٱلْءَايَٰتِ لِقَوْمٍ يَعْلَمُونَ ۝ ﴾ يونس: ٥

"It is He Who made the sun to be a shining glory, and the moon to be a light of beauty, and measured out stages for it, that you might know the number of years and the count of time. Allah did not create this except in truth. And He explains His signs in detail, for those who understand." [Surat Younus 10: 5].

Hadeeth Shareef

عن ابن عمر رضي الله عنه: قال رسول الله ﷺ:

"الشهر تسعة وعشرون أو ثلاثون"   رواه مسلم وأحمد

Ibn Omar رضي الله عنه reported that Rasoolullah (s) said: "A month is twenty nine or thirty days."
Reported by Imams Muslim and Ahmad

C11

© 2002 eCUIP, The Digital Library Project, Chicago, IL. Image created in part with photos from the Adler Planetarium and Astronomy Museum.

The Islamic Month

﴿ إِنَّ عِدَّةَ ٱلشُّهُورِ عِندَ ٱللَّهِ ٱثۡنَا عَشَرَ شَهۡرٗا فِي كِتَٰبِ ٱللَّهِ ﴾ التوبة: ٣٦

" The count of months [in the year] for Allah are twelve in the book of Allah." [9 :36]

There are twelve months in the Islamic year, just like in the Gregorian year. The following table lists all the Islamic months in the lunar year.

	Arabic	Month (English)	Main Events
1	مُحَرَّم	Muharram	Ashuraa'
2	صَفَر	Safar	
3	ربيع الأول	Rabee'-ul-Awwal	- The birth of Prophet Muhammad
			- The death of Prophet Muhammad
4	ربيعُ الثاني	Rabee'-uth-Thani	
5	جُمادى الأوَّل	Jumadal-Awwal	
6	جُمادى الثاني	Jumada-Thani	
7	رَجب	Rajab	Israa' and Mi'raaj
8	شَعْبان	Sha'ban	
9	رمَضان	Ramadan	The month of fasting (1st through 29th or 30th)
10	شَوَّال	Shawwal	Eid-ul-Fitr (1st through 3rd)
11	ذو القِعْدة	Dhul-Qi'dah	
12	ذو الحِجَّـة	Dhul-Hijjah	- Hajj
			- Eid-ul-Adha (10th through 13th)

C12

When Do We Start Fasting?

In this section we will take a look at the start and finish of Ramadan. How should we begin Ramadan, and how should its beginning be calculated?

The Arrival of Ramadan

Every year the beginning of Ramadan brings new challenges to the Muslim community. Should Ramadan begin with the sighting of the moon locally? Should we start when Saudi Arabia starts? Should we begin with the beginning of Ramadan in Pakistan? Do we rely on the calculations of the new moon by an observatory? These and many other questions are often asked at the beginning of Ramadan here in North America.

This generally goes back to a few main problems that we have here in the West. The first being problem is that we have no Islamic central authority like in most Muslim countries. No official muftis or councils exist with enough power to encourage the Muslim community as a whole to follow one authority. Second, many Muslims do not understand the fine details that go into the beginning of Ramadan according to the books of Islamic Fiqh. Third, a feeling of nationalism has also clouded the collective judgments of the Muslim community here in the West based along national lines. Unfortunately, some of us feel that various interpretations of Islamic law are inherently better since they coincide with the views of my fellow countrymen! This attitude is very detrimental to the community as a whole, and does not conform to Islamic ideals!

In this section, we will take a look at the beginning of Ramadan and how it should begin including sighting the moon and issues related to astronomical calculation.

Sighting the Moon

The month of fasting starts with the beginning of the lunar month of Ramadan. This event is confirmed traditionally by sighting the new crescent moon by the sunset of the 29th day of the lunar month of Sha'ban. If the crescent moon is not seen, Muslims wait until the thirty days of Sha'ban are completed, then they start fasting the first day of Ramadan.

Abu Hurayrah reported that the Prophet instructed: "Fast after you have seen it [the new crescent] and end the fast [at the end of the month] when you see it. If it is hidden from you, then wait until the thirty days of Sha'ban have passed." *Reported by Al-Bukhari and Muslim.*

According to the majority of imams, the report of only one pious person is accepted to decide the beginning of Ramadan. Ibn 'Umar

The hilal signals the beginning of Ramadan

said: "The people were looking for the new moon and when I reported to the Messenger of Allah that I had seen it, he fasted and ordered the people to fast." Reported by Abu Dawud, al-Hakim, and Ibn Hibban.

Given these reports, the scholars have differed regarding them. Tirmidhi states, "Most knowledgeable people act in accordance with these reports. They say that it is correct to accept the evidence of one person to determine the beginning of the fast. This is the opinion of Ibn al Mubarak, ash-Shafi'i, and Ahmad. An-Nawawi says that it is the soundest opinion.

Concerning the new moon of Shawwal [which signifies the end of the fast], it is confirmed by sighting the crescent moon by the sunset of the 29th day of Ramadan or by completing thirty days of Ramadan. Most fuqahaa', or jurists, state that the new moon of Shawwal must have been reported by at least two pious witnesses. However, other scholars do not distinguish between the new moon of Shawwal and the new moon of Ramadan. In both cases, he accepts the evidence of only one pious witness. Witnesses may be male or female.

What about Astronomical Calculations?

We are blessed to live in a world that has been made easy through the marvels of modern science. Science and technology have enhanced the quality of life as well as taught mankind about the intricacies of the world around him. Physics, chemistry, biology, and other earth sciences have unlocked the answers to many of our questions that only a century ago could not have been answered.

One of those sciences that has been developed and has answered some of those questions has been the study of astronomy. Through astronomy, we have been able to learn precise details regarding the natural

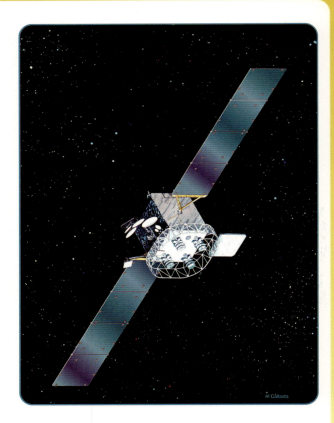

occurrences of the positioning of the sun and moon with great certainty. Should these vast sciences be overlooked? In fact, a convenient marriage between astronomy and the Sunnah of our beloved Messenger ﷺ is possible in order to rid ourselves of the problems regarding the start and end of Ramadan.

Using advanced technology, we can now know accurate details about the beginning and end of solar and lunar months. Many contemporary scholars have started to accept accurate astronomical information to determine the beginning and end of Ramadan, and other Islamic lunar months. The Fiqh Council and the Islamic Society of North America have recently decided to declare the beginning and end of Ramadan based on accurate astronomical reports. The use of astronomical data is now acceptable to many contemporary scholars, Islamic religious organizations and countries. There are still many other scholars and entities who are still studying this issue, or prefer to base their decision on the actual observation of the crescent moon in the beginning and end of Ramadan.

What exactly is fasting?

Sawm is the abstaining from food, drink, and sexualrelations from dawn until sunset, with the explicit intention of doing so for the sake of Allah. Fasting can be broken down into five separate types or categories:

1. Fard فَرْض **:** This is fasting done during the whole month of Ramadan, once a year.

2. Wajib واجِب **:** This refers to fasts that are made to:
- fulfill a nathr, or a vow on a specific day or date for the sake of Allah, upon the fulfillment of someone's wish or desire.
- Make up for a day or more you missed fasting in Ramadan.
- Fasting as a kaffarah, or expiation, to expiate a religious mistake, for example, a broken oath,, a killing by mistake, or other incidents.

3. Sunnah سُنَّة **:** This refers to fasts that are made according to the noble example of Rasoolullah, like fasting 'Aashouraa' on 10th of Muharram, or the Day of 'Arafah, on the 9th of Thul Hijjah.

4. Mustahabb مُسْتَحَب **:** This refers to all fasts that are encouraged outside the obligatory fasts such as fasting on Mondays and Thursdays, and the 13th, 14th and 15th days of every lunar month.

5. Haram حَرَام **:** Such as fasts on the first days of Eid ul Fitr, Eid ul Adhaa, and the days of Tashreeq during Hajj (11th, 12th and 13th days of Thul-Hijjah) for the pilgrims.

The Obligatory Actions of Fasting

1. Niyyah: The intention to fast

The sincere intention to fast is a necessary act of fasting. Even if a person were to stay away from all the things that nullify fasting without a sincere intention, then this would not be considered a fast and that person would not gain the spiritual benefit of fasting. Sincere intention allows you to put away the troubles of the world and concentrate solely on fulfilling Allah's سبحانه وتعالى orders.

It is not necessary to express the intentions verbally, because sincere intention is placed in the heart. However, it is permissible, though not mandatory, to express intention verbally also. In this way, you can combine sincere intention in both heart and mind.

Additionally, intentions should be made the night before each day "that tomorrow I will fast." The Maliki madhhab states that intention made at the beginning of the month of Ramadan is sufficient for the whole month, but the majority of scholars and mathahib agree that intention should be made on a nightly basis. The voluntary fasts, those that are not obligatory, can be intended up until the time of the early morning until noon. After which, a voluntary fast would not count if intention was made after noon.

2. Imsaak: Abstaining from Eating, Drinking and Sexual Relation During the Day.

Allah commanded that the fast starts from dawn and ends at sunset every day. During that time Muslims must refrain from eating, drinking and consuming substances like smoking, medicine, or drugs.

Allah says in Surat-ul-Baqarah,

﴿ وَكُلُوا وَاشْرَبُوا حَتَّىٰ يَتَبَيَّنَ لَكُمُ ٱلْخَيْطُ ٱلْأَبْيَضُ مِنَ ٱلْخَيْطِ ٱلْأَسْوَدِ مِنَ ٱلْفَجْرِ ۖ ثُمَّ أَتِمُّوا ٱلصِّيَامَ إِلَى ٱلَّيْلِ ۚ ﴾ البقرة: ١٨٧

"And eat and drink until the whiteness of the day becomes distinct from the blackness of the night at dawn, then complete the fast till night." [Surat-ul-Baqarah 2:187]

Sahabi 'Adiyy Ibn Hatim said "When the ayah "Eat and drink until the white thread becomes distinct to you ..." was revealed, I took two threads; a black and white threads and placed them underneath my pillow. During the night I looked at them to distinguish between them. In the morning I went the Messenger of Allah and mentioned that to him and he said: 'It is the black of the night and the white of the day.'" [Bukhari and Muslim].

Therefore, the fasting time is only during the time between Fajr (dawn) and Maghrib (sunset). A Muslim stops eating slightly before Fajr and breaks the fasting immediately at sunset.

Du'aa for breaking the fast

دُعَاءُ الإِفْطَار

"اللهُمَّ لَكَ صُمْتُ وعلى رِزْقِكَ أَفْطَرْتُ ذَهَبَ الظَّمَأُ وابتلَّتِ العُرُوقُ وثَبَتَ الأجْرُ إن شاءَ الله"

رواه أبو داوود

Allahumma laka sumtu, wa 'ala rizqika aftartu, thahaba-thama'au wabtallatil urooqu, wa thabat-al-ajru insha'Allah.

"O Allah I fasted for you alone, and broke my fast by eating what you have given me. Thirst is over, my flesh is watered, and my reward for fasting is approved by the will of Allah."

Recommended Actions During Fasting

The following actions discussed in this section refer to the acts that are considered mustahabb, or recommended, by Prophet Muhammad ﷺ. These acts, if done, bring the person who does them great thawab, or rewards. Thus, they are important, but not mandatory. Those actions are as follow:

- **Suhoor:** سُحور Suhoor is a pre-dawn meal that takes place right before the fasting begins before fajr prayer. It was an established Sunnah of Allah's Messenger ﷺ and those companions who followed him.

- **Delaying the suhoor:** Not only is it sunnah to have a pre-dawn meal, it is also sunnah to do so as late as possible without eating after the Fajr athaan has been called. This helps during the day to avoid hunger and fatigued. It also helps the person who is fasting to perform his religious obligations with vigor and not feel sluggish throughout the day.

- **Immediately breaking fast:** It is the Sunnah of Allah's Messenger ﷺ to break his fast immediately when hearing the athaan of the Maghrib prayer upon sunset at the end of the day. You shouldn't delay breaking fast. This is a reward from Allah that we may eat immediately after completing our daily fasting during Ramadan.

- **Breaking the fast with dates:** Breaking the fast with dry fresh dates is also the Sunnah of Allah's Messenger ﷺ. If dates are not available, then something else can be used, even a cup of water.

- **Making Intention during the night:** It is also mustahabb to make your intentions during the night. Remember, during Ramadan intention needs to be made before the Fajr time. However making intention during the night to fast the next day, safely allows you to do so without missing the time to make intention.

The previously mentioned acts can bring the person who does them great rewards and can help protect him/her from falling into bad deeds during the fasting period. Keep these simple and easy things in mind, because they can make your fast that much better!

Fasting Outside of Ramadan

Ramadan is not the only time when Muslims are encouraged to fast. There are other voluntary fasts that a Muslim is encouraged to perform. In this section, we will examine the optional fasts that were regularly observed by Allah's Messenger ﷺ. They bring great reward to those who fulfill them.

Fasting the First Six Days of Shawwal

Shawwal is the month that immediately follows Ramadan. It has been narrated that any six days during that month are recommended to fast.

Abu Ayyuob al-Ansari (Allah be pleased with him) reported that Rasoolullah said: "He who observed the fast of Ramadan and then followed it with six (days) of Shawwal; it would be as if he fasted forever."

Therefore, the person that fasts these six days after Ramadan, it's as if he fasted his whole life. Scholars interpreted this hadeeth saying that fasting the thirty days of Ramadan are rewarded as if one is fasting three hundred days since Allah rewards each good deeds tenfold. Then fasting the six days of Shawwal is rewarded also tenfold, which means that they will be considered as one fasts sixty days. The tital reward of both fasts will be as if you fast 360 days which amount to around one year. If a Muslim keeps the habit of doing that every year, he or she will be considered as fasting forever.

Fasting on the Day of 'Arafah

Other hadeeth have been mentioned regarding fasting on the day of 'Arafah. Let's look at the following hadeeth on this point.

Abu Qatadah al-Ansari (Allah be pleased with him) reported that Rasoolullah ﷺ was asked about fasting on the day of 'Arafah (9th of Dhu'I-Hijja), whereupon he said: "It expiates the sins of the preceding year and the coming year." He was asked about fasting on the day of 'Ashuraa (10th of Muharram), whereupon be said: "It expiates the sins of the preceding year." *(This has been reported by Imam Muslim).*

The Fast of 'Ashuraa

In a hadeeth related by Ibn Abbas (R) when the Messenger of Allah came to Madinah, he found the Jews fasting the day of Aashuraa'. He inquired why they did so. They replied that it was a good day, the day in which Allah delivered Prophet Musa and the Children of Israel from their enemy, Pharaoh. As gratitude Musa fasted that day. The Prophet responded:' "I'm closer to Musa than you." He then fasted the day and commanded the believers to fast." *(Bukhari and Muslim)*

The Jews fasted only on the 10th of Muharram and the Muslims were asked to fast one extra day. Thus one can fast either the 9th and 10th, or the 10th and 11th of the month.

Narrated by Salim's father: The Prophet said, "Whoever wishes may fast on the day of 'Ashuraa'."

Narrated By Ibn 'Abbas: I never saw the Prophet seeking to fast on a day more (preferable to him) than this day, the day of 'Ashuraa', or this month, i.e. the month of Ramadan.

According to the above mentioned hadeeth, it is very meritorious to fast on the day of 'Ashuraa or the 10th of Muharram.

Fasting on Mondays and Thursdays, As Well As Three Days Every Month

Fasting on Mondays and Thursdays was also mentioned in numerous ahadeeth, and it is an established practice of the Prophet ﷺ. Likewise, it was also recommended by Allah's Messenger ﷺ that Muslims fast at least three days a month. The following hadeeth illustrate this point.

Abu Qatadah Ansari (RA) reported that Allah's Messenger ﷺ was asked about fasting on Monday, whereupon he said:" It is (the day) when I was born and revelation was sent down to me." Reported by Muslim.

Osamah ibn Zayd narrated that the Prophet of Allah ﷺ used to fast on Monday and Thursday. When he was asked about it, he said: "The works of the servants (of Allah) are presented (to Allah) on Monday and Thursday." *Related by Tirmidhi*

Hunaydah ibn Khalid narrated from his wife on the authority of one of the wives of the Prophet ﷺ who said: The Apostle of Allah used to fast the first nine days of Dhul-Hijjah, Ashuraa' and three days of every month, that is, the first Monday (of the month) and Thursday. *Related by Tirmidhi*

Narrated By Hafsah, Ummul Mu'minin : The apostle of Allah ﷺ used to fast three days every month: Monday, Thursday and Monday in the next week.

Umm Salamah once said: "Rasoolullah ﷺ used to command me to fast three days every month beginning with Monday or Thursday." *Reported by Tirmithi.*

CHAPTER REVIEW

Projects and Activities

1. Participate with your class or family in a field trip to sight the Hilal at the beginning of Ramadan, or any other lunar month.

2. Participate with your class or family in a field trip to an observatory in your city. Learn some astronomical information about how the lunar month starts and ends.

3. Create a poster of the Islamic lunar year, which includes all the twelve months of the year.

Stretch Your Mind

1. What are the similarities and differences between lunar and solar years?

2. Compare and contrast Islamic and Christian fasting.

Study Questions

1. Define: a. Suhoor   b. Imsaak   c. 'Aashouraa'   d. Niyyah
2. What is the lunar year made of? Support your answer with an ayah.
3. How many days in the lunar month? Support your answer with a hadeeth.
4. What are the types of siyam?
5. What are the mandatory actions of siyam?
6. How does a Muslim observe the niyyah of fasting?
7. What should a fasting Muslim abstain from?
8. What are some of the optional fasting opportunities outside Ramadan?

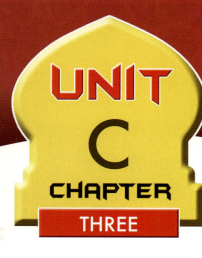

Mubtilaat-us-Siyam: The Nullifiers of Fasting

CHAPTER OUTLINE

1. Learn the main nullifiers of fasting.
2. Understand the wisdom behind easing the fasting rules on people with medical conditions.
3. Understand how a broken fast can be made up.
4. Learn some common actions that do not nullify the fast.
5. Learn some common actions that are discouraged while fasting.

VOCABULARY

Mubtilaat-us-Siyaam مُبْطِلاتُ الصِّيام

Qadaa' قضاء

Kaffarah كفارة

Fidyah فدية

In this section, we will take a good look at the actions that nullify fasting, as well as those actions that don't. Likewise, we will take a look at those actions that are recommended by the Prophet and those actions that are discouraged.

Mubtilaat-us-Siyam: The Nullifiers of Fasting

The nullifiers of siyam are those acts that break the fast and render it void. Just like in salah, there are actions that invalidate the fast and they should be avoided at all costs. There are two procedures to make up for the missed days of fasting:

1. **Qadaa'** قَضاء : It is a process that is called qadaa', or to make up. It refers to a fast that is made in place of one that is broken intentionally.

2. Kaffarah كَفَّارة : It is a penalty for missing a day of fasting in a certain manner, as explained later.

Let us learn now the main Mubtilaat-us-Siyam, or the Nullifiers of Fasting.

1. Eating and Drinking. Deliberate eating, drinking and consuming of substances (medicine, smoking, drugs etc.) break fasting. These actions nullify the fast if done willfully.

However, if a person eats or drinks forgetfully or accidentally or is forced to do it, the fasting will stay intact. That day should not to be made up and the person should continue his or her fasting. If someone forgets that he or she was fasting and eats or drinks, then he must stop eating and drinking as soon as he remembers, then continue his or her fasting.

Abu Hurayrah reported that the Prophet (S) said: "Whoever forgets he is fasting, and eats or drinks, is to complete his fast, as it is Allah who fed him and gave him something to drink." [Reported by Al-Bukhari, Muslim and others]. Ibn Abbas also reported that the Prophet (S) said: "Allah has excused for my ummah: mistakes, forgetfulness, and what they are forced to do."
[Reported by At-Tahawee, al-Hakim and Darqutni]

Similarly, if a person breaks the fast before the actual Maghrib (sunset), or after Fajr, because of a mistake in time recognition, he is not to make up the day.

While smoking and taking drugs is obviously prohibited, according to most contemporary scholars, smoking and consuming substances also breaks the fast.

2. Intentional Vomiting. Abu Hurayrah reported that the Prophet (S) said : "Whoever is overcome and vomits is not to make up the day. Whoever vomits intentionally must make up the day." [Reported by Ahmad, Abu Dawood, at-Tirmithi and Ibn Majah]

3. Sexual Intercourse. Just like eating and drinking, sexual relations invalidate one's fast. Allah only allows such activity during the nights of Ramadan, but not during the day. Allah says in Surat-ul-Baqarah,

"Permitted to you, on the night of the fasts, is the approach to your wives. They are your garments and ye are their garments." [2:187]

Sexual intercourse not only breaks the fast, but also requires the two partners to offer a kaffarah , or expiation. The Kaffarah is a penalty on the person who breaks their fast intentionally through such prohibited actions, during the day of fast. The kaffarah is to do one of the following actions in the order displayed below:

a. Releasing a slave,
b. Fasting sixty consecutive days
c. Feeding sixty needy individuals.

Intimate relation between couples is the only action, according to most scholars, which requires making up the nullified day and a kaffarah must be performed.

Related Story

Abu Hurayrah reported that a man came to Rasoolullah and said: "I am destroyed!" The Prophet asked: "What has destroyed you?" He said, "I had intercourse with my wife during a day of Ramadan." The Prophet asked: "Are you able to free a slave?" He said, "No". "The Prophet asked: "Is it possible for you to fast for two consecutive months?" He said, "No." The Prophet asked: "Is it possible for you to feed sixty poor people?" He said, "No." The Prophet said: "Then sit." A basket of dates was brought to the Prophet and he said to the man: Give this in charity." The man said: "To someone poorer than us? There is no one in Madinah who is poorer than us!" The Prophet laughed until his molar teeth could be seen, and he said: "Go and feed your family with it." [Reported by Al-Bukhari, Muslim and others] Most scholars say that both husband and wife have to perform the acts of expiation (kaffarah) if they intentionally have intercourse during a day of Ramadan on which they had intended to fast.

Contemporary Fiqh

Medical Injections

Medical injections were not available at the time of the Prophet {P}. Presently, medical injections are necessary medical tools to help patients recover. What do contemporary scholars say about them? Do they break the fast or not?

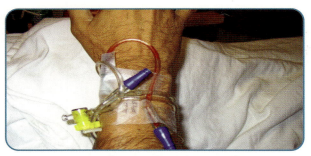

Injections Containing Nourishment
When a seriously ill person cannot eat food or keep it in his or her stomach, doctors order that nourishment must be injected into his or her veins. The injection reaches the bloodstream then it likewise breaks the fast since it is being used in place of food and drink. Though this urgent type of action breaks the fast thus falls generally under intentional eating and drinking, it is not considered as a sin if given to a sick person in need of it. As a matter of fact, a person who reaches this stage must break his fast to stay well and alive. All what is needed is to make up the day later. This is similar to the use of drips containing glucose and saline solutions, and inhalers used by people sick of asthma.

Other Medical Injections. Medical injections taken in the arm or the hip, do not invalidate the fast according to the stronger opinion of the contemporary scholars. Nose, ear and eye drops can also be taken during the fast without a problem. Just in case, if the drops are felt toward the throat coming from the nasal canals or from the ears, the fasting Muslim should spit them out. Non-nutritious medical injections and drops in general are not considered food, and they are not usually taken through the mouth into the stomach.

Regular Medicine. Medicine taken through the mouth into the stomach, like pills or syrup, does invalidate the fast.

May Allah relieve all sick believers.

Things That Do Not Break Your Fast

Now that we know what breaks the fast, both intentionally and unintentionally, let's look at what doesn't break the fast. The following items are commonly thought to break the fast, but they don't. Those items are as follows:

1. To eat or drink unintentionally (accidentally drinking water or eating a piece of food)
2. Water entering ears or nose
3. Dust or dirt going down the throat
4. Swallowing one's own saliva
5. Taking an injection (a shot)
6. Applying kohl or other cosmetics to the eyes
7. Taking a bath to keep cool.
8. Rubbing oil onto the body or hair
9. To vomit unintentionally
10. Applying perfume (however it is not permitted to inhale the smoke of incense while fasting. It is also not permissible to smoke cigarettes or inhale their smoke)
11. Brushing the teeth without toothpaste (i.e. using a miswak)
12. A wet dream, which makes ghusl obligatory, does not break the fast

Discouraged Actions During Fasting

The following actions are religiously makrooh, or discouraged during fasting, because they could eventually lead to breaking one's fast. These few actions could put one's whole fast in jeopardy; therefore, they should be avoided at all costs. Those actions are as follows:

1. Chewing Flavorless Gum, Rubber, Plastic Items, or Other Such Things:

If the gum is flavored, then you have in fact broken your fast. Gum chewing will break your fast during Ramadan, especially if it is flavored. Even though the gum is not swallowed, the flavoring is, and will invalidate fasting. Something has gone down your throat and is ingested by the body!

2. Using Toothpaste:

Toothpastes or powders shouldn't be used during fasting either. Should any tooth-

paste or tooth powder reach the back of the throat it could possibly invalidate the fast. In fact, many scholars recommend not using the miswak, even though it is an established Sunnah of Allah's Messenger ﷺ for the simple fact that mistakes in using them could lead to breaking the fast.

3. Tasting Any Article of Food or Drink Despite Spitting It Out, for no Good Reason:

This too is highly disliked, because it can lead to breaking the fast. Remember, anything that goes down the back of the throat will in fact break the fast because the body is being nourished. However, Muslim scholars allowed a mother or a cook to taste the food they are cooking for family of customers when it is necessary.

4. Trying to Quench Thirst by Swallowing saliva:

Naturally saliva will pass through the back of the throat during fasting. This fact is undeniable, however what is mentioned here is purposely gathering saliva in the mouth to try and quench thirst. According to some scholars, this in itself will break the fast because it signifies that the person fasting has the intention to break it.

5. To Complain of Hunger or Thirst:

The purpose of fasting is to develop taqwa (God-consciousness) through personal struggle. Constantly complaining about thirst and hunger doesn't aid in learning the lessons of Ramadan and fasting.

6. To Use Too Much Water up the Nostrils and Gargle In Wudu:

Despite the fact that these are established Sunnah of the Prophet ﷺ in wudu', we should strive not to use too much water during wudu' in Ramadan for the simple fact that you could possibly break your fast.

7. Quarreling, Fighting, and Arguing:

Bickering, arguing, and fighting are filthy acts that should be abstained from both inside and outside of Ramadan. However, it is even worse during the month of Ramadan, the month of mercy and increased religious practice and reflection.

8. Backbiting, Lying, and Swearing:

Additionally, foul words and poisons of the tongue, including backbiting, gossiping, lying, and swearing should be avoided at all costs. Ramadan should help us learn patience, and help us to stay away from these evils.

Exemptions from Fasting During Ramadan

Allah سبحانه وتعالى in his mercy, has made Islam very easy for those who wish to practice it. Sometimes the hardships of life demand some ease in the acts of worship that are obligatory on Muslims including prayers and fasting. Allah exempts certain people from fasting when it is not possible. Those individuals that are exempted from fasting are so because of one of the following conditions:

1. Illness

Sick people who fear their health will be badly affected by fasting. They should make up the loss, everyday, when they recover after Ramadan if possible. If it is feared that fasting will lead to death, it is obligatory to break one's fast.

2. Travel

A traveler is also exempted from fasting, however it is better for him to fast if his/her journey is not tiresome.

﴿ فَمَن شَهِدَ مِنكُمُ ٱلشَّهْرَ فَلْيَصُمْهُ وَمَن كَانَ مَرِيضًا أَوْ عَلَىٰ سَفَرٍ فَعِدَّةٌ مِّنْ أَيَّامٍ أُخَرَ يُرِيدُ ٱللَّهُ بِكُمُ ٱلْيُسْرَ وَلَا يُرِيدُ بِكُمُ ٱلْعُسْرَ ﴾ البقرة: ١٨٥

"Whoever of you is present in the month, he shall fast therein, and whoever is sick or upon a journey, then (he shall fast) a (like) number of other days; Allah desires ease for you, and He does not desire for you difficulty." [Surat-ul-Baqarah 2:185]

3. Aging

The elderly or terminally ill people that have no strength to fast or will not be cured of their illness after Ramadan. They will have to give fidyah, or compensation for everyday they don't fast.

﴿ وَعَلَى ٱلَّذِينَ يُطِيقُونَهُ فِدْيَةٌ طَعَامُ مِسْكِينٍ ﴾ البقرة: ١٨٤

"and those who are not able to do it [aging and permanently ill] may effect a redemption by feeding a poor man." [Surat-ul-Baqarah 2:184]

4. Pregnancy and Breast Feeding

Expecting and nursing mothers are exempting from fasting if they deem fasting harmful to their health or to their babies.

5. Menses (A woman's monthly menstruation)

This period usually last for seven days every month.

6. Nifaas (Post Child-berth Bleeding)

This period usually lasts for 40 days.

7. Insanity and Unconsciousness

Insane or unconscious individuals are exempted from fasting because they are not required to perform religious obligations for their lack of mental health.

Fidyah (فِدْيَة)

Fidyah, or atonement refers to a compensation that is paid due to the inability to fast. This is paid by the elderly or terminally ill people who cannot perform a full fast and will not be healed of their illnesses after the passing of Ramadan.

Those individuals who cannot fast at all should do one of the following to expiate the obligation of fasting upon him/her.
(1) To give 3.5 lbs + approx. 1.6 kg of wheat per every missed day of fasting, or 7 lbs – approx. 3.2 kg of barley per every missed day of fasting.

(2) Or……..the equivalent of the above in cash per every missed day of fasting.

If, however, an old or sick person gains the strength or recovers from their sickness after Ramadan, he/she must make up the missed number of fasts. Whatever he gave as charity, will be an additional blessing from Allah سبحانه وتعالى

CHAPTER REVIEW

Projects and Activities

Create a poster or a Powerpoint presentation about Mubtilat-us-Siyam, or Nullifiers of Fasting. Include the discouraged actions during fasting.

Stretch Your Mind

How do the rules of Islamic fasting witness to the kindness of Allah and the easiness of the Islamic religion?

Study Questions

1. List the actions that are classified as Mubtilat-us-Siyam, or nullifiers of fasting? Support your answer with the related ayaat and hadeeth.
2. Who is exempt from fasting ? Support your answer with the related ayaat.
3. What do you need to do if you miss a fast by eating or drinking?
4. What is the kaffarah for breaking the fast through sexual relations?
5. Indicate if the following actions break the fast:

   a. To eat and drink forgetfully

   b. Food put in the mouth by force of a fasting person

   c. Water going down the throat while gargling,

   e. Intentionally Swallowing a pebble, a piece of paper, or any item that is not used as food or medicine

   f. Using medical ear or eye drops

   g. Inhaling snuff into the nostrils

   h. To eat and drink after the Fajr prayer or to break the fast before sunset due to a cloudy sky or a faulty watch, etc., and then realizing one's fault

   i. A woman give birth to her child during a day of Ramadan.

   j. A woman gets into her menses period during a day of Ramadan

   k. To apply or smell perfume   l. Smoking

   L. while being conscious of one's fast, to vomit at least a mouthful intentionally

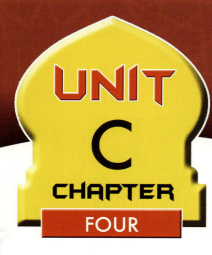

Hajjat-ul-Wadaa'
Prophet Muhammad's Farewell Pilgrimage (Part One)

CHAPTER OUTLINE

1. Learn about the preparations the Prophet made for his Farewell Hajj.
2. Learn the rituals of Hajj that the Prophet performed before reaching Makkah.

VOCABULARY

- The Farewell Pilgrimage حَجَّة الوَداع
- Miqaat ميقات
- Ihram إحْرام
- Talbiyah تلبِية

Islam Spread Peacefully Over Arabia

There were no wars a military expeditions after Tabook. There was peace across Arabia from one end of the peninsula to the other. During the 9th and 10th years A. H., the Prophet was extremely busy receiving delegations representing the various tribes from all over Arabia. Historians cite more than seventy tribes and nations that dispatched delegations to Madinah to learn about and accept Islam. The tribes of Daws, Taqeef, Fazarah, and Haneefah were among the many that came to meet the Prophet and pledge their allegiance. At least two Christian delegations came and declared their acceptance of Islam; delegations from Najran and another from Tai' under the leadership of Udayy Ibn Hatim At-Ta'ee also visited the Prophet. Prophet Muhammad was also extremely busy sending out instructors and messengers to teach those tribes and others the religion of Islam.

The Prophet Plans for Hajj

Allah prescribed the Hajj in the 9th year A.H. The Prophet made the decision not to go for Hajj during the 9th year A. H. This was because many Arabs still hadn't embraced Islam and they would have come to Makkah to make Hajj according to their faulty, traditional ways. Some of them would have done Hajj naked, while others would have brought their idols with them. Therefore, Rasoolullah sent Abu Bakr with a few hundred Muslims to perform Hajj the right way demonstrating to the Arabs how to perform it properly. He ordered Abu Bakr and Ali Ibn Abi Talib to teach the Quraysh and the Arabs Surat-ut-Tawbah which invited all Arabs to become Muslims. It also called upon them not to come to Al-Masjid-ul-Haram as long as they worship other than the one true God.

When the month of Thul-Qi'dah came in the 10th year A.H., the Prophet ﷺ prepared for Hajj and ordered the people of Madinah to do likewise. The Prophet sent messengers to all parts of Arabia asking the Muslims to join him in the Greater Pilgrimage.

Fast Facts

Prophet Muhammad performed Hajj only one time after he became a prophet. That was Hajjat-ul-Wadaa'.

He performed 'Umrah twice. The first was in the seventh year of Al-Hijrah, which is called 'Umrat-ul-Qadaa'. He performed it with many of the Sahabah based on the agreement with the Quraysh in Al-Hudaybiyah. Rasoolullah performed the second 'Umrah along with Hajjat-ul-Wadaa' in the tenth year of Al-Hijrah.

Responding to the Call of Prophet Ibraheem

In doing so, Prophet Muhammad was carrying out the command given to Ibraheem (عليه السلام) nearly 2500 years before Muhammad's birth.

﴿ وَأَذِّن فِي ٱلنَّاسِ بِٱلْحَجِّ يَأْتُوكَ رِجَالًا وَعَلَىٰ كُلِّ ضَامِرٍ يَأْتِينَ مِن كُلِّ فَجٍّ عَمِيقٍ ﴾ الحج: ٢٧

"And proclaim amongst mankind the pilgrimage. They will come to you on foot and upon all kinds of lean camels coming from every remote land." [22: 27].

The Prophet responded to Ibraheem's (عليه السلام) call not with hundreds or thousands, but with more than one hundred thousand believers.

Preparing for the Great Hajj

The tents were pitched outside Madinah. Thousands of Muslims from many tribes and localities of Arabia came to join the Prophet on his first Hajj. They poured down from the

Al-Masjid An-Nabawi

mountains and out of the valleys, from deserts, towns and villages. Now they knew what brotherhood in Islam actually meant.

In the recent past, these same people were tearing each other to pieces. They had been addicted to the evils of drinking, gambling, adultery and discrimination. But now they were acting as if they had but one soul and one sense of purpose: to respond to their Lord's call to visit His Sacred House.

Prophet Muhammad ﷺ ensured that the rituals of Hajj were very clear to the Muslims. During the Farewell Hajj, he practiced before the pilgrims everything that he preached. God saw that he did not miss conveying anything to his followers. It was for God to command and for Muhammad to obey.

Prophet Muhammad ﷺ had a very effective method of preaching. He ensured that his followers promptly acted upon his teachings. He forgave all his former enemies—Abu-Sufyan, Ikrimah Ibn Abi Jahl, Malik Ibn Awf, 'Uyaina Bin Hisn, and countless more. Indeed, in this pilgrimage there were thousands who had fought him as enemies, but they were now his friends and followers. They had gone through some difficult experiences before finally reaching the conclusion that he, Muhammad, was nothing but a true messenger. Thus they showed their appreciation of his virtues by their presence at Madinah, in the tenth year of Hijrah.

25th of Thul-Qi'dah: The March of Pilgrims

The Prophet ﷺ and tens of thousands of Muslims set off toward Makkah at the end of Thul-Qi'dah (25th). By doing so the Prophet ﷺ had in mind teaching the people the Hajj rites according to his Sunnah. He had all his nine wives with him so that women could learn about their rites as well.

When the Prophet ﷺ reached Thul-Hulayfah, he encamped and spent the night there. Thul-Hulayfah is the Miqaat ميقات, the marker point for pilgrims who come for Hajj from the north. Those wishing to perform pilgrimage cannot pass through the Miqaat without having made their intention for Hajj and putting on the Hajj uniform which is called Ihram إحْرام .

The next morning the Prophet and his followers prayed Salat-ul-Fajr. Then he told them all the revelation he had received instructing him about the rituals and rules of Hajj. He ordered: "Wear your Ihram here and make your intention for Hajj." So he washed, wore his Ihram and before he made the intention for Hajj, Ai'shah gave him some fragrant musk to wear. He then prayed two rak'aat, which are called Sunnat-ul-Ihram.

The pilgrim's garb, the ihram, is very simple and consists only of one piece of white cloth tied round the waist with another similar piece covering the upper part of the body. The head and arms are left uncovered. The companions and followers eagerly followed the example of their Prophet and donned the ihram too in the same way.

The Wisdom Behind the Mandate of Ihram

In this garb, all men stand before their Lord as equals. Kings cannot be distinguished from poor men, nor noblemen from laborers. Ihram provides a visual picture of equality of human beings. This is a striking reality check for many people. It instills a real dose of humility especially to those who are vulnerable to having a superiority complex based on their position in society. Here is unity and equality carried out in practice and not merely preached as a theory in textbooks.

Fiqh Point

When in state of ihram, pilgrims cannot do the following:

1. Cut hair or clip nails
2. Wear perfume
3. Men cannot wear regular clothing
4. Hunt
5. Cut branches of trees in Makkah
6. Have Sexual relations with a spouse.

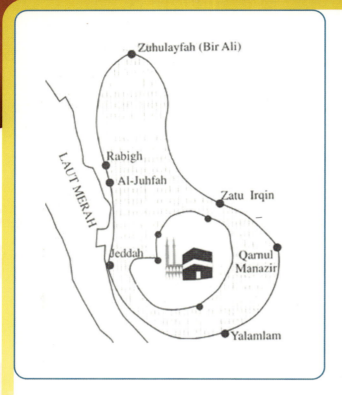

Map shows the locations of the miqaats for beginning Hajj from all directions. Pilgrims must adhere to Ihram clothes and rituals in the Haram area as they perform Hajj or 'Umrah.

The Hajj

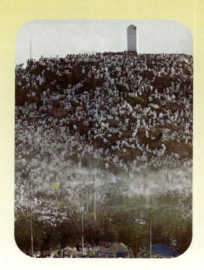

By Him whose House the loving pilgrims visit,
Responding with ihram at the appointed limit,
Uncovering their heads in total humility
Before One to Whom faces bow in servility.
They exclaim in the valleys, "We have responded to You -
All Praise is Yours, and Kingdom too!"
He invited and they answered, with love and pleasure;
When they called upon Him, nearer came the Divine treasure.
You see them on their mounts, hair dusty and disheveled,
Yet never more content, never happier have they felt;
Leaving homelands and families due to holy yearning,
Unmoved are they by temptations of returning.
Through plains and valleys, from near and far,
Walking and riding, in submission to Allah.

Source: Awdah-ul-Masalik ila Ahkam-il-Manasik. The poem is by Imam Ibn Qayyim al-Jawziyyah. It is translated into English by Usama Hassan. Other parts of the poem are inserted in the appropriate places throughout this and the following chapter.

Starting the Hajj

With their bodies washed clean, their hearts purified, and clothed in the white garb, the Muslims followed their leader. Their beloved brother in faith, Prophet Muhammad ﷺ led Salat ul-Thuhr. After that he mounted his camel, Al-Qaswaa', and gave the signal to make تلْبِيَة Talbiyah:

لَبَّيْكَ اللهُمَّ لَبَّيْكَ ، لَبَّيْكَ لا شَرِيكَ لكَ لَبَّيْكَ
إنَّ الحَمْدَ والنِّعْمَة لكَ والمُلكَ ، لا شَرِيكَ لكَ

"Labayk-allahumma Labayk. Labayka La Sharika laka Labayk Innal-hamda wan-ni'mata laka wal-mulk, la shareeka lak…"

(Here I am at your service. Here I am, O God! I am here and declare that there is no partner with you. I am here at your service. All praise, thanks, and blessings belong to you. You have no partner, O God!

This is the most direct form of response to God's call of service. Man speaks to God directly and God speaks to mankind without any intermediary or intercession. It makes man a free man. The soul of man realizes its greatness by standing in the presence of God, his only Lord, and it is emancipated from all evil thoughts.

Spiritual Awakening

As Prophet Muhammad ﷺ said the Talbiyah at each stop, he was followed by thousands of voices in unison repeating what he said. The hills and deserts echoed their passionate calls to their Lord.

Those men and women who have experienced Hajj report that they feel an intense spiritual awakening. Indeed there is something about Hajj that can raise even the meanest of men to nobility and devotion. It is like being drowned in the sea of God's Love.

Hajj indeed is a symbol of sacrifice in which the soul of man sacrifices worldly comforts, luxuries, and joys for the sake of pleasing God. Although Hajj has some physical difficulties and financial burdens, pilgrims still love it for its spiritual gratification. There are Muslims, who have performed pilgrimage a score of times are still not satisfied and wish to perform more. It is the most fascinating and spiritual journey for a Muslim.

CHAPTER REVIEW

Projects and Activities

1. Borrow two pieces of ihram, and wear them as the Hujjaj usually do. Take pictures, and share them with your classmates and friends.

2. Watch a documentary about Hajj.

Stretch Your Mind

What is the wisdom behind having the points of Miqaat around Makkah?

Study Questions

1. Define: a. Miqaat   b. Ihram   c. Talbiyah
2. What is the ayah where Allah orders the believer to come for Hajj? Write the ayah in Arabic and its meaning in English.
3. What is the wisdom behind the ihram uniform? What restrictions apply when a Muslim is in the ihram situation?
4. Write the Prayer of Talbiyah in Arabic along with its meaning in English.
5. What are the actions a pilgrim cannot do after starting his or her ihram, and making the niyyah for Hajj?
6. Provide brief answers to the following questions:
    a. Name the two Christian delegations the Prophet received and hosted in Madinah?
    b. When did Allah make Hajj an obligatory worship?
    c. When did Prophet Muhammad perform Hajj?
    d. How many times did the Prophet perform Hajj after he became a Prophet?
    e. How many times did the Prophet perform 'Umrah after he became a Prophet?
    f. What is the name of the Miqaat point the Prophet passed through in his way to Hajj?

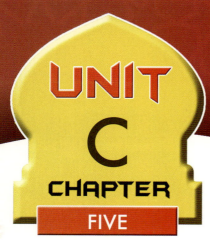

Hajjat-ul-Wadaa':
Prophet Muhammad's Farewell Pilgrimage (Part Two)

CHAPTER OUTLINE

Learn about the events of Prophet Muhammad's Farewell Hajj.
Learn the rituals of Hajj.
Appreciate and value the spiritual importance of Hajj.
Learn and appreciate the Prophet's final message to Arabs and mankind

VOCABULARY

- Tawaf-ul-Qudoom طواف القدوم
- As-Safa الصَفا
- Al- Marwah المَروَة
- Sa'i سَعي
- Mina منى
- Arafaat عَرَفات
- Al-Muzdalifah المُزدَلِفَة
- Tawaf-ul-Ifadah طواف الإفاضة
- Tawaf-ul-Wadaa' طواف الوَداع
- Yawm-ut-Tarwiyah يومُ التَروية
- Yawm-un-Nahr يَومُ النَحْر

The Fourth of Thul-Hijjah:
The Tawaf of Arrival

Before the Prophet reached Makkah on the 4th day of Thul-Hijjah, he encamped at Thee-Tuwa valley (a place close to Makkah) and spent the night there. He prayed Fajr, and then made ghusl before entering Makkah. As soon as he reached Makkah he hastened to Al-Ka'ba, kissed Black Stone, and made seven circuits around Al-Ka'bah. This action is called Tawaf-ul-Qudoom طواف القدوم, or the Arrival Tawaf.

This is the first Hajj ritual a pilgrim should perform when he enters Makkah. During the first three rounds he jogged lightly and the remaining four he went somewhat easy. Then he prayed two rak'aat at Maqam Ibraheem. Then he recited,

﴿ وَاتَّخِذُوا مِن مَّقَامِ إِبْرَاهِيمَ ﴾ البقرة: ١٢٥

"And make the stand of Ibraheem a place to pray." (2:125).

Later, he drank water from the spring of Zamzam before going to make Sa'i.

Performing Sa'i السعي Between As-Safa and Al-Marwah

The Prophet (pbuh) proceeded to the Hill of As-Safa الصفا. On his approach, Rasoolullah recited the Qur'anic verse:

﴿ إِنَّ الصَّفَا وَالْمَرْوَةَ مِن شَعَائِرِ اللَّهِ فَمَنْ حَجَّ الْبَيْتَ أَوِ اعْتَمَرَ فَلَا جُنَاحَ عَلَيْهِ أَن يَطَّوَّفَ بِهِمَا وَمَن تَطَوَّعَ خَيْرًا فَإِنَّ اللَّهَ شَاكِرٌ عَلِيمٌ ﴿١٥٨﴾ ﴾ البقرة: ١٥٨

"Behold! As-Safa and Al-Marwa are among the symbols of Allah. So, those who perform Hajj or 'Umrah should walk around them" [Surat-ul-Baqarah 2:158]

Rasoolullah then climbed As-Safa until he could see Al-Ka'bah from where he stood. He faced Al-Ka'bah and thrice proclaimed Allah's Oneness and glorified Him. Then he said Takbeer followed by La Illaha ilallah, Wahdahu La Sharika Lah, Lahul Mulku Walahul Hamdu wahuwa Ala Kulli Shay'in Qadeer."

"There is no deity worthy of worship except Allah. He has no partners. To Him belong the kingdom and all praise. He alone grants life and death. He has power over all things. There is no god but He. He has fulfilled His promise, given victory to His servant, and He alone defeated the confederates."

Then he descended toward Al-Marwah الْمَرْوَة. Half way through when he came to the bottom of the hill, he jogged then slowed down. Climbing the Hill of Al-Marwah, he faced the Qiblah and made takbeer and repeated what he had said on As-Safa. At Al-Marwah on his seventh round the Prophet commanded all those who had no 'hadiy', or cattle for sacrifice, to offer to shave their heads or shorten their hair and free themselves from the restriction of ihram for the time being.

At the Ka'bah

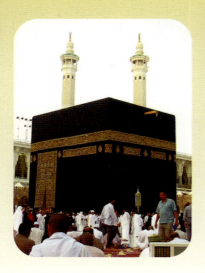

When they see His House - that magnificent sight
By which the hearts of all creatures are set alight -
It seems they've never felt tired before,
For their discomfort and hardship are no more.
Now the eye of the lover drowns in its stream.
It sees through its tears the goal of its dreams;
Now for Allah, how many tears are issued,
Each one being followed by a multitude?
When the eye perceives the House, its darkness clears,
And from the sorrowful heart, pain disappears;
Vision cannot encompass this beautiful sight:
Each glance returns with greater delight!
No wonder at this, for when the Merciful preferred
The House for Himself, it became most honored.
He clothed it in majesty, a magnificent garment;
Embroidered it with beauty, a wonderful ornament!
The hearts all love the House, therefore,
Awed and humbled, in respect and honor.

The Eigh of Thul-Hijjah: The Day of Tarwiyah

On the eigth of Thul-Hijja (the day of Tarwiyah تروية), the Prophet left Makkah for Mina and reached there at noon. All the Muslims joined the Prophet at Mina and stayed there over night.

The Ninth of Thul-Hijjah: Arriving at Arafaat

After the Fajr prayer on Friday, the ninth of Thul-Hijjah, the Prophet rode his camel Al-Qaswaa' to 'Arafaat. 'Arafaat, also called Arafah, is a plain near Mina which has a small mount that is called "Jabal-ur-Rahmah," or the Mount of Mercy.

The one hundred thousand pilgrims followed the Prophet to 'Arafaat. The Prophet's tent was pitched at a place called Namirah to the east of 'Arafaat. Soon after midday, riding his camel, he went to the center of Arafaat and delivered his famous sermon.

Historians estimate that one hundred thousand pilgrims observed Hajj with the Prophet in the ninth year of Al-Hijrah, and listened to his sermon.

Famous Sermon

After thanking God, the Prophet addressed the people saying: "O People! Listen to me very well, because I do not know that after this year I will ever meet you again in this place.

O People, (from now onwards) until you meet your Lord, your blood and your properties are as sacred as are this day and this month.

And surely you will meet your Lord and He will ask you about your deeds, and I have conveyed His message to you.

"He who is entrusted with property belonging to another should deliver his trust to whom it belongs.

"And all that is lent on usury is cancelled but your capitals are yours. Do not do injustice to others, nor let injustice be done to you."

"God has decided that there is no usury. And all interest due to 'Abbas bin Abdul-Muttalib is cancelled."

"And all compensation for bloodshed in the Time of Ignorance (Jahiliyyah) is abolished."

"Therefore, Oh, people, understand well my sayings. I am conveying Allah's message to you. I have left with you something that if you take hold of, you will never go astray, namely the Book of God and my Sunnah. Don't become kuffar (Non-believers) after me, beheading each other.

Oh, people, listen to my speech and make sure that you understand it. You are taught that each Muslim is a brother of every other Muslim and Muslims form one brotherhood. It is not lawful for a man to take anything of his brother's except what is given with one's own free will. Therefore, do not do injustice to one another.

Oh, God! Have I conveyed my message?" They all shouted with one voice, yes.

The Completion of the Message

When the Prophet had finished his sermon he stepped down from his camel. Bilal made 'athan and the Prophet ﷺ combined the prayers of Thuhr and 'Asr with one 'Athan and two Iqamahs (Qasr and Jami')

As he did so, God revealed to him,

﴿ ٱلْيَوْمَ أَكْمَلْتُ لَكُمْ دِينَكُمْ وَأَتْمَمْتُ عَلَيْكُمْ نِعْمَتِي وَرَضِيتُ لَكُمُ ٱلْإِسْلَٰمَ دِينًا ۚ ﴾ المائدة: ٣

"This day, I have perfected for you your Faith, and completed My blessing upon you, and have accepted for you Al-Islam as a religion." [Surat-ul-Ma'idah 5: 3]

The Prophet immediately recited this verse to all present.

Reading Between the Lines

When Abu Bakr رضي الله عنه heard the verse about faith being perfected, he wept! He realized that when the message was completely delivered, the Messenger would depart. He sensed that the day when the Prophet ﷺ would meet his Lord and depart this life leaving his companions was not far off.

Then the Prophet ﷺ mounted his camel and rode until he reached a spot where he turned to face the Qiblah. He made thikr and du'aa' there until sunset.

Arafat

Now to 'Arafaat, hoping for Mercy and Forgiveness
From the One overflowing with Generosity and Kindness;
Now for Allah is that Magnificent Standing
Like, though lesser than, the Day of Reckoning.
The Irresistible draws near, His Majesty manifest,
Boasting to His angels, for He is the Mightiest,
"My slaves have come to Me so lovingly,
I'll be Generous and Merciful, willingly.
I have forgiven their sins, - to this you are witness -
Fulfilled their hopes, and showered them with goodness."
So joyous news! O people of that standing,
When sins are forgiven and mercy is spreading;
How many slaves are set completely free?
Whilst others seek a cure, and heal will He.
Now Satan is never known to lose such face:
He's blameworthy, rejected, in utter disgrace.
For he sees a matter that enrage him must:
He flees, slaps his face and covers it in dust!
Such forgiveness he never did see
As granted by the Lord, and such Mercy!
He built his edifice from every temptation available
Till he thought it was complete, unassailable;
Then Allah struck his building at its very foundation,
So it fell upon him, tumbling in devastation;
What worth has his structure, this evil ploy,
That he does build, and the Lord does destroy?

Praying at Al-Muzdalifah

After sunset, the Prophet left this place and traveled on to Al-Muzdalifah. There he spent the night praying Maghrib and Ishaa' prayers. He again combined them, with one 'athan and two iqamahs. In this case he prayed three rak'aat of Maghrib, and shortened Ishaa' to two rak'aat. The Prophet slept there in Muzdalifah.

On the morning of the tenth day of Thul-Hijjah, the Prophet prayed Fajr in Muzdalifah. This day is the first day of Eid-ul-Adha. Before the sun came up, he mounted his camel. He went on his way until he reached al-Masha'ril Haram. He faced the Qiblah and made du'aa' until it was almost daylight. The Prophet pushed his camel on to Mina, passing by the road leading to Jamrat-ul-Aqabah in Mina.

The Tenth of Thul-Hjjah

During the tenth day of Thul-Hijjah, the Prophet performed a few Hajj rituals:

1. Throwing the Stones

Prophet Muhammad performed this ritual of Hajj in Mina at a place called Jamrat-ul-Aqabah. It is in commemoration of an event that happened thousands of years ago when Iblees tried to stop Ibraheem from carrying out Allah's order to sacrifice his son Isma'eel. This had happened three times, in three adjacent spots in Mina. Prophet Ibraheem ﷺ, of course refused to disobey Allah. He threw stones at Iblees and went ahead to fulfill the vision he saw.

Prophet Muhammad commemorated the actions of his great grandfather, Prophet Ibraheem. He threw seven pebbles at each of the three symbols there saying "Allahu

Jamraat in Mina

Akbar," after throwing each one. Muslims learn through this rite that true believers must reject Shaytan. They must take him as their greatest enemy and reject his calls to disobey Allah if they are to be successful in this life and the Hereafter.

In this day. Prophet Ibraheem only threw seven stones on one of the spots where Iblees appered tp Prophet Ibraheem. It is called Jamrat-ul-Aqabah Al-Kubra.

2. The Sacrifice

The Prophet had brought one hundred camels to sacrifice at Mina on the tenth day of Thul-Hijjah, which is the first day of Eid-ul-Adha. This day is also called Yawm-un-Nahr يَوْمُ النَّحْرِ, or the day of slaughtering because the pilgrims start slaughtering their sacrifices on that day. Rasoolullah sacrificed 63 camels: one for each year of his life, and hegave the remainder to 'Ali. 'Ali then sacrificed these camels. In doing this, the Prophet commemorated the great obedience that Prophet Ibraheem demonstrated when he was willing to follow Allah's order to slaughter his son Isma'eel. He distributed the meat among the poor and the pilgrims.

The Prophet then shaved his head and wore his regular clothes. His companions were around him while he was having his head shaved, competing to collect each single hair before it would fall to the ground.

Muzdalifah and Mina

Now to Muzdalifah, to spend the night
In the Sacred Area, then Prayer at first light;
Now on to the Great Pillar, which they need
To stone at the time of the Prayer of Eid;
Now to their tents for the sacrifice prepared,
Reviving the tradition of a Father revered.
If sacrificing themselves were Allah's demand,
They would respond, submitting to the command;
Just as they'd expose their necks in Jihad
To Allah's enemies, till these stream with blood;
They discipline themselves, presenting the head for a shave:
Bringing humility and happiness to the obedient slave.

3. Shaving and Removing Ihram.

After performing the above rituals, the Prophet shaved his head and changed his ihram clothes. He now wore his regular outfits.

4. Tawaf-ul-Ifadah

After shaving, the Prophet took off his Ihram and wore ordinary clothes and musk perform. He rode to Makkah and made Tawaf-ul-Ifadah طواف الإفاضة. He started from the Black Stone and made seven circuits. This is a very important rukn, or pillar of Hajj. It is the main tawaf in the Hajj rituals, and for that it is also called Tawaf-ul-Hajj, or the Tawaf of the Pilgrimage. If a pilgrim neglects to perform it, his or her Hajj will not be valid until it is performed.

Tawaf-ul-Ifadah

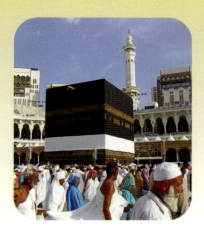

So when they've removed those natural growths,
Completed their rites, and fulfilled their oaths,
He invites them again to visit His House:
What honor and welcome this visit allows!
By Allah, they visit it in so much splendor,
Receiving their rewards and plenty of honor;
There Allah bestows Grace, Favor, and Kindness,
Showing Generosity, Mercy and Forgiveness.

11th - 13th of Thul-Hijjah: The Remaining Days of Eid-ul-Adha

The Prophet ﷺ remained during the second, third and fourth days of Eid-ul-Adha in Mina. These three days are called in Fiqh books "Ayyam-ut-Tashreeq." On each of these blessed days, he threw seven stones on each of the three Jamraat in the following order:

1. Jamrat-ul-Aqabah Al-Kubra
2. Jamrat-ul-Aqabah Al-Wusta
3. Jamrat-ul-Aqabah As-Sughra

On the afternoon of the eleventh day of Thul-Hijjah, which is the second day of Eid-ul-Adha, he stoned the three Jamraat at sunset, each with seven pebbles, making Takbeer with the throw of each stone. He stopped and made du'aa' after throwing at the first and the second one. He threw at the third one, but did not stop.

He made a speech on that day at Al-Jamraat mounting his camel. Imam Ahmad reported in his Musnad that the Prophet ﷺ delivered a speech. He was riding his camel and said:

The Farewell Sermon

"Oh people, On what day are we? And in what month, and what country?"
They said: " This is a sacred day, a sacred month, a sacred country."
He said: "Your blood and your property and your honor are as sacred as this day, this month and this country, until you meet your God."
He told them that usury is prohibited by God and then recited the verses: "The year is twelve months—four of them are sacred, Shawal, Thul-Q'idah, Thul-Hijjah, and Rajab."
"And after that, you men! You have your rights on your wives and they have their rights on you. And instruct each other to be good to your women-folk, for they are assigned to you, and have no control over anything by themselves. And you have taken them as God's trust, and they have been made lawful to you by the Word of God."
"Listen to me well. Do not commit injustice. Do not commit injustice. Do not commit injustice. All blood money and usury in Jahilyyah are cancelled from now on."
The Prophet threw the stones in the same manner in the third and fourth days of Eid.

Mina

Then they return to Mina, each to his tent,
Every minute, wishes is granted, and they are content;
They stay there a day, then another, then a third,
They're allowed to depart early, but to stay is preferred;
They stone the pillars daily after the sun's decline,
With a slogan of takbir in the presence of the Divine!
If only you could see their standing there:
Palms outstretched, hoping for Mercy's share!
"O Lord! O Lord! Knowing as You do
That we hope for no one, only You!
Then grant our wish, O You All-Knowing,
We pray for Your Mercy overflowing."

13th of Thulhijjah: Tawaf-ul-Wadaa', The Final Hajj Rite

The Prophet ﷺ concluded by throwing the stones in Mina on the 13th of Thul-Hijjah, which is the fourth day of Eid-ul-Adha. After Maghrib time, he moved to Makkah where he performed the final rite of Hajj, which is called Tawaf-ul-Wadaa' طواف الوداع. This tawaf was not different from the others.

The Farewell Tawaf

When they've achieved at Mina all their gains,
Once more they fill the valleys and plains:
To the Ka'bah, the Sacred House, by the end of the day,
To circle it seven times, and then to pray.
When departure nears and they are certain
That the bond of proximity is about to loosen,
There's only a last stand for a final farewell:
Now for Allah are the eyes that swell,
And for Allah are the heavy hearts that turn
Into cauldrons of desire, where fire does burn;
And the passionate sighs whose heat so vigorous
Nearly melts the lover, ecstatic, rapturous!
Now you see those bewildered, perplexed in the throng,
Whilst others chant their sorrowful song:
"I depart, but there remains for You my yearning,
My fire of grief is raging and burning;
I bid farewell, but longing pulls my reins -
My heart is encamped in Your eternal plains!"
No blame today for saying what you feel:
No blame for expressing what you used to conceal!

This Hajj is called "The Farewell Pilgrimage حجة الوداع," because it was the first and last time the Prophet performed Hajj after he became a prophet.

Table of Hajj Rituals That the Prophet Performed

Thul Hijjah Days	Major Hajj days	Eid-ul-Adha days	Place	Rituals
8th	Day of Tarwiyah		Mina	Staying in Mina
9th	Day of Arafah		Arafah/ Muzdalifah	Staying in Arafah until Sunset, overnight in Al-Muzdalifah
10th	Day of Sacrifice	1st	Mina	Sacrifice/ Throw stones/ Tawaf-ul-Ifadah/ Remove Ihram uniform
11th	Day of Tashreeq 1	2nd	Mina	Throw stones
12th	Day of Tashreeq 2	3rd	Mina	Throw stones
13th	Day of Tashreeq 3	4th	Mina	Throw stones (If stayed in Mina)

CHAPTER REVIEW

Projects and Activities

1. You are a publisher and want to publish a guide for pilgrims, or Hujjaj. Help them perform Hajj as the Prophet did.

2. Create a Powerpoint or flash presentation about the rituals of Hajj.

3. Develop a poster which includes beautiful quotations from the Prophet's Farewell Sermon.

Stretch Your Mind

1. Create a Month of Thul-ul-Hijjah Calendar, then enter the following occasions and ritual in the proper days:
    a. Yawm-ut-Tarwiyah
    b. Yawm-Arafah
    c. The Night at Al-Muzdalifah
    d. Yawm-un-Nahr
    e. Days of Tashreeq
    f. Days of Eid-ul-Adha

Remember that some of the above rituals and occasions may overlap. Try to be creative in designing and organizing your calendar.

2. Infer the wisdom behind the following Hajj rituals:
    a. Wearing the ihram uniform
    b. Tawaf
    c. Sa'i
    d. The sacrifice
    e. Throwing the stones in Mina

Study Questions

1. When did Prophet Muhammad perform Hajj?
2. How many times did the Prophet perform hajj after he became a prophet?
3. Define:

Miqaat	Ihram
Tawaf-ul-Qudoom	Tawaf-ul-Ifadah
Sa'i	Yawm-ut-Tarwiyah
Yawm Arafah	Jamrat
Yawm-un-Nahr	Ayyam-ut-Tashreeq

4. Describe what the following places are, and explain why they are significant:

As-Safa and Al-Marwah	Mina
Arafah	Muzdalifah

5. What is the wisdom behind the ihram uniform? What restrictions apply when a Muslim is in ihram situation?
6. Where did the Prophet deliver his Khutbat-ul-Wadaa', or Farewell Sermon? List five main ideas that came in the sermon.
7. List the Hajj rituals the Prophet performed from the beginning to the end.

UNIT D

Islam Prevails over Arabia

Chapter One	Ghazwat Tabook	D2
Chapter Two	Honesty Saves: The Story of the Three Who Missed Tabook	D10
Chapter Three	Surat-ul-Munafiqoon	D16
Lesson 1	Surat-ul-Munafiqoon: Verses (1-4)	D17
Lesson 2	Surat-ul-Munafiqoon: Verses (5-8)	D21
Lesson 3	Surat-ul-Munafiqoon: Verses (9-11)	D25
Chapter Four	Prophet Muhammad Passes to Jannah	D28

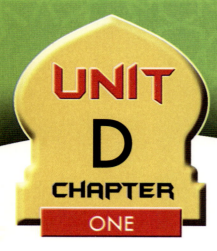

Ghazwat Tabook: Fifty Days in the Harsh Desert

CHAPTER OUTLINE

1. Learn about the real cause of the expedition to Tabook.
2. Learn about the events that took place -on the way to Tabook.
3. Appreciate the virtue of giving for the cause of Islam.
4. Appreciate the virtue of being active and exerting great effort for the cause of Islam.
5. Learn about the retreat of the Romans and their Arab allies.
6. Learn about the events during the return from Tabook.
7. Understand the phenomena of nifaq and the munafiqeen.

VOCABULARY

- Nifaaq نفاق
- Munafiqeen منافقين
- Jaysh-ul-Usrah جيش العسرة

The Great Threat from the North

After the Battle of Hunayn, the only real threat that remained for the Muslims came from the Roman Empire in the north. There were rumors claiming that the Roman Emperor was planning a campaign against the Muslims. Though the Prophet had liberated most of Arabia, he and his companions knew that there was still a threatening presence on their northern borders. According to the rumors, the Arab tribes on the Syrian frontier had joined forces with the Romans in preparation for confrontation with the Muslims.

Reports of an imminent attack were carried to Madinah by the traders coming from Syria. They told of an enormous well-equipped army of about forty thousand fighters in addition to the Arabian tribes of Lukham, Judham, and other tribes who had allied with the Byzantines. The news was that they had reached Al-Balqaa', an area in present day Jordan.

The news from Syria brought back memories of the experience of Ghazwat Mu'tah that you learned about last year. In that battle, the Romans and their Arab allies in Syria assembled around two hundred thousand fighters. Zaid Ibn Al-Harithah and other Muslim leaders and soldiers who were martyred during that battle were not forgotten.

Swift Action

Prophet Muhammad didn't want to take any chances, so he began assembling his largest army ever. He was worried that the Byzantines with their huge army maight attack the Islamic regions, or go as far as Madinah. If this happened, it would surely leave awful effects on Islam and Muslims. With a clear view of what was at stake, the Prophet was determined to proceed up north to face the Byzantines and fight a decisive battle at their own borders.

The Battle of Tabook was to be the last of the Prophet's military expeditions.

Jaysh-ul-Usrah: The Army of Hardship

It was summer, and the blazing desert heat was enough to discourage anyone from traveling. It was in the month of Rajab, in the ninth year of Hijrah. Allies of the Muslims began arriving in Madinah by the thousand to join the Muslim army. Wealthy Muslims contributed large amounts of money for the army. Uthman Ibn Affan رضي الله عنه donated enough money to equip ten thousand troops. The army was thirty thousand men strong with ten thousand horses.

At-Tirmithi reported that Abdul-Rahman Ibn-ul-Khattab said: "The Prophet was encouraging the Sahabah to pay charity and fundraise for this Ghazwah battle. "Uthman Ibn Affan donated nine hundred saddled-camels, a hundred horses, two hundred ounces of gold as charity, and a thousand dinars. The Messenger of Allah looked at them and said: "From this day on nothing will harm 'Uthman regardless of what he does."

Abdur-Rahman Ibn Awf also gave two hundred silver ounces. Abu Bakr gave all his money to the campaign and left nothing for his family. When he was asked why he hadn't left anything for his family he said, "I left for them Allah and his Prophet." Omar donated half of his fortune. Al-'Abbas gifted a lot of money too. Talhah, Sa'd Ibn 'Ubadah and Muhammad Ibn Maslamah gave money for the welfare of the jihad. 'Asim Ibn 'Adi offered ninety camelloads. People raced each other to donate large amounts of money or goods. One person would give a bushel or half a bushel that he owned; women contributed to the fundraising competition too by giving jewelry and other items they owned. They all donated with utmost generosity toward the effort except, of course, for the hypocrites.

Despite such generosity, the army still fell short of being perfectly equipped. There remained a serious shortage of money, equipment and mounts. Eighteen men had to take turns, sharing one camel. That's why the army was called "The Army of Hardship," or "Jaysh-ul-Usrah."

The Muslim Army Heads North

The Prophet set up his camp at Thaniyyat el-Wadaa'. The people of Madinah were witnesses to the stunning scene of the Prophet at the head of his huge army of 10,000 horsemen and 20,000 other soldiers on camelback and on foot.

It was a habit of the Prophet not to disclose where he was going for ghazwaat, or battles. But for this ghazwah, the Prophet specified that he was going to Tabook because of the great distance and the long duration of the trip. He wanted everyone to prepare emotionally and physically for this long and difficult journey.

Before his travel, the Prophet commanded that Muhammad Ibn Maslamah Al-Ansari should be appointed the amir over the city of Madinah during his absence. This was the greatest Muslim army ever assembled during the lifetime of the Prophet. The thirty-thousand strong Muslim army marched northwards to Syria under the scorching Arabian sun. Despite the hardship, the hearts of the Muslims were filled with love and dedication to the service of Allah and His Messenger.

The Hypocrites

The munafiqeen, or the hypocrites, were a group in Madinah who claimed and outwardly appeared to be Muslims. However, they were really disbelievers in their hearts. Their action is called in Arabic "nifaaq", or hypocrisy. Since the Prophet's arrival in Madinah from Makkah, the munafiqeen conspired against the Muslims and collaborated with their enemies. They just acted as traitors within the early Muslim society.

The hypocrites this time tried to scare the believers away from fighting the Romans. The munafiqeen warned them: "Do you really believe that fighting those people is as easy as fighting a few Arabs? By God, we can see that tomorrow you will be dragged in chains."

Experiences like this easily helped the Muslims to figure out who was sincere among them, and who was not sincere. The hypocrites also said to Muslims: "Do not travel in this heat." To which God replied in the Qur'an: "The fire of Hell is stronger in heat." [9:81]. Nevertheless, many of them came to the Prophet making excuses to avoid traveling with him. The Prophet knew that

Map of Saudi Arabia, and Tabook

they were liars and hypocrites, so he didn't bother to argue with them. He kept tolerating them, hoping that God at some time would guide them to the straight path. However, a number of the hypocrites planned to join the Muslim army for evil purposes, as you will learn later.

While in Northern Arabia, the army passed by the ruins of Thamood, the people of Prophet Salih, at the village of Al-Hijr. The place is now called Mada'in Salih, in the northwestern part of present Saudi Arabia. As you learned in your elementary years, Allah destroyed Thamood because the people disobeyed Allah, and disbelieved in the message of Prophet Salih عليه السلام. When they were near that place, Prophet Muhammad asked his followers to hurry up while passing through the area. He also prevented them from drinking, eating or making ablution from the wells in that place.

Imams Al-Bukhari and Muslim reported that the Prophet ﷺ said: "Don't enter upon those punished people unless you are crying as I fear that you may be hit with what they

Mada'in Saleh

were inflicted with." And he covered his head with his cloak and accelerated his stride.

D5

The Muslims in Tabook

Halfway between Madinah and Jerusalem, the army set up camp at a place called Tabook in present day Saudi Arabia. The journey took several weeks to complete. The army remained in Tabook for twenty days, searching for information about the advance of the Roman army. The enemy army never showed up!

The Romans had their spies and were informed of the Prophet's preparations for war and knew he had come for them. Upon hearing about the Muslims' march, the Byzantines and their allies were terrified. The Romans quickly retreated to their own frontiers. Once inside their territories they scattered. It seems that they had recalled their experience in Mu'tah and realized that they would not be able to defeat the huge Muslim army. The Prophet, who had come to defend Arabia, had no desire to invade Syria and confront its army, but he was prepared for both possibilities: war and peace.

The Muslims gained an awesome military reputation in the mid and outlying lands of the Arabian Peninsula. The gains achieved by such a reputation were far better than those made through military confrontation. The Arab tribes, who allied themselves with the Byzantines, became quite certain that their dependence on their former masters had come to an end. They realized that the Muslims had become more powerful than ever, and that they had better come to terms with them before it was too late. So they became pro-Muslim and the Islamic state was able to expand its borders out to the Byzantine borders.

Prophet Muhammad realized that the mission was accomplished. He could disperse the great threat of the huge Roman army and their Arab allies. He also made his enemies realize that they could not defeat the Muslims easily.

After he had achieved all of the above, the Prophet decided to travel back to Madinah.

The Return Journey to Madinah

Before he returned to Madinah, the Prophet ﷺ called some of the tribes to Islam and established alliances with friendly tribes in the area.

Some of the munafiqeen tried to kill the Prophet during the journey. They thought they could seize the opportunity when the Prophet was on his camel near the edge of a cliff. They attempted to cause him to fall off that cliff, but Allah warned His Prophet about their wicked plot. The Prophet was guarded by Ammar Ibn Yaser and Huthayfah Ibn-ul-Yaman who struck the heads of the attackers' camels causing them to flea. Ammar and Huthayfah managed to protect the Prophet and recognize the masked men. So, they asked the Prophet for permission to capture and kill these wicked culprits. The Prophet refused and said, "I don't want the Arabs to think that I kill my companions."

Miracles on the Way

1. Ibn Ishaaq said: "The people woke up with no water and complained to the Prophet. He implored Allah, Who sent a cloud that rained on them until they quenched their thirst and they took with them their supply of water."

2. When the Prophet was on his way he lost his she-camel. Zaid Ibn Al-Luseet, a hypocrite, said: "Muhammad claims that he is a Prophet and informs you about the news of Heaven, and yet he does not know where his she-camel is?"

Then the Prophet said: "There is a man saying so and so…By God I know only what Allah has taught me; and He informed me that she is in the valley entrapped in her tether by a tree trunk. Go and fetch her." They went and found her in the valley exactly as the Prophet described.

3. Imam Muslim reported that before the Prophet had dismounted in a place where the water was scarce, he told his followers that by the grace of Allah the next day they would pass by Tabook spring. He warned them not to touch it before his arrival. Two men had arrived before him and touched the water and it became just a thin trickle. The Prophet scolded the two men for not listening to him. Then his companions gathered what little water was left and gave it to the Prophet. He washed his hands and face then he poured the water back to the spring making Du'aa'. The spring gushed with water. And he told them:" Whoever lives of you will hear that this valley will be the most fertile."

Abu Tharr Al-Ghifari: A Role Model in Faithfulness

On the road, the camel of Abu- Tharr Al-Ghifari slowed him down. So he placed his belongings on his back and followed in the footsteps of the Prophet on foot. A while later the Prophet stopped to rest for a while. Someone looked around and glimpsed a man walking from afar and exclaimed: "O Prophet! There is a man coming alone." The Prophet said: "Let him be Abu-Tharr." When the people looked hard they shouted: "O Prophet! By God, he is Abu-Tharr." The Prophet said: "Allah, have mercy on Abu-Thar. He walks alone, he dies alone, and he will be resurrected alone."

Abu Tharr was a leader in his tribe Ghifar and had embraced Islam early on in Makkah. He called his tribe to Islam and many had become Muslims. Prophet Muhammad loved him for his truthfulness, clean heart and diligence. One time, Abu Tharr asked the Prophet to appoint him as an amir, or a leader. The Prophet declined and told him that it was a big responsibility and a trust that he could not handle. Abu Tharr accepted what the Prophet told him and never asked again. He continued to be a sincere and faithful follower of the Prophet as this story illustrates.

After he had stayed twenty days in the area of Tabook the Prophet headed back south toward Madinah. The Muslims arrived in Madinah during the month of Ramadan after a long trip that had lasted for fifty days.

A Lesson in Fiqh

The Prophet and the Muslims prayed Salat-ul-Musafir, or the Traveler's Prayer, during the campaign to Tabook. The Prophet combined Thuhr and Asr prayers during the time of Thuhr. The Maghrib and Ishaa' prayers were also combined during the time of Maghrib. This is called جَمْعُ تَقْديم Jami' Taqdeem, or advanced combination. A Muslim can also pray the same two combination of prayers during the time of the later one. This is called جَمْعُ تَأخير Jami' Ta'kheer, or delayed combination.

The Prophet also shortened the four-rakaat prayers (Thuhr, Asr and Ishaa) to two rakaat during travel. The shortening of a prayer is called قَصْر Qasr in Arabic.

We learn from the above that a traveler can combine and shorten the prayers as long as he or she is traveling.

FAITH IN ACTION

★ Always participate in the life and activities of your Muslim community. Be among the first people to do what your community asks you to do. Do not procrastinate in Islam's work.

CHAPTER REVIEW

Projects and Activities

1. Write a journal on the campaign of Tabook. Include in the journal a map showing the city's location, and some pictures.

2. Create a field model of Mada'in Salih.

D8

Stretch Your Mind

1. What were the root causes of the possible attack of the Romans against the Muslims?
2. Imagine you are one of the Muslims in Madinah at the time of the campaign to Tabook. What would you do if you heard the Prophet calling upon you to travel for a month or two, in the severe heat of the desert? Explain the reasons for your reaction?
3. Most of the Sahabah responded to the call of the Prophet, although they knew that they would suffer, or may even be killed, if they did so. What, do you think, made them decide to go?
Read the following hadeeth and then write a paragraph explaining what the Prophet meant by it. Give examples that show you understand the hadeeth very well.

عن أبي هُرَيْرةَ رضِيَ اللهُ عنه قال : قالَ رَسولُ اللهِ صلى اللهُ عَلَيْه وسَلَم :
"إنَّ شَرَّ النّاسِ ذو الوَجـهَيْن ، الذي هؤلّاء بِوَجْه و هؤلاء بِوَجْه."
رواه البخاري ومسلم

Abu Hurayrah narrated that Rasoolullah said:
"The worst of people is the one who is double-faced, he comes to some people with a face, and he comes to others with a different face."

(Reported by Al-Bukhari and Muslim)

Study Questions

1. When and where did the Campaign to Tabook take place?
2. Why did the Prophet advance toward Syria?
3. Describe the military powers of the Muslims and the enemies during that military campaign?
4. Who were the enemies of the Muslims in Tabook?
5. How did the campaign to Tabook end?
6. Who was among the people who followed the Prophet and traveled alone through the desert? What lesson can we learn from him?
7. What was the greatest lesson the Muslims learned in the course of the battle?
8. Who are the munafiqeen?
9. By the end of the campaign, there was a threat on the Prophet's life. Describe what happened.
10. Briefly describe at least two of the miracles demonstrated by the Prophet during the journey to Tabook.
11. Describe how a traveler can combine and shorten the prayer.

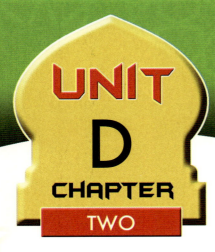

Honesty Saves: The Story of the Three Who Missed Tabook

CHAPTER OUTLINE

1. Learn Ka'b Ibn Malik's experience.
2. Appreciate the importance of honesty and truthfulness.
3. Understand the danger of procrastination in performing important work.
4. Learn and understand ayaat 17-20 of Surat At-Tawbah.

PEOPLE TO REMEMBER

- Ka'b Ibn Malik — كَعْبْ بن مالك
- Murarah Ibn-ur-Rabee' — مرارة بن الربيع
- Hilal Ibn Umayyah — هلال بن أميَّة

Prophet Muhammad Calls All Muslims for Tabook

Ka'b Ibn Malik said, "I stayed behind on the expedition to Tabook. I had never been stronger or wealthier than I was at that time. Never before did I have two camels. When the Prophet ﷺ, would go out on an expedition, he would always indicate another destination until the army actually left. Rasoolullah ﷺ, made this long journey at a time of intense heat, through a waterless desert, yet even though he had a great enemy to face. However, he made the whole thing quite clear to the Muslims so that they could make the necessary preparations for the expedition. He told them the direction of his travel. The Muslims, with the Messenger of Allah, were so numerous. A recording book or a register (was incapable) of including all of them.

D10

Ka'b Fails to Travel with the Prophet and the Muslims

Anyone wanting to absent himself from the expedition thought that would go unnoticed unless a revelation was sent down about him from Allah about his failure to attend.

Ka'b: "The Messenger of Allah was to make the expedition when the fruit was ripe and there was plentiful shade. Because of this, I really wanted to stay at home. Rasoolullah and the Muslims with him made their preparations, and I would go out to do the same but then I would return without having accomplished anything, saying to myself, 'I can do it any time I wish.' I went on like this until the people were fully prepared. Then the Messenger of Allah set out with the Muslims, but I had still not completed any of

my preparations. I continued like this until the expedition had left. The Prophet left on the expedition of Tabook on a Thursday. He liked to set out on Thursdays.

I intended to set off and catch up with them, and I wish that I had done so, but that was not decreed for me. When I saw the people who stayed after the Prophet ﷺ had left, it saddened me that they were either hypocrites, or had been excused by the Prophet for being sick or old.

The Messenger ﷺ did not mention me until he reached Tabook. While he was sitting among the people at Tabook, he said, "What has Ka'b ibn Malik done?" A man said, "O Rasoolullah, he has been held back by his two cloaks and self-conceit.' Mu'ath ibn Jabal رضي الله عنه, said to him, "What an evil thing to say! By Allah, O Rasoolullah , we only know good things about him!" Rasoolullah ﷺ was silent.

Related Wisdom

Do not put off until tomorrow what you can do today.

The Prophet Returns to Madinah and Ka'b Tells Him the Truth

"When I heard that the Prophet, was on his return journey from Tabook, I became very upset and began to think up lies. But I resolved to stick to the truth. The Messenger ﷺ arrived in the morning. Whenever he came back from a journey, he would first go to the mosque and pray two rak'aat there and then he would sit to receive the people. When he did that, those who had stayed behind went to him making their excuses, swearing that they were telling the truth to him. There were about eighty such men in all. He accept-

ed what they claimed and asked Allah to forgive them. When I greeted him, he gave me an angry look and said,
"Come here."
I walked up and then sat down in front of him. He said to me,
'What kept you back? Didn't you buy a camel?'
I said, 'Oh Messenger of Allah, by Allah, if I was sitting with anyone else in the world I would think that I could escape his anger by making some excuse. I am gifted in argumentation, but, by Allah, I know that if I were to tell you a false story today that might satisfy you with regard to me, Allah would soon make you angry with me. If I tell you the truth, you will be angry with me, but I hope for a good outcome from Allah, the Almighty. By Allah, I do not have any

excuse. By Allah, I have never been stronger nor wealthier than when I remained behind you.'"

Rasoolullah ﷺ said, "This one has spoken the truth. Get up until Allah decides about you." Some men followed me and said to me, 'By Allah, we have not known you to commit a wrong action before this! You could have offered an excuse to the Prophet ﷺ like the others who stayed behind. The Prophet's prayer for forgiveness would have erased your wrong action. By Allah, they continued to reproach me until I wanted to return to the Prophet and deny what I had said. Then I said to them, 'Has anyone received the same treatment from Rasoolullah as I did? They said, ' Yes, Murarah ibn-ur-Rabee' al-'Amiri and Hilal ibn Umayyah al-Waqifi." They mentioned to me two righteous men of good character who had been present at Badr. When they mentioned them to me, I was determined to remain truthful."

The Prophet and the Muslims Ostracize Ka'b

"The Prophet ﷺ forbade people from speaking to the three of us out of all those who had remained behind. So the people avoided us. The Earth seemed strange to me and it was not the same Earth I used to know. We remained under this boycott for fifty days. My two companions were depressed and stayed in their homes, weeping. I was the youngest of them and was tougher. I used to go out and attend the prayer with the Muslims. I would walk in the markets, but no one would speak to me. I went to the Messenger of Allah, may Allah bless him and grant him peace, and greeted him while he was in his assembly after the prayer. I would say to myself, "Did he move his lips to return the greeting, or not?" Then I would pray near him and sneak a look at him and he would look at me while I attended to my prayer. But when I turned towards him, he would turn

away from me. When that harshness of the Muslims had gone on too long for me, I climbed over the wall of Abu Qatadah's garden. He was my cousin and the dearest of people to me. I greeted him, and, by Allah, he did not return the greeting to me. I said to him, "Abu Qatadah, I ask you by Allah, do you not know that I love Allah and His Messenger?" He was silent. I repeated my question and he was still silent. I again repeated my question and he said, "Allah and His Messenger know best." My eyes overflowed with tears and I turned and climbed back over the wall.

A Great Test

While I was walking in the market of Madinah, a farmer from Syria, who had brought some food to sell in Madinah, said, "Who will direct me to Ka'b ibn Malik?" The people led him to me and he handed me a letter from the King of Ghassan, a Tribe in Northern Arabia. I was a scribe, so I read it. It said, "It has reached us that your companion (Prophet Muhammad) has been harsh to you. Allah has not put you in a place to be humiliated. Join us and we will support you." When I had read it, I said, "This is also part of the test," and I threw it in the oven to burn it up.

The Situation Worsens

When forty of the fifty days had passed, and revelation had still not been conveyed, a messenger from the Prophet ﷺ came to me and said, "Rasoolullah commands you to withdraw from your wife." I said, "Am I to divorce her, or what?" He said, "No, just withdraw from her, and do not go near her." He sent the same message to my two companions. I said to my wife, "Join your family and stay with them until Allah decides about us." I remained like that for ten days until fifty days had passed from the time when speaking to us was first prohibited.

The Good News: Allah Forgives Ka'b

"Then on the morning after the fiftieth day, I prayed Fajr on the roof of my house. While I was sitting up there I heard someone shouting at the top of his voice from the top of Sal' hill: "Ka'b ibn Malik, good news for you!" I fell down in prostration (Sujood-ush-Shukr) and felt a wave of relief sweep over my body. Rasoolullah ﷺ announced to the people that Allah had turned towards us after he had prayed the Fajr prayer. The people came to bring us the good news. They also went to my two companions with the good news. One man spurred on his horse to reach me and one of the Aslam tribe ran towards me and climbed the mountain. His voice reached me quicker than the horse. When the one whose voice I had heard approached me, I removed my garments and put them on him out of gratefulness and happiness with the good news he had brought. By Allah, that day I had no other garments than those that I was wearing. I had to borrow two garments to wear to go before the Messenger of Allah. Crowds of people met me to congratulate me on Allah's turning towards me. They were saying to me, "Enjoy the turning of Allah towards you!" until I entered the mosque. The Messenger of Allah was sitting surrounded by people. Talha ibn 'Ubaydullah رضي الله عنه, got up, hurrying to shake my hand and congratulate me. By Allah, not one of the Muhaijreen got up except him. I will never forget what Talhah did.'

Ka'b to Give Sadaqah

"Ka'b said, 'When I greeted the Messenger ﷺ his face was shining with joy and he said, "Rejoice in the best day that has come to you since your mother bore you!" I said, "Is it from you, Messenger of Allah, or from Allah?" He said, "Indeed it is from Allah, the Mighty and Exalted!" When the Messenger ﷺ was happy, his face would shine as if it were a part of the moon. We used to recognize that in him. When I sat down in front of him, I said, 'Messenger of Allah, part of my repentance is that I give out all of my property as sadaqah for Allah and His Messenger." The Messenger said, "Keep part of your property for yourself. That will be better for you." So I said, "I will keep my share at Khaybar."

Honesty Helps

I said to Rasoolullah, "Oh Rasoolullah, Allah Almighty has saved me because I was honest, and part of my repentance is that I will speak nothing but the truth for as long as I live." By Allah, I do not know of anyone among the Muslims whom Allah Almighty has tried more. By Allah, I have not tempted to lie from the time I said that to Rasoolullah ﷺ, until this very day, and I hope that Allah Almighty will protect me during what remains of my life.'

'Allah Almighty then sent down the following ayaat (see next page) of Surat-ut-Tawbah :

The End of the Leader of the Hypocrites

Briefly after the Prophet returned to Madinah from Tabook, Abdullah Ibn Ubayy Ibn Abi Salool, the leader of the munafiqeen, died. The Prophet, who had a kind heart, asked Allah to forgive him. But Allah said in the Qur'an that He would not forgive him.

Understood Meaning

[9:117] Allah turned with favor to the Prophet, the Muhajireen, and the Ansar,- who followed him in a time of hardship, after the hearts of some of them had nearly went astray, but He turned to them (also): for He is Most Kind, Most Merciful with them.

[9:118] (He turned in mercy also) to the three who were left behind; (they felt guilty) to such a degree that the earth seemed tight to them, for all its spaciousness, and their (very) souls seemed strained to them, - and they perceived that there is no fleeing from Allah (and no refuge) but to Himself. Then He turned to them, that they might repent: for Allah is all forgiving, Most Merciful.

[9:119] O ye who believe! Fear Allah and be with those who are truthful.

[9:120] It was not fitting for the people of Madinah and the Bedouin Arabs of the neighborhood, to refuse to follow Allah's Messenger, nor to prefer their own lives to his: because nothing could they suffer or do, but was considered as a credit and a good deed for them whether they suffered thirst, or fatigue, or hunger, in the cause of Allah, or took paths to defeat the Unbelievers, or overcome the enemy: for Allah will not waste the reward of those who do good;-

D14

CHAPTER REVIEW

Projects and Activities

1. Write a play that describes the story of Ka'b and perform it with your classmates in front of your school.

2. Ka'b said that he was a scribe. Research and find out what Ka'b used to write for the Prophet.

3. Write an essay of 700 words about the negative effects of "Procrastination", using Ka'b's story as an example.

Stretch Your Mind

1. How many days did the campaign to Tabook last? For how many days did the Prophet and the Muslims ostracize Ka'b and the other two companions who had lagged behind? What lessons can you learn from that?

2. Imagine you are one of the Muslims in Madinah at the time of the campaign to Tabook. What would you do if you heard the Prophet calling upon you to travel for a month or two in the severe heat of the desert? Explain the reasons for your reaction.

3. Compare the hardship Abu Tharr Al-Ghifari went through, when he followed the Muslims alone in the desert, with the hardship that Ka'b went through after the Muslims returned to Madinah. Indicate which hardship you would rather go through if you had to choose between

Study Questions

1. Who were the believers who stayed in Madinah behind the Prophet without a good excuse?
2. What made Ka'b رضي الله عنه stay behind?
3. What did Ka'b tell the Prophet when he explained why he stayed behind?
4. What did the hypocrites tell the Prophet? Did he believe them?
5. What punishment did Ka'b and his two counterparts receive from Allah?
6. How did the ordeal of Ka'b end?
7. What was the greatest lesson Ka'b learned during the course of the ordeal he went through?
8. Who died shortly after the Prophet returned to Madinah? Describe what the Prophet did about that.

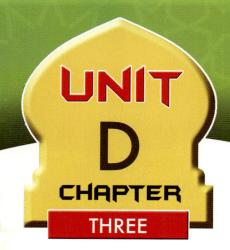

Surat-ul-Munafiqoon
سورة المنافقون

CHAPTER OUTLINE

1. Learn and memorize Surat-ul-Munafiqoon.
2. Understand the danger of nifaaq, and the negative role that the munafiqeen played in the early Muslim society.

Introduction

Surat-ul-Munafiqoon was revealed in Madinah, and it is 11 verses long. The Muslims in Madinah were living with a difficult problem: that problem was the Al-Munafiqoon, or the hypocrites. These people didn't want to become Muslims, but when they saw that the majority of the people in the city were accepting Islam, they calculated that it would be in their interests to pretend to be Muslims and be on the side of the majority. So, they were disbelievers in their hearts, but they acted as if they were Muslims. Therefore, Allah called them "Al-Munafiqoon," the hypocrites.

The munafiqoon were around 300 men. In the time leading up to the arrival of the Prophet and his followers to Madinah, the leader of the Munafiqoon, Abdullah Ibn Abi Salool had ambitions to become the king of Madinah. However, when most of the people in Madina became Muslim, naturally, the Prophet became the de facto leader of the city. This caused Ibn Abi Salool to become jealous of the Prophet, and he became his hidden enemy.

Surat-ul-Munafiqoon addresses the issue of hypocrisy and the hypocrites. Prophet Muhammad ﷺ was polite and courteous with the hypocrites, and be tried to set a good example to encourage them to become true believers. At the same time, he was not naive about their bad intentions. Therefore, he was very careful to take measures to limit their harm on his beloved Muslim community.

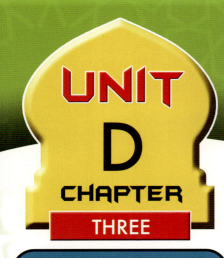

UNIT D
CHAPTER THREE
LESSON ONE

سورة المنافقون

Surat-ul-Munafiqoon: Verses (1-4)
The Characteristics of the Hypocrites

LESSON OUTLINE

1. Learn and memorize ayaat 1-4 of Surat Al-Munafiqoon.
2. Understand that what is in the heart is what Allah values the most.
3. Learn and memorize the hadeeth of this lesson.
4. Learn and understand the danger of Al-Yameen Al-Ghamamoos, or swearing to a lie.

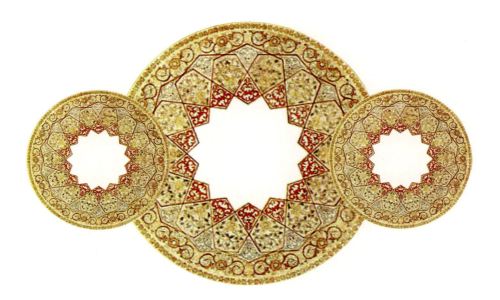

Understood Meaning

(63:1) When the hypocrites come to you they say, "We testify that you are the Messenger of Allah." Allah knows that you are His Messenger, but Allah testifies that the hypocrites are lying [about their claim].

(63:2) They use their oaths as a mean of protection and then they try to prevent people from following Allah's path; what they are doing is terrible.

(63:3) This is because they pretend to be believers but in reality they disbelieved. So a seal was put on their hearts so they will not understand.

(63:4) When you see them their outward appearance they will impress you and when they speak you listen to them because of their eloquence. However, they sit [in the masjid] like wood logs leaning against the wall [without any spirit or understanding]. They think that every call is against them. They are the enemy so beware of them. Allah will destroy them, how can they turn away from truth to falsehood?

Lessons Learned

Allah searches the hearts and watches the deeds. It is not enough for one to just say "I am a Muslim." One must truly believe it in the heart, so that it shows in his or her actions. Prophet Muhammad has said in a well-known hadeeth:

عَن أبي هُرَيْرَةَ رضِيَ اللهُ عَنْهُ قال: قال رسولُ اللهِ ﷺ:
"إنَّ اللهَ لا يَنْظُرُ إلى صُوَرِكم وأموالِكم ولكن يَنظُرْ إلى قُلوبِكُم وأعْمالِكم."

رواه مسلم

Abu Hurayrah narrated that Rasoolullah said:
"Allah doesn't look only at your looks and wealth, but he looks at your hearts and deeds."   Reported in Muslim.

1. The Hypocrites Committed Three Terrible Actions:
a. They swore to the lie that they were Muslims.
b. They hid behind the lie to protect themselves from being held accountable for working against Islam.
c. They tried to turn people away from Islam.

Major Sin

اليَمينُ الغَموس Al-Yameen Al-Ghamoos, is the "Drowning Oath." It is one of the major sins in Islam to swear on something while you know you are a liar. It is called the "Dipper Oath," because it causes the person who does it to plunge in sin and Hellfire.

2. Their Hearts Are Sealed.
Because the hypocrites chose to hide their disbelief, Allah put a seal on their hearts so they would not be able to truly understand the significance of prayer, fasting, or worshiping Allah. If they truly understood and believed in their hearts, it would show in their actions.

3. They Are Double-faced.
The hypocrites kept a nice outward appearance to hide the fact that they were rotten on the inside. The leader of the hypocrites, Abdullah ibn Ubay ibn Abi Salool, was a particularly good looking man who spoke very well. People would listen to him because he appeared very impressive. Yet in the masjid, he was like a log leaning against the wall because he was dead on the inside.

4. They Are Cowards.
The hypocrites did not have the courage to declare that they were indeed disbelievers, nor did they have the courage to truly submit as Muslims. Their deception meant that they lacked self confidence. This led them to be very hypersensitive and they would be paranoid that anything that was said must be directed against them.

5. They Are Real Enemies of Islam.
Allah cursed them by denying them His guidance and He sealed their hearts. When someone commits many major sins or insists to disbelieve, although he had learned the truth, Allah may seal his heart and deprive him of His guidance. And this is exactly what happened to the munafiqeen. In fact, Allah places the munafiqeen in a lower level than the disbelievers. While the disbelievers openly act according to their beliefs, the hyp-

ocrites see the truth of Islam. They pretend to pray with the Muslims, but their hearts are full of disbelief and hatred toward Islam and Muslims.

They are enemies to the Muslims. Allah commands us to recognize that the hypocrites are enemies whom we should be cautious with in our dealings. We should note that the Messenger of Allah, peace be upon him, was always very polite with the hypocrites, but at the same time, he did not rely on them for any critical functions.

They are losers. We can observe from the life story of Rasoolullah that the hypocrites failed to destroy the unity of the Muslims. All they managed to do was to make false promises and spread rumors. Because they were so weak in character, they could offer nothing of benefit to the Muslims or to the disbelievers.

PUTTING THE QUR'AN IN ACTION

★ Take a personal inventory of yourself. Do you live according to your beliefs? Develop some short-term and long-term goals to improve the relationship between what you say and what you do.

★ Think of a time when you put too much trust in people because they dressed or talked in an impressive manner. If you had a chance to do it again, what would you do differently? This is an important lesson to learn for the rest of your life. Many people get stuck in bad business deals or even bad marriages because they became so impressed with external attractiveness that has blinded them to the signs of a rotten core.

CHAPTER REVIEW

Stretch Your Mind

1. Were the munafiqeen brave or cowards? Defend your answer.
2. What are the differences betweena hypocrite and an ordinary sinner.

Study Questions

1. Who are the munafiqeen? List their main attitudes.
2. What are the main serious mistakes of the Munafiqoon?
3. Allah investigates what is in the heart of the individual. Do you agree? Support your answer with a hadeeth.
4. What is Al-Yameen Al-Ghamous?
5. Why did Allah seal the hearts of the hypocrites?

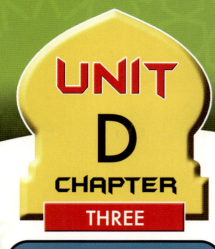

UNIT D
CHAPTER THREE
LESSON TWO

سورة المنافقون

Surat-ul-Munafiqoon: Verses (5-8)
The Evil Cause of the Hypocrites

LESSON OUTLINE

1. Learn and memorize ayaat 5-8 of Surat Al-Munafiqoon.
2. Understand some evil attitudes the hypocrites had.
3. Learn and memorize the hadeeth of this lesson.

Understood Meaning

(63:5) If it is said to them: "Come and Allah's Messenger will pray for your forgiveness" they will turn their heads away and you will see them oppose this in arrogance.

(63:6) It is the same for them if you pray for forgiveness for them or you do not ask for forgiveness for them. Allah will not forgive them. Allah does not guide those who are rebelliously disobedient.

(63:7) They are the ones who say: "Do not spend on the Muhajireen who are with the Messenger of Allah until they split away from him." Allah owns all of the sustenance and wealth in the Heavens and the Earth but the hypocrites do not understand that Allah does not need them to support the Muhajireen.

(63:8) The hypocrites say, "When you return to Madinah we swear that the honorable people will expel the pathetic from the city." Allah owns all honor and honor is for His Messenger and for the believers, but the hypocrites do not know what is good for them.

Background Story

Prophet Muhammad ﷺ went out with his companions on the military expedition called Ghazwat Bani Al-Mustaliq. They engaged in a minor battle with the people of Bani Al-Mustaliq, which they won. Then they went to an oasis in the area. There, one of the servants of 'Omar Ibn Al-Khattab named Jahjah, was leading the horses to water. The people were all eagerly crowding around the watering hole, so Jahjah kicked one of the Ansar as a joke. The man from the Ansar became very mad, and he started calling out to his fellow Ansar to come and help him. Jahjah then started to call for the Muhajireen for help against the Ansar. A big fight was about to break out when the Prophet ﷺ came. He became angry and said, "What is wrong with you behaving like the ignorant pagans?" So he was told what had happened, and then he said, "Stop behaving this way, because it is terrible (and forget about this)."

The news of this quarrel reached the leader of the hypocrites, Abdullah Ibn Ubay and his circle of friends. Abdullah saw an opportunity to exploit this conflict and create disunity and enmity between the Muhajireen and the Ansar. He said, "How could the Muhajireen call each other against us? They come to live in our land, take our wealth, and still want to fight with us. It is true, 'Fatten your dog, and it will eat you.' I swear by Allah, when we return to Madinah the great one will kick out the weak." Then he turned to those around him saying, "This is what you did to yourselves. You invited the Muhajireen to your land, and you shared your land and money with them. I swear by Allah if you stop giving to them, they will leave your property to go somewhere else."

Zayd ibn Al-Arqam, a young boy, heard what Abdullah ibn Ubay had said. Zaid became very angry and told the Prophet what had happened. 'Omar Ibn Al-Khattab suggested that Abdullah ibn Ubay should be killed. But Rasoolullah ﷺ said, "If we do this, 'Omar, then people will think that Muhammad kills his followers. No…Instead, tell the people to go."

Meanwhile, Abdullah ibn Ubay was brought to the Prophet and he swore with his friends that he had never said anything, and that Zayd was lying. Many people believed Abdullah ibn Ubay, and they started to blame Zayd. Rasoolullah ﷺ even thought that Zaid might have made a mistake. Zayd felt very hurt by this, and he was upset that the people were not believing him.

The Muslims began their return journey to Madinah. Rasoolullah had them travel all day and all night and then half way into the next day before stopping. After setting up camp they all fell asleep. By keeping the people busy traveling and tiring them out, Rasoolullah was able to prevent them from spreading the news about the negative events which had occurred.

Allah revealed Surat Al-Munafiqoon declaring that Zaid had been telling the truth and that the hypocrites were indeed lying. So the hypocrites were called to ask the Messenger of Allah to pray for their forgiveness, but Abdullah ibn Ubay turned away saying, "We did not do anything wrong. You told me to believe and I believed. You told me to give zakah and I did. All that is left is for me is to make sujood to Muhammad."

When the son of Abdullah ibn Ubay heard what had happened he went and stood with his sword in front of his father and he said, "You will not enter Madinah until you admit that you are the weak one and Rasoolullah is the great one." Abdullah ibn Ubay became very upset that his own son was against him, but he did what his son insisted on.

From then on, every time Abdullah ibn Ubay would try to do something, his own people would turn against him. Later, 'Omar ibn Al-Khattab realized that the Prophet was wiser than he was when he refused to use violence against Abdullah Ibn Ubay.

'Omar said, "I realize by Allah that the opinion of the Messenger of Allah has more blessings in it than my opinion." (Seerat Ibn Hisham, Bukhari, Muslim, Tafseer Al-Tabarri)

Lessons Learned

1. One of the signs of hypocrisy is that the person is too arrogant to admit mistakes and ask for forgiveness.

2. There is nothing that we can do for the disbelievers or the hypocrites. Allah will not forgive them, so we are not supposed to pray for them when they die. When they are alive, we can pray that Allah will guide them and open their hearts to Islam.

3. Allah will not guide those who are committed to disobeying Allah.

4. The hypocrites lack so much in understanding that they thought they could influence the Muslims, because the Muslims were dependent on their money. If they truly had understanding, they would have realize that Allah owns all of the treasures in creation and He does not need the hypocrites to take care of the Muslims.

5. The hypocrites thought that they were great and the Muslims were pathetic. The fact is that the reverse is actually true. Anyone with knowledge could have seen this. It doesn't take much to see how pathetic, cowardly, and arrogant the hypocrites were.

Fast Facts

When the verse (9:80) was revealed, "Pray for their forgiveness or do not. Even if you pray for their forgiveness seventy times Allah will not forgive them," the Messenger of Allah, peace be upon him, said, "I will do more than seventy, maybe Allah will forgive them. So Allah revealed, (63:6) "It is the same for them if you pray for forgiveness for them or you do not ask for forgiveness for them."

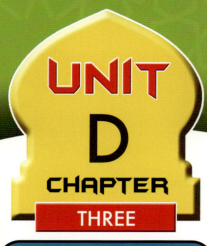

UNIT D
CHAPTER THREE
LESSON THREE

سورة المنافقون

Surat-ul-Munafiqoon: Verses (9-11)
Giving for the Sake of Allah

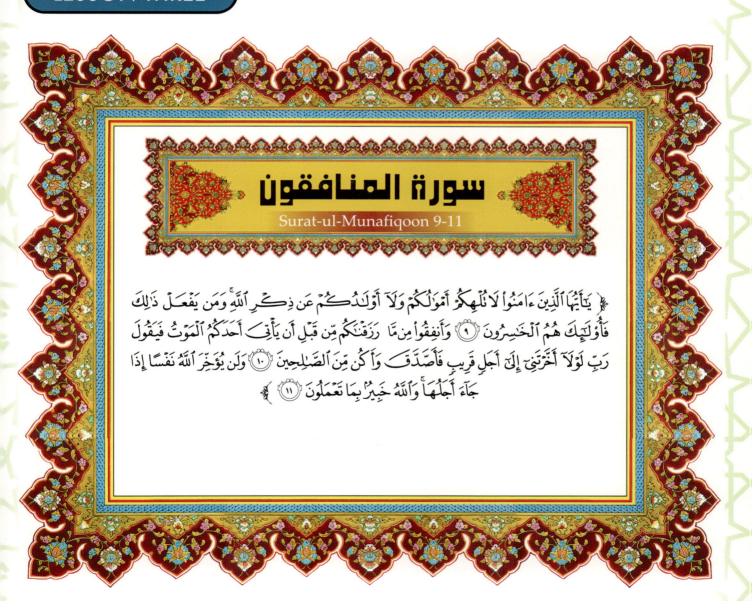

Understood Meaning

(63:9) O believers, do not let your money or your children distract you from making remembrance of Allah. Those who do this will be the losers.

(63:10) And give from what I have blessed you with before death comes to you and you say, "O Lord, why don't you please give me a little more time so that I can give charity and be among the good people?"

(63:11) Allah will not postpone death for any soul if its time has come. So remember Allah knows all of the little things you do.

Lessons Learned

1. The losers in life let their money and children distract them from their obligations towards Allah. This is what the hypocrites do, and as believers, we need to be careful not to fall into this mistake.

2. If we have any obligation, we should do it or pay it as soon as possible. Don't be like the person who waits until death comes and then asks for more time.

3. Once a person's time comes it will not be postponed. So we should ask for forgiveness and be as good as possible at all times, because Allah knows everything that we do.

Hadeeth Shareef

Ibn Abbas said, "Whoever has enough money to go to make Hajj to Allah's house, or he owes zakah and does not take action, will ask to go back at the time of death." A man asked, "O Ibn Abbas, fear Allah, because the only person who asks to come back is the disbelievers. Ibn Abbas said, "I will recite to you some Qur'an on this topic (63:10) And give from what I have blessed you with before death comes to you and you say, "O Lord, why don't you please give me a little more time so that I can give charity and be among the good people?*(Tirmithi)*

PUTTING THE QUR'AN IN ACTION

★ Imagine that the Angel of Death came to you right now. Make a list of all of the things you would feel regretful for not doing before meeting your Lord. Then go and do those things as soon as possible.

CHAPTER REVIEW

Stretch Your Mind

1. What did the hypocrites do that made Allah refuse to forgive them?

2. The munafiqeen were internal enemies of Islam. Do you agree? Support your answer with some historical incidents.

Study Questions

1. What are the main lessons that you can learn from the ayaat of this lesson?
2. What does Allah order the believer concerning money and wealth?

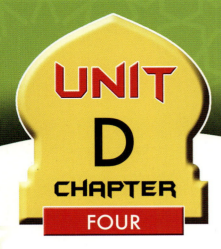

Prophet Muhammad Passes to Jannah

CHAPTER OUTLINE

1. Learn about the events before the passing away of Prophet Muhammad ﷺ.
2. Understand how Allah and Prophet Muhammad prepared the Muslims for this sad event.
3. Appreciate the high level of love and devotion given to Rasoolullah by the Sahabah.

VOCABULARY

Ar-Rafeeq-ul-A'la الرَّفِيقُ الأَعْلَى

Prophet Muhammad had successfully completed his mission of teaching and spreading the message of Islam. By the year 632, Islam had become triumphant in all of Arabia, and he was even now taking a foothold in Syria, Africa and other places. Indeed, great change had come about across the region. Idols in Makkah and Arabia had been destroyed. The people started worship Allah alone and a new society had been fashioned based on tawheed (belief in God alone), belief in Prophethood, and life after death. A true feeling of human unity through brotherhood and sisterhood had developed.

As the Qur'an says in Surat-us-Saff:

﴿ هُوَ ٱلَّذِىٓ أَرْسَلَ رَسُولَهُۥ بِٱلْهُدَىٰ وَدِينِ ٱلْحَقِّ لِيُظْهِرَهُۥ عَلَى ٱلدِّينِ كُلِّهِۦ ۚ وَلَوْ كَرِهَ ٱلْمُشْرِكُونَ ۝ ﴾ الصف: ٩

"He is the One Who sent His Messenger (Muhammad) with Guidance and the Religion of Truth (Islamic Monotheism) to make it victorious over all (other) religions even though the polytheists, pagans, idolaters and disbelievers hate (it)." [61:9]

When Allah had purified the Ka'bah from desecration, and the idols were destroyed, the Muslims yearned to perform Hajj again. The mission of the Messenger ﷺ of Allah was also nearing completion. It was also necessary for him to bid farewell to his loving companions. So Allah gave permission to His Messenger ﷺ to take them for Hajj. It was the first Hajj for him since he have began his mission. You learned about the Prophet's Hajj in the earlier unit.

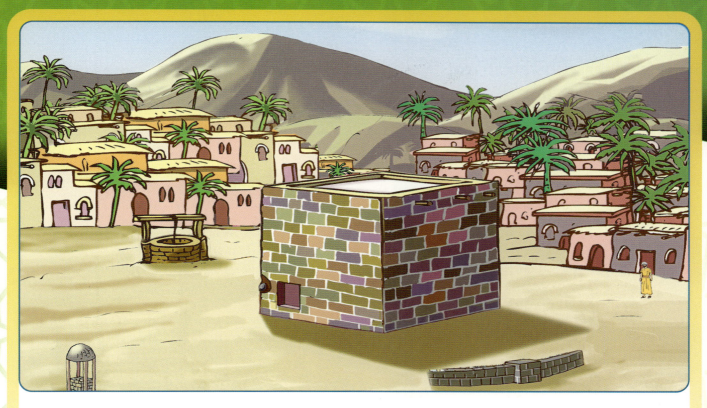

Prophet Mohammad left Madinah for many reasons: to perform Hajj; to meet Muslims from far and near; to teach them their faith and its rituals; to bear witness to the truth; to hand over the trust; and to give his final instructions. He would administer an oath binding on the Muslims to follow his teachings and to be rid of the last traces of Jahiliyyah, or the ignorance of the pagan era. More than a hundred thousand Muslims performed Hajj with him. This is known as Hajjat al-Wada' (the 'Farewell Hajj') and Hajjat al-Balagh (the Hajj of Conveying').

The Prophet ﷺ made farewell to all the Muslims and accompanied by the Muhajireen and Ansaar returned to Madinah. He refused to stay in Makkah and leave the people of Madinah who supported him. When Muhammad ﷺ first saw Madinah on his return from Makkah, he recited the Takbeer three times and then said:

"There is no god but Allah, alone with no partner. His is the kingdom and His is the praise. He has power over all things. We are returning, repenting, worshipping, prostrating to our Lord, and praising Him. Allah has been true to His promise and has helped His slave and defeated the enemies alone.'

He ﷺ entered Madinah in broad daylight.

Allah Prepares Muslims for the Prophet's Departure

Allah the All-Wise knew that the Prophet's departure from this world would not be easy on the Prophet's family and companions. Therefore, Allah gradually prepared the Muslims for such sad event. First, Allah ordered the Prophet to perform the Hajj with about one hundred thousand of the Muslims from Madinah, Makkah, and all Arabia. He could see them, and they all saw him. During his sermons, he told them all,
"I might not be able to meet you after this year."

Allah also revealed this ayah of Surat-ul-Ma'idah:

﴿ ٱلْيَوْمَ أَكْمَلْتُ لَكُمْ دِينَكُمْ وَأَتْمَمْتُ عَلَيْكُمْ نِعْمَتِي وَرَضِيتُ لَكُمُ ٱلْإِسْلَٰمَ دِينًا ﴾ ﴿٣﴾ المائدة: ٣

" Today, I have completed for you your religion, and granted you the last of My blessings, and I have chosen Islam as your way of life." [Surat-ul-Ma'idah 5:3]

When Omar Ibn-ul-Khattab رضي الله عنه heard this ayah, he wept. He was asked what had made him weep and he replied: "After perfection there can only be decrease." Probably he felt the death of the Prophet ﷺ was near.

Selected Story
Very Young, But Smart

Omar bin Al-Khattab used to let Ibn Abbas sit beside him, so 'AbdurRahman bin 'Auf said to Omar, "We have sons similar to him." Omar replied, "(I respect him) because of his status that you know." Omar then asked Ibn 'Abbas about the meaning of this Holy Verse:-- "When comes the help of Allah and the conquest of Mecca . . ." (110.1)

Ibn 'Abbas replied, "That indicated the death of Allah's Apostle, which Allah informed him of." Omar said, "I do not understand of it except what you understand."

Prophet Muhammad Falls Ill

Two months after performing the Farewell Hajj, Prophet Muhammad ﷺ fell ill. During the first part of the month of Rabi'-ul-Awwal of the 11th year of Hijrah, the Prophet's illness intensified. He ﷺ was suffering the pains of sickness and enduring them with dignity and patience. During that time, Allah revealed the last ayah of the Qur'an:

﴿ وَٱتَّقُوا۟ يَوْمًا تُرْجَعُونَ فِيهِ إِلَى ٱللَّهِ ۖ ثُمَّ تُوَفَّىٰ كُلُّ نَفْسٍ مَّا كَسَبَتْ وَهُمْ لَا يُظْلَمُونَ ﴿٢٨١﴾ ﴾

البقرة: ٢٨١

"And fear the Day when ye shall be brought back to Allah. Then shall every soul be paid what it earned, and none shall be dealt with unjustly." [Surat-ul-Baqara 2:281]

The Prophet ﷺ was at the house of Maymoona رضي الله عنها, one of his wives, and the pain increased to such a level that he could no longer go out. The Prophet's wives, wanting the best care for him, agreed that he would be more comfortable and best cared for at the house of A'ishah رضي الله عنها. The companions Al-Fadl ibn al'Abbas and Ali ibn Talib brought him ﷺ to A'ishah's home, as he was quite weak and unable to walk. Holding onto them for support, and with his head bandaged, he ﷺ dragged his feet along the ground until they reached the house.

The Last Sermon

The Prophet ﷺ became so weak that he found it difficult to move, but he continued to lead the congregational prayers for some time. Despite his sickness, it was important for him to continue to fulfill his mission. On Thursday, the eigth of Rabi'-ul-Awwal he learned that the Muslims were worried for him, so he felt the need to speak to them. He wanted to remind them of the fundamentals of Islam one last time before he departed this world. He was so resolute to lead his brothers and sisters to Paradise. Before he left home, he asked his wives to pour on him seven containers of water to ease his severe him from fever and the hot weather. On that occasion, he told his companions:

You seem worried for me…There is a slave among the slaves of Allah to whom God has offered the choice between this world and that which is with Him, and the slave has chosen that which is with God.

Upon hearing this, Abu Bakr رضي الله عنه wept as he understood that the Prophet ﷺ was talking about himself, and that the choice Rasoolullah had made meant that his death was imminent. Abu Bakr then said,

"We would truly sacrifice our wealth, our fathers and mothers to save you if we could."
Then the Prophet responded ,
"I paid back the favors of everyone toward me, except for the favors of Abu Bakr. I leave that to Allah."

Then the Prophet preached to the Muslims for the last time. He said:
"I am not worried on you that you may live as poor. Rather, I am concerned that you will compete on dunya, or the worldly life, like the nations before you did. So it will ruin you, as it did destroy them. I advise you to take good care of your women. And take care of your prayer, take care of your prayer, take care of your prayer.

Abu Bakr Appointed to Lead the Prayer

When the Prophet Muhammad felt so weak, he appointed Abu Bakr رضي الله عنه to lead the prayers. This was an implicit indication from the Prophet that if he left, Abu Bakr should lead the Muslims after him.

The Prophet ﷺ spent the rest of his illness in the home of his beloved wife A'ishah رضي الله عنها. Sometimes he was overcome with an urge to be with his companions, and would exert his weak body and go to the mosque. On one occasion, Abu Bakr رضي الله عنه who was already leading the prayer, realized that the Prophet was approaching. He stepped back without turning his head, but the Prophet ﷺ pressed his hand on his shoulder to let him know to continue leading. The Prophet ﷺ sat left to Abu Bakr رضي الله عنه and completed the prayer while seated.

Later the Prophet's sickness and pain became unbearable. His fever was so high that he started to say:

يا الله إن للمَوْتِ سَكرات

"O Allah, death has sharp pains."

Selected Story

The Prophet Whispers to Fatimah

Fatimah, the Prophet's only living daughter, used to visit him every day. Whenever she entered his room, the Prophet used to stand and greet her by saying "Welcome, my daughter." He would also kiss her on the forehead and seat her. But this time, he couldn't stand and receive her as he usually did. When she saw him so frail and in pain, she cried and said, "Oh, the terrible pain my father is suffering!" At this time the Prophet said, "Your father will suffer no more pain after this day." The Prophet then asked her to sit by him on his bed and whispered to her twice, first making her cry and then making her laugh. A'ishah wanted to learn what the Prophet had whispered to Fatimah. Fatimah kept the Prophet's whispers secret until after he had passed away. The Prophet first told her that he will die soon, so she cried. Then she laughed when he told her that she will follow him shortly, and that Allah will make her join him in Jannah.

The Prophet's Final Hours

In the early morning of the 12th of Rabi' al-Awwal, the Prophet's ﷺ fever abated a little and he looked into the mosque from A'ishah's room. He was pleased to see the Muslims praying Fajr prayer in congregation, but he couldn't join them. He was still very concerned about the affairs of his ummah, but he appeared to take pleasure in observing the sincerity of their worship. Anas رضي الله عنه said, "I had never seen the Prophet ﷺ in a better shape than he was at that moment." The companions thought that their beloved Prophet ﷺ had recovered, and that they were to continue to enjoy his leadership and companionship.

The Prophet's ﷺ apparent recovery did not last. A'ishah said that Rasoolullah ﷺ that morning had lain down and placed his head on her lap. Abdur-Rahman, the son of Abu Bakr's رضي الله عنه came in with a green toothbrush (miswak) in his hand. The Prophet ﷺ stared at his hand and she understood that he wanted it, so she gave it to him. He brushed his teeth harder than he had ever done before, then he put it down.

Shortly after, the Prophet began to lose his consciousness. He opened his eyes again an hour later saying to A'ishah:

" No Prophet is taken by death until he has been shown his place in Paradise and then offered the choice to live or to die."

A'ishah then felt Allah's Messenger ﷺ heavy in her lap and she looked at his face. His eyes were fixed and he was saying his last words, in an answer to a question which was unheard by those around:

بل الرفيقُ الأعْلى

"O Allah, [I want] the supreme companion [in Heaven].

The Prophet Passes Away

On the morning of Monday, the 12th of Rabi'-ul-Awwal of the 11th year of Hijrah, corresponding with 632 A.D, the Prophet ﷺ departed this world while lying in the lap of his beloved wife A'ishah رضي الله عنها.

The fateful news that the believers never wanted to hear spread out to the community. It was such a painful blow, causing the Sahabah anguish and mental turmoil. Prophet Muhammad ﷺ was the one who had led them from the dark of jahiliyyah, or ignorance, to the light of Islam and true knowledge. What were they to do now?

Omar Ibn-ul-Khattab رضي الله عنه, who was known for his passionate and strong personality, entered a state of denial. He refused to accept that his beloved Muhammad ﷺ had passed away. He unsheathed his sword vowing to put down the "hypocrites" who would claim that his beloved Muhammad ﷺ was dead. He wanted to believe that Muhammad ﷺ had simply absented himself for a period of time, as Musa عليه السلام had done before. He wanted to believe that Muhammad ﷺ would return to his people again.

> Prophet Muhammad died at the age of 63 (in lunar years), or 61 (in solar years).

Abu Bakr Pronounces the Prophet's Passing Away

When Abu Bakr رضي الله عنه heard the sad news, he came to the door of the mosque where Omar رضي الله عنه was speaking, though he did not pay attention to him. He entered the house of A'ishah رضي الله عنها where the Prophet ﷺ was shrouded in a corner. He cried, uncovered his head, kissed him, and said,

"O Rasoolullah, you have tasted the death which Allah has decreed for you. Now you will never be afflicted with death after that."

He then went to the mosque and asked Omar رضي الله عنه, who was still quite agitated, to stop. He then turned to the people and began by praising Allah سبحانه وتعالى then spoke the following noble words, which must have come as a great comfort to the grieving companions:

"أيُّها النّاسُ مَنْ كانَ يَعْبُدُ مُحَمَّداً فإنَّ مُحَمَّداً قَدْ مَاتَ وَ مَنْ كانَ يَعْبُدُ اللهَ فإنَّ اللهَ حَيٌّ لا يَمُوتُ"

"O People! If Muhammad is the one whom you worship, then know that he is dead. But if it is Allah (The One God) you worshipped, then know that He does not die."

He then recited the following verse from the Qur'an, 3:144, which was revealed after the Battle of Uhud:

"Muhammad is no more than an apostle: many were the apostles that passed away before him. If he died or were slain, will you then turn back on your heels? If any did turn back on his heels, not the least harm will he do to Allah; but Allah (on the other hand) will swiftly reward those who (serve Him) with gratitude." [3:144]

Abu Bakr Becomes the Leader of the Muslims

Prophet Muhammad ﷺ had recognized the leadership qualities of his friend Abu Bakr رضي الله عنه. He implicitly indicated this in his appointment to lead the salah when he was too ill to do so himself. Abu Bakr رضي الله عنه certainly rose to the challenge of leadership when his community needed it at this time of bereavement and emotional turmoil at the loss of their beloved Muhammad ﷺ.

Muslims later on Monday met in a place called Saqeefat Bany Sa'idah, a meeting area, to decide who would lead the Muslims after the Prophet. Some of Al-Ansar wanted to have one of them to become the leader. However, the majority of Muslims at that meeting chose Abu Bakr As-Sidddeeq to become the Khaleefah, or the successor leader of Muslims after Prophet Muhammad ﷺ. Later all Muslims met in the mosque and approved Abu Bakr as their future leader, after the Prophet.

﴿ وَمَا مُحَمَّدٌ إِلَّا رَسُولٌ قَدْ خَلَتْ مِن قَبْلِهِ الرُّسُلُ أَفَإِن مَّاتَ أَوْ قُتِلَ انقَلَبْتُمْ عَلَىٰ أَعْقَابِكُمْ ۚ وَمَن يَنقَلِبْ عَلَىٰ عَقِبَيْهِ فَلَن يَضُرَّ اللَّهَ شَيْئًا ۗ وَسَيَجْزِي اللَّهُ الشَّاكِرِينَ ﴾ ﴿١٤٤﴾ آل عمران: ١٤٤

> Abu Bakr was the first man named Khaleefah, which means a successor leader after the Prophet.

Abu Bakr was instrumental in enabling an agreement to be reached about the place of burial. The Prophet ﷺ was buried on Tuesday, the 13th of Rabi'-ul-Awwal. The place of his burial was decided by his saying as related by Abu Bakr: "Allah does not cause a prophet to die, but in the place where he is to be buried." Therefore, the Prophet was buried in A'ishah's room next to the mosque, the same place where he died.

Reflections

The Prophet ﷺ lived a most simple, austere, and modest life. He and his family used to go without cooked meals for several days and months at a time, relying often on only dates, dried bread, and water. During the day, Prophet Muhammad ﷺ was the busiest of men performing his duties in many roles. All at once, he functioned as a head of state, a chief justice, a commander-in-chief, an arbitrator, a teacher and a family man. He was the most devoted man at night. He used to spend one to two thirds of every night in prayer, reflection and du'aa'. He endured the hardship of losing all of his children before his death, except for his daughter Fatimah عنها رضي الله, who died only six months after he passed away. All of the Prophet's ﷺ wives (known as Ummahaat-ul-Mu'mineen, i.e., mothers of the faithful) remained widows for the remainder of their lives, as commanded by Allah.

The Prophet ﷺ, even though he was the virtual ruler of Arabia, possessed only simple mats, blankets, jugs, and other items required for everyday life. He ﷺ left nothing to be inherited except a white mule (a gift from Muqawqis, the king of Egypt), some modest clothes, and a piece of land that he had received as a gift during his life time. Among his last words were:

"نحْنُ معاشِرُ الأنبياء لا نُورَثْ ، ما تَرَكْناهُ صَدَقة"

"We, the Community of Prophets, are not inherited from. Whatever we leave is for charity."

He ﷺ did not own the luxurious and decadent items one associates with those in positions of kings or leaders. This life on Earth was not his focus. His goal in life was to please Allah سبحانه وتعالى through worship and by sharing the religion of Islam with his brothers and sisters. So the Prophet ﷺ left more than the richest ruler ever did in inheritance. His legacy was the new Islamic nation that he had assembled from clusters of warring tribes. Muhammad ﷺ was the exemplar of the teachings of the Qur'an, which, for centuries, has guided us in our thoughts and actions, and will continue to do so.

Prophet Muhammad was a transformational leader. He transformed all Arabia from savage Bedouins into noble citizens. Further, they became kind brothers and sisters in Islam. He protected women against infanticide, rape, and other unfortunate forms of subjugation. Equal to men, women after Islam became respected citizens of the Muslim society.

The Prophet's ﷺ actions and words were remembered and later recorded (known as hadeeth), so that Muslims in future generations, to the end of time, could try to act and speak as he did. He has served as an example for all Muslims, in all periods to modern times. He will remain a model example for all of humanity.

Spread of Islam in Arabia

When Muhammad ﷺ passed away in 632, the western half of Arabia was Muslim. Two years later, the entire peninsula had been brought to the faith, and Muslim armies had moved up into the desert between Syria and Mesopotamia.

The people of the Christian cities of Syria and Palestine accepted Islam in rapid succession after AD 635. In the year 635 AD, Damascus came into the fold of the Muslim nation, followed by Antioch in 636. In 638, the great city of Jerusalem also came under Muslim rule.

Decades later, North Africa, Iraq, Khurasan, or Iran, and many other lands joined the Muslim realm.

Islam after the Prophet continued to be accepted and celebrated by millions of people, and in vast and faraway regions. In present times, around 1.5 billion people around the world profess Islam as their way of life. They follow the message of the Prophet, who once day was alone in Makkah. His profound faith and trust in Allah enabled him to achieve the miracle of uniting billions of people, of different generations and backgrounds, across the world, under the shade of Islam.

Time Line

1.	Beginning of the Prophet's fatal disease.	End of Safar, 11 A. H.
2.	Period of seriousness of disease. Stay in A'ishah's room.	7 days, up to the time of passing away.
3.	Last congregational prayer at the mosque, and last sermon.	5 days before passing away, Thursday, Thuhr prayer.
4.	Passing away.	12 Rabi' I, 11 A. H. Monday, mid-morning.
5.	Burial in A'ishah's room.	13 Rabi' I, 11 H, Tuesday.

In Praise of the Prophet

Attributed to Hassan Ibn Thabit

When I saw his light shining forth,
In fear, I covered my eyes with my palms,
Afraid for my sight, because of the beauty of his form.
So I was scarcely able to look at him at all.

The lights from his light are drowned in his light
and his face shines out like the sun and moon in one.

A spirit of light lodged in a body like the moon,
a mantle made up of brilliant shining stars.

I bore it until I could bear it no longer.
I found the taste of patience to be like bitter aloes.

I could find no remedy to bring me relief
other than delighting in the sight of the one I love.

Even if he had not brought any clear signs with him,
the sight of him would dispense with the need for them.

Muhammad is a human being but not like other human beings.
Rather he is a flawless diamond and the rest of mankind is just stones.

Blessings be on him so that perhaps Allah may have mercy on us
on that burning Day when the Fire is roaring forth its sparks.

FAITH IN ACTION

★ Devote your life for the service of Allah and His religion, as the Prophet did.
★ Express your love toward the Prophet by following his Sunnah and kind manners.
★ Always send your greetings to the Prophet by saying, "Sallallahu Alayhi Wasallim."

CHAPTER REVIEW

Projects and Activities

1. Write a poem or a essay about the feelings in your heart concerning the passing of Prophet Muhammad.

2. Create a timeline of the events that took place shortly before and after the passing away of the prophet.

Stretch Your Mind

1. Why do you think Allah chose that such a great Prophet like Muhammad died and did not live forever? Infer some lessons.

2. In what way did Abu Bakr demonstrate special leadership qualities?

3. Why do you think the Prophet highlighted the point of taking good care of women in his last sermon?

Study Questions

1. When and where did the Prophet pass away?
2. Describe the events that preceded the Prophet's passing away.
3. Where was the Prophet buried and why?
4. Why was Abu Bakr رضي الله عنه a natural choice to be the leader of the Muslims after the passing away of Muhammad ﷺ?
5. Who was the only living offspring of the Prophet when he passed away? Describe her last visit to him.
6. What was the content of the Prophet's last sermon to the Muslims?
7. What was the age of the Prophet when he passed away?

D37

UNIT E

As-Sunnah: The Other Divine Revelation

Chapter One	As-Sunnah: The Prophet's Way	E2
Chapter Two	The Basics of Uloom-ul-Hadeeth	E10
Chapter Three	The Recording of the Hadeeth	E16
Chapter Four	The Major Books of Hadeeth (Part I)	E22
Chapter Five	The Major Books of Hadeeth (Part II)	E30

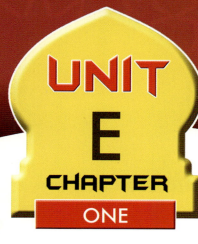

As-Sunnah: The Prophet's Way

UNIT E CHAPTER ONE

CHAPTER OBJECTIVES

1. Understand what the Sunnah is, and how it relates to Al-Qur'an.
2. Appreciate the important place of the Sunnah in Islam.
3. Receive a basic overview of the history of collecting and analyzing hadeeth.
4. Learn the basic terminology and methodology of the science of hadeeth.
5. Gain a respect for the enormous amount of work and sacrifice that was put into preserving the hadeeth.
6. Learn about the most important books of hadeeth, along with their unique characteristics.
7. Get an introduction to the authors of the main books of hadeeth.
8. Learn and memorize the hadeeth on obeying the Prophet ﷺ.

VOCABULARY

- Sunnah — السُّنَّة
- Sunan — سُنَن
- Hadeeth — حَديث
- Ahadeeth — أحاديث
- Wahy — وَحْي

A rare picture of the Prophet's grave, inside the Prophet's Mosque in Madinah.

What Is the Sunnah?

In the Arabic language, the term "Sunnah" refers to a habit or custom or a way of doing things. The sunnah of any person is the way that a person conducts his or her life. An example of the linguistic usage of the word can be found in the following hadeeth: "Whoever establishes in Islam a good sunnah gets its reward, and the reward of all those who follow it. And whoever establishes a bad sunnah in Islam gets its sin, and the sins of all those who follow it..." (Muslim). Therefore, sunnah in the Arabic language is a way, a conduct or a lifestyle of a person or people.

Muslim scholars define the Sunnah in the following manner:
"The Sunnah is any speech, action, approval, or attribute of the Messenger of Allah ﷺ." Here are some examples:

A. **Speech:** In Arabic, قَوْل qawl, which means everything the Prophet said after he became a Prophet. An example of that is the hadeeth of the Prophet ﷺ:

"إنَّما الأعمالُ بالنِّيّات"

"Actions are judged according to the intentions." (Al-Bukhari)

B. **Action:** In Arabic, فِعْل fi'l. This means everything the Prophet did after he became a Prophet. The actions of the Prophet ﷺ, can be subdivided into three categories:

- Actions intended to demonstrate some part of the religion, like how he prayed and how he performed Hajj, etc.

- Actions demonstrating parts of the religion that are unique to him. For example, he would sometimes fast for several consecutive days without eating or drinking. We are not permitted to fast in this manner.

- Actions that relate to him as a human being. For example, he liked certain foods, or he stood up, sat down or went to sleep in certain places. We are not required to follow this

E3

category of action, but a few companions like Ibn 'Omar used to do so out of their love for the Messenger of Allah ﷺ.

C. **Approval:** In Arabic, تَقْرِير taqreer, which means everything the Prophet approved of. An example of this is when one of the Sahabah said the following statement after he rose from rukoo' during salah:

"رَبَّنَا وَلَكَ الْحَمْدُ كَمَا يَنْبَغِي لِجَلَالِ وَجْهِكَ وَعَظِيمِ سُلْطَانِكَ"

"Oh our lord, we praise you, as Your majestic face and great kingdom deserve."

After salah, the Prophet commended and approved of what the man had said.

Another example of this is the incident when some of the Sahabah prayed two rak'aat between the athan and iqamah during the Maghrib and Ishaa times. The Prophet did not object, so it was considered an approved Sunnah. Otherwise, had Rasoolullah objected to these two actions, they would not be considered Sunnah.

D. **Attribute:** In Arabic, صِفَة sifah. This means all the reports about him, i.e. about what he was like. For example, he was described as a man who was neither overly tall, nor short.

The Sunnah is the Prophet's way of worshipping Allah and practicing Islam.

What is The Difference Between the Sunnah and the Qur'an?

The Qur'an contains the message, teachings, and laws of Allah, that are conveyed by the words of Allah. The Sunnah contains the message, teachings, and laws of Allah, conveyed in the words and actions of the Messenger, peace be upon him. Allah says this in Surat-un-Najm in the Qur'an about the Messenger of Allah, peace be upon him;

﴿ وَمَا يَنطِقُ عَنِ ٱلْهَوَىٰ ۝ إِنْ هُوَ إِلَّا وَحْىٌ يُوحَىٰ ۝ ﴾
النجم: ٣-٤

"He does not speak according to his desires, he speaks only the Wahy, or divine revelation." [53:3-4]

Based on the above ayah, the hadeeth of the Prophet is part of Wahy, or divine guidance and revelation. That is because every time Rasoolullah ﷺ said or did anything, it was with the approval of Allah. So in this way, both the Qur'an and the Sunnah are messages from Allah. The difference between the two, however, is that the words of the Qur'an are the actual words of Allah, while the wording of the hadeeth are those of the Prophet.

There is a type of hadeeth, however, that relates exact words of Allah that are not part of the Qur'an. This is "Hadeeth Qudsi." The Prophet usually says in the beginning of the Hadeeth Qudsi "Allah says," and then he mentions the saying of Allah.

Table: Similarities and Differences among Qur'an, Hadeeth, and Hadeeth Qudsi

	Type of Revelation	Meaning revealed by	Words chosen by	Can be recited in Qiyam position during prayer and as a worship	Can be Authentic or unauthentic
1	Al-Qur'an	Allah	Allah	Yes	No, it can only be authentic
2	Hadeeth	Allah	Prophet Muhammad	No	Yes
3	Hadeeth Qudsi	Allah	Allah	No	Yes

The Roles of Sunnah in Islam

1. The Sunnah Tells Us How to Implement Al-Qur'an. If we only had the Qur'an alone, we would not know exactly how to apply it to our lives. So Allah has taught us, through His Messenger, how to properly understand and implement the Qur'an.

The Qur'an is sometimes brief and non-specific regarding matters of fiqh. The role of the Prophet was to describe in detail how we should worship Allah. For example, Allah ordered the Muslims to pray, but He did not detail in Al-Qur'an how many times a day we should pray. Nor did Allah state how many rak'aat we should perform in each prayer. Al-Qur'an instructed us to give zakah, fast, and perform Hajj. However, Allah did not explain in detail how to perform all of the pillars of Islam. This was the role assigned to Rasoolullah ﷺ. He explained and demonstrated to the early muslims all details of worship and etiquette in Islamic life.

Allah also ordered us in Al-Qur'an to demonstrate noble characteristics such as honesty, truthfulness, kindness, mercy, and courage, along with many other qualities. He sent Rasoolullah to show us through his actions how we could achieve a high level of character in our daily lives.

2. The Sunnah Clarifies the Qur'an. There are many phrases and concepts in Al-Qur'an that needed clarification. Although the early Muslims understood much of the Qur'an, they could not understand everything in it without the help of Rasoolullah. Therefore, Rasoolullah was the teacher who explained Allah's message to his followers

﴿ وَأَنزَلْنَآ إِلَيْكَ ٱلذِّكْرَ لِتُبَيِّنَ لِلنَّاسِ مَا نُزِّلَ إِلَيْهِمْ وَلَعَلَّهُمْ يَتَفَكَّرُونَ ﴾ النحل: ٤٤

"And I have sent down to you the Qur'an so that you will clarify to the people what has been sent to them." [16:44]

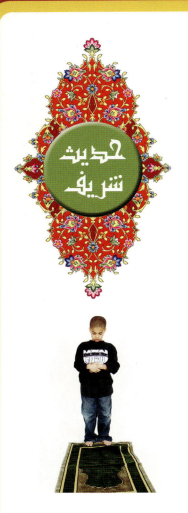

Hadeeth Shareef

عن مالك بن الحُوَيْرِث رَضِيَ اللهُ عَنْهُ قال: قالَ رَسولُ الله ﷺ:

"صَلوا كَما رَأيْتُموني أُصَلّي."

رواه البخاري

Malik Ibn-ul-Huwayrith narrated that the Prophet said:

"Pray like you see me pray."

(Reported by Imam Al-Bukhari)

عن جابر بن عبد الله رَضِيَ اللهُ عَنْهُ قال: قالَ رَسولُ الله ﷺ:

"لِتَأخُذوا عَنّي مَناسِكَكُم."

رواه مسلم

Jabir Ibn Abdullah narrated that the Prophet said:

"Learn from me your rituals."

(Reported By Imam Muslim)

3. The Sunnah Is the Second Source of Religious Knowledge, after Al-Qur'an. As was explained in the above points 1 and 2, the Sunnah teaches Muslims additional details about Islam that are not found in the Qur'an. However, all scholars of Islam understand that Al-Qur'an remains the first source of knowledge for us, and the Sunnah comes second. In fact, learning the Qur'an alone, without learning the Sunnah, may lead to misinterpreting Allah's directions in Al-Qur'an. Allah sent Prophet Muhammad to teach us how to practice the Qur'an. Much of the details of Islamic teachings can be found in the Sunnah, but they were not mentioned in the Qur'an. Therefore, the Sunnah is the second source of religious knowledge in Islam.

The more we follow the Sunnah of Prophet Muhammad, the more we act like him. Many of the things that the Prophet told us to do are mandatory. However, many others are not mandatory, but they are recommended.

Obeying Prophet Muhammad is Mandatory in Islam

Obeying the Prophet and following his Sunnah is mandatory in Islam. In many ayaat, Allah stressed the importance of obeying Prophet Muhammad and following his Sunnah and his great example. Let's explore what Al-Qur'an says about obeying Prophet Muhammad.

a. Allah granted Prophet Muhammad many great attributes and manners that are the perfect example for all mankind. The lifestyle of Prophet Muhammad is Allah's choice for those who seek to please Him and win His Jannah on the Day of Judgment. Therefore, the Sunnah and the lifestyle of the Prophet is the one that is favored by Allah.

﴿ لَّقَدْ كَانَ لَكُمْ فِى رَسُولِ ٱللَّهِ أُسْوَةٌ حَسَنَةٌ لِّمَن كَانَ يَرْجُوا۟ ٱللَّهَ وَٱلْيَوْمَ ٱلْءَاخِرَ وَذَكَرَ ٱللَّهَ كَثِيرًا ﴿٢١﴾ ﴾

الأحزاب: ٢١

"Certainly you have in the Messenger of Allah an excellent role model for those who seek the pleasure of Allah and the latter day and remembers Allah much." [33:21]

b. Obeying the Prophet is mandatory in Islam. Allah orders all Muslims in Surat-Al-Imran to obey Allah and His Prophet,

﴿ وَأَطِيعُوا۟ ٱللَّهَ وَٱلرَّسُولَ لَعَلَّكُمْ تُرْحَمُونَ ﴿١٣٢﴾ ﴾

آل عمران: ١٣٢

"Obey Allah and His Messenger so that you will receive mercy."[3:132]

c. Allah confirmed that whoever obeys the Prophet, he or she will be obeying Allah. The way we do this today is by following the Sunnah. Allah says in Surat-un-Nisaa',

﴿ مَّن يُطِعِ ٱلرَّسُولَ فَقَدْ أَطَاعَ ٱللَّهَ ﴿٨٠﴾ ﴾ النساء: ٨٠

"Whoever obeys the Messenger has obeyed Allah."[4:80]

d. Allah has made obedience of His Messenger a way to winning the love of Allah. Allah says in Surat Al-Imran,

﴿ قُلْ إِن كُنتُمْ تُحِبُّونَ ٱللَّهَ فَٱتَّبِعُونِى يُحْبِبْكُمُ ٱللَّهُ وَيَغْفِرْ لَكُمْ ذُنُوبَكُمْ وَٱللَّهُ غَفُورٌ رَّحِيمٌ ﴿٣١﴾ ﴾ آل عمران: ٣١

"Say (O Muhammad): If you truly love Allah, then follow me and Allah will love you and forgive you your sins."[3:31]

e. During the life of the Prophet, Allah has made submission to the decisions of the Messenger of Allah a precondition for belief. Allah says in Surat-un-Nisaa',

﴿ فَلَا وَرَبِّكَ لَا يُؤْمِنُونَ حَتَّىٰ يُحَكِّمُوكَ فِيمَا شَجَرَ بَيْنَهُمْ ثُمَّ لَا يَجِدُوا۟ فِىٓ أَنفُسِهِمْ حَرَجًا مِّمَّا قَضَيْتَ وَيُسَلِّمُوا۟ تَسْلِيمًا ﴿٦٥﴾ ﴾ النساء: ٦٥

"I swear by your Lord they will not believe until they make you decide the disputes between them, and then they do not find any objection in themselves to your judgment and they submit completely."[4:65]

Don't Take the Sunnah Lightly

Rasoolullah was once sitting in the masjid with his companions. He told them that there would come a day when some people would claim that the Sunnah is not important. He said: "I have been given the Qur'an and its equivalent with it. A time is about to come when a man will sit back in his chair and say, "Only follow the Qur'an. Whatever you find in it that is permissible, consider it permissible and whatever you find in it that is forbidden, consider it forbidden." The Prophet then said "I say, whatever the Messenger of Allah forbids is like what Allah forbids."

Then the Prophet gave examples of the things that he prohibited, although it is not mentioned in the Qur'an. He said, "It is prohibited for you to eat the meat of donkeys and wild animals. It is also prohibited to enter the houses of the People of the Book (Christians and Jews) without their permission, to take their food or belongings without their permission, and to hurt their families."

(This narration is reported in Abu Dawood, At-Tirmithi, Ibn Majah and Ahmad)

Hadeeth Shareef

عن أنس بن مالك رَضِيَ اللهُ عَنْهُ قال: قَالَ رَسُولُ الله ﷺ:
"مَنْ رَغِبَ عَنْ سُنَّتِي فَلَيْسَ مِنِّي"
رواه البخاري

Anas Ibn Malik narrated that the Prophet ﷺ said:
"Whoever neglects my Sunnah is not one of my true followers."
Reported by Imam Al-Bukhari and others

عن أبي هريرة رضي الله عنه قال : قال رسول الله ﷺ :
"كلُّ أُمَّتي يَدْخُلونَ الجَنَّةَ إلا مَنْ أَبَى.
قالوا: يا رَسُولَ اللهِ وَمَنْ يَأْبَى؟
قال: مَنْ أطاعَني دَخَلَ الجَنَّةَ وَمَنْ عَصَاني فَقَدْ أَبَى"
رواه البخاري

Abu Hurayrah narrated that the Messenger of Allah, ﷺ, said:
"Everyone from my ummah (nation) will enter Paradise, except those who refuse."
He was asked, "Oh Rasoolullah, who would refuse?"
He said, "Whoever obeys me enters Paradise and whoever disobeys me has refused."

Reported in Al-Bukhari

Projects and Activities

Write a story that shows how the Sahabah or the early scholars of Islam were sincere and motivated to follow the Sunnah of the Prophet.

Stretch Your Mind

List some similarities and differences between Al-Qur'an and As-Sunnah.

Study Questions

1. What does the term "Sunnah" mean in Arabic?
2. Define the term "Sunnah."
3. Discuss at least three reasons for obeying the Prophet and following his Sunnah.
4. Can Muslims understand the Qur'an without the help of the Prophet? Explain your answer.
5. "Following the Sunnah leads to Jannah." Is this true? Support your answer with a hadeeth.
6. State five examples that illustrate why Muslims need the "Sunnah" if they are to follow Islam correctly.
7. State one hadeeth that shows the importance of As-Sunnah.

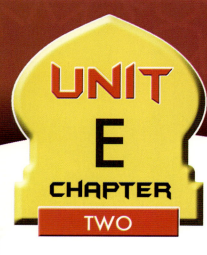

The Basics of Uloom-ul-Hadeeth

CHAPTER OBJECTIVES

1. Develop awareness of the importance of Uloom-ul-Hadeeth
2. Understand the basic terms of Uloom-ul Hadeeth
3. Learn the basic classifications of hadeeth: Al-Hadeeth-us-Saheeh and Al-Hadeeth-ul-Hasan. Al-Hadeeth-ud-Da'eef and Al-Hadeeth-ul-Mawdoo'.

VOCABULARY

Uloom-ul-Hadeeth	علوم الحديث	Sihaah	صحاح
Sanad	سَند	Hasan	حَسَن
Asaneed	أسانيد	Hisaan	حسان
Matn	مَتْن	Da'eef	ضَعيف
Matn is	مُتون	Di'aaf	ضعاف
Raawi	راوي	Mawdoo'	موضوع
Saheeh	صحيح	Mawdoo'aat	مَوضوعات

E10

Definition of Hadeeth

A hadeeth is a report of the sayings or actions of Prophet Muhammad together with the list of its chain of narration. عُلومُ الحَديث 'Uloom-ul-Hadeeth, or the science of hadeeth, is all of the technical knowledge we learn about the narration of hadeeth.

Why Is This Important?

As we learned in the previous chapters, Allah has promised to protect this religion. From this promise, we can be sure that Allah has protected the hadeeth of His Messenger, peace be upon him. We cannot personally see our Prophet to follow his example, but we have been instructed by Allah to follow the Sunnah. The ahadeeth are therefore a key to our understanding and following his Sunnah.

Allah Almighty inspired generations of scholars from the time of the companions to the present day to work on preserving the ahadeeth. These scholars have developed a whole intricate science to screen and classify the ahadeeth. Through hard work and dedication over hundreds of years, they separated the authentic Hadeeth of the Prophet from the faked and inaccurate narrations that were falsely attributed to the Prophet. These great scholars produced many great collections of ahadeeth of the Prophet. In this chapter, we will learn some of the basic terminology of this science and look at some examples of how these terms are used in practice.

Basic Terminology:

1. **Sanad** سَنَد : This word refers to the chain of narrators of a particular hadeeth. (i.e. the list of people who transmitted the narration originating from the Prophet.) The plural of "sanad" is أسانيد "asaneed."

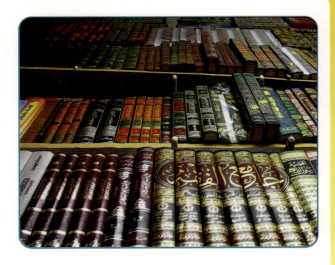

2. **Matn** مَتْن : The actual text of the hadeeth. The plural of matn is مُتون mutoon.

4. **Raawi** راوي : Is one of the narrators in the chain of narration. The word means "narrator." The plural of raawi is رُواة ruwaah.

5. **Saheeh** صَحيح : This is the overall higher grade for the sanad and the matn. It means "sound and correct." The plural of saheeh is صِحاح sihaah.

6. **Hasan** حَسَن : This is an overall good grade hadeeth that is slightly less than Saheeh. The hasan hadeeth is acceptable to use as evidence. The plural of hasan is حِسان hisaan.

7. **Da'eef** ضَعيف : This is an overall low grade hadeeth, that means there is a significant weakness in the chain or in the text of the hadeeth, that makes it unusable as religious knowledge. The plural of da'eef is ضِعاف di'aaf.

8. **Mawdoo'** موضوع : This means that proof is available to show that the hadeeth is fabricated, or has untrue naration. The plural of mawdoo' is مَوْضوعات mawdoo'aat.

Hadeeth's Place in Islam

We learn Islam through two main sources of knowledge: Qur'an and Sunnah. We have to follow all ayaat and sound ahadeeth and recognize them as part of our religion. The hadeeth is recognized as part of our religion if it is saheeh or hasan. The Da'eef Hadeeth or the Mawdoo' narration cannot be considered part of Islam.

Some scholars, however, say that we can use da'eef hadeeth in matters of manners, and when it encourages us to love Allah and worship Him. The majority of the scholars do not follow that opinion. They say that the Qur'an and the sound hadeeth, saheeh and hasan, have thousands of verses and ahadeeth that motivate us to do good deeds. Therefore, we don't need to look for such motivation among weak ahadeeth. Finally, all scholars of Islam assign no religious value to mawdoo' hadeeth. A hadeeth of this category is simply a lie and cannot be attributed to Rasoolullah.

Al-Hadeeth-us-Saheeh الحديث الصحيح : The Authentic Hadeeth

To identify a hadeeth as saheeh, it must pass five tests:

1. The chain of narration must be connected. Each narrator has actually learned the hadeeth from the earlier narrator.
2. The narrators must be known for their high ethical and religious standards.
3. The narrators must be known for their precision in regards to their memory and accuracy of transmission. This is because a saheeh hadeeth is a verbatim report, i.e. a word for word report, of what the Prophet ﷺ actually said.
4. The text of the narration cannot contradict another text that has a more reliable chain of transmission.
5. There cannot be any logical problem with the hadeeth that would throw doubt on its authenticity.

Example:

Imam Bukhari and Imam Muslim said: "Qutaybah told us that Jareer told him that he heard from Umara who heard from Abi Zar'ah who heard from Abu Hurayrah that:"

A man came to the Messenger of Allah, peace be upon him, and said, "O Messenger of Allah, who is most deserving of my good companionship?" He said, "Your mother" The man said, "Then who?" He said, "Your mother." The man said, "Then who?" He said, "Your mother." The man said, "Then who?" He said, "Your father."

The section in bold is called the sanad. The section that follows it is called the matn. In this hadeeth, the chain of narration is connected. Also, all of the narrators in the chain are known among scholars of hadeeth for being very reliable, trustworthy and precise. This chain of narration is also well known among scholars of hadeeth and it doesn't contradict any other narration. The text of the hadeeth itself is understandable and is consistent with the rest of the Qur'an and Sunnah. So this hadeeth has been categorized as saheeh, or absolutely sound.

Al-Hadeeth-ul-Hasan الحديث الحسن : The Fine Hadeeth

The criteria for grading a hadeeth as hasan are the same as those used in the grading of a saheeh hadeeth, with one exception. A hasan hadeeth will have one or more narrators in the chain who have been found to be a little weak in their precision, but not to the degree that they are considered unreliable. Because these narrators are not as precise, they will often convey the correct meaning of the hadeeth, but some or all of it will be in their own words, rather than verbatim.

Example:

Imam Ahmed said Yahya told me that he heard from Bahiz who heard from his father who heard from his father that:

He said to the Messenger of Allah, peace be upon him, "O Messenger of Allah, who should I be good to?" He said, "Your mother" I said, "Then who?" He said, "Your mother" I said, "Then who?" He said, "Your mother, then your father, then your relatives in order of closeness to you."

This chain of narration is connected and there are no problems with the text. All of the narrators in the chain are considered reliable except Bahiz. Some scholars considered him reliable and some felt that he made mistakes. But he is definitely truthful, and he is used as a narrator of hadeeth by At-Tirmithi, An-Nasa'ee, Ibn Majah and Abu Dawood. However, Bukhari and Muslim, who are known to have employed the highest standards, chose not to use him. So the chain of narration for this hadeeth is considered hasan. It is still usable as evidence, but it does not meet the highest standards of a Saheeh hadeeth.

Al-Hadeeth-ud-Da'eef الحديث الضعيف : The Weak Hadeeth

A hadeeth can be Da'eef, or weak, for one or more of the following reasons:
1. The chain of narration is broken in some way. One or more of the narrators did not learn it directly from the earlier narrator.
2. The text contradicts something that has been transmitted in a more reliable manner like the Qur'an or another stronger hadeeth.
3. The narrator is known to make so many mistakes that what he says is completely unreliable.
4. The narrator is found to be so sinful that his integrity cannot be trusted.
5. There is a logical problem with the Hadeeth that clearly indicates a mistake was made.

It is important to note that the grading of a single chain of narration as da'eef doesn't mean the matn itself is weak. It does happen that a single hadeeth can have multiple chains of narration. These multiple narrations have varying degrees of weakness, but when considered together the overall chain of narration can be considered hasan.

Example:

Imam Al-Tirmithi said that Muhammad said to him that Wakeea' said to him that Yazeed said to him that he heard from Ibn Mubarak, who heard from Suhaib, that the Messenger of Allah, peace be upon him, said:

"A person who makes permissible what the Qur'an has forbidden has not believed in the Qur'an."

This chain of narration has several problems:
1. It is broken because Ibn Mubarak never met Suhaib.
2. Ibn Mubarak's quality as a narrator is unknown.
3. Yazeed is generally considered a weak narrator of hadeeth.

4. The son of Yazeed relates from his father this hadeeth with a different chain of narration. The son of Yazeed is also not a good narrator of hadeeth.

However, the meaning of the text is correct and supported by many verses from the Qur'an. So we can conclude that the hadeeth is weak, but the meaning is correct.

Al-Hadeeth-ul-Mawdoo' الحديث الموضوع : The Fabricated Hadeeth

A hadeeth can be mawdoo', or fabricated, when one or more of the narrators in the sanad is a known liar and fabricator of hadeeth. That can be combined with a clear religious deviation from the Qur'an or the other saheeh hadeeth.

When the scholars, or ulamaa', label a certain hadeeth as mawdoo', this means that the Prophet never said what is being reported. In other words, one narrator has lied and fabricated the hadeeth. In fact, there was a period in time when there were many spurious ahadeeth spread around by mischief makers and those with ill motivations. A notorious fabricator, Abd-ul-Kareem Abu'l-Auju, admitted to fabricating thousands of hadeeth that declared the halal haram and the haram halal. It was therefore very important that the scholars of hadeeth sort through the material to make it clear to the Muslims which ahadeeth were accurate and which were not.

Mawdoo' is the lowest level possible of a hadeeth narration. The meaning of the text might be correct, but the Prophet didn't say it. Someone else has said it. Therefore, the hadeeth has no religious value.

Example:

"اطْلبوا العلمَ وَلو بالصين"

"Seek knowledge even if you have to go to China."

Hadeeth Shareef

عن أبي هريرة رضي الله عنه قال : قال رسول الله ﷺ :
"من كذبَ عليَّ متعمّداً فليَتَبَوَّأْ مقعَدَهُ مِنَ النار."

رواه مسلم وأحمد وأبو داود والترمذي وابن ماجة

Abu Hurayrah رضي الله عنه narrated that Rasoolullah said: "Whoever lies on me deliberately should pick his place in Hell Fire."

Reported by Muslim, Abu Dawood, At-Tirmithi and Ibn Majah

FAITH IN ACTION

★ Always make sure that you learn the saheeh and hasan, or authentic, ahadeeth of the Prophet, and practice them. Avoid following the mawdoo', or fabricated ahadeeth, or the ones with a weak chain of narrators.

CHAPTER REVIEW

Projects and Activities

1. Open a volume of Saheeh-ul-Bukhari or Saheeh Muslim and copy one hadeeth. Point out the sanad and the matn of the hadeeth.
2. Open Sunan-un-Tirmithi and copy one hadeeth that is hasan. Point out the sanad and the matn of the hadeeth.
3. Open a book on the weak and fabricated ahadeeth, and copy one hadeeth that is daíeef and another that is mawdoo'.

Stretch Your Mind

What is the difference between hadeeth saheeh and hadeeth daíeef?

Study Questions

1. Define: Sanad, Matn, Raawi.
2. What is the hadeeth saheeh? Write an example.
3. What is the hadeeth hasan? Write an example.
4. What is the hadeeth daíeef? Write an example.
5. What is the hadeeth mawdoo'? Write an example.
6. What types of ahadeeth are acceptable as religious guidance?

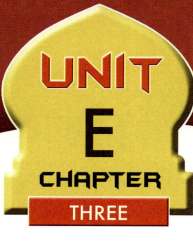

The Recording of the Hadeeth

CHAPTER OBJECTIVES

1. Learn about the early attempts to write down the hadeeth.
2. Learn an overview of the history of hadeeth.
3. Recognize the categories of hadeeth books and references.

Allah says in Surat-ul-Hijr:

﴿ إِنَّا نَحْنُ نَزَّلْنَا ٱلذِّكْرَ وَإِنَّا لَهُۥ لَحَٰفِظُونَ ۝ ﴾ الحجر: ٩

"I have sent down the thikr (the Qur'an) and I am preserving it." (15:9)

The word 'thikr' here includes both the Qur'an and the Sunnah.

As we have seen, the Sunnah is the second most important part of the religious guidance after the Qur'an. Without it one cannot understand the Qur'an properly. So, to keep His promise to protect the Qur'an, Allah also preserved the Sunnah. In this chapter we will begin to see how this happened.

The Companions Started the Tradition of Writing Hadeeth

The recording of hadeeth started at the time of the Prophet ﷺ with his companions. Imam Bukhari relates that Abu Hurayrah said, "There is not a companion of Rasoolullah ﷺ who relates more hadeeth from him than me, except Abdullah ibn Amr. He used to write what he heard, and I cannot write."

In Sunan Abu Dawood, Abdullah ibn Amr said, "I used to write everything I heard from Rasoolullah ﷺ because I wanted to memorize it. Then the Quraysh told me not to write it. They said, "How can you write everything he says when he is a human who speaks when he is happy and when he is angry? So I stopped writing and asked

Rasoolullah ﷺ about this. He said as he pointed to his mouth, "Write… I swear by Allah nothing comes out of it except the truth."

Therefore, some of the Ahadeeth were written down by Abdullah Ibn Amr during the early years of Islam.

Ahadeeth were written by Abdullah Ibn Amr for his own personal use. He was the only one permitted to write them down. The Prophet generally discouraged the Sahabah from writing them at that time. He feared that people would mix them with the Qur'an, and become confused between the two. After the revelation of the Qur'an was completed, the Prophet passed away.

Khaleefah Abu Bakr ordered the collection of the Qur'an in one volume. Later on, Khaleefah Uthman made seven copies of Al-Qur'an and distributed them to the major cities of the Muslim nation at that time.

The fear that people might mix hadeeth with the Qur'an had now diminished and a stronger focus was placed on collecting and writing the hadeeth. The companions were also very careful when they narrated the hadeeth, because they knew that it was a major sin to attribute speech to Rasoolullah incorrectly. So they taught the next generation to pay close attention to the trustworthiness of the people they learned hadeeth from. This idea became a common saying among the following generations in the phrase, "The ahadeeth are part of our religion, so be careful who you take them from."

The Ahadeeth Were Also Memorized:

The Messenger of Allah ﷺ was teaching people their religion when he spoke. He was the greatest teacher on Earth. He was a fluent and eloquent speaker and would repeat himself often. He was also careful not to tire his students out. A'ishah, may Allah be pleased

A very old manuscript

with her, said, "Rasoolullah ﷺ did not talk continuously like you talk. Instead, he would talk in a clear and distinct manner that would be easily memorized by the person sitting with him." *(Tirmithi)*

The companion Abu Sa'eed Al-Khudri was once asked by one of his students if he would write down the ahadeeth that he knew. He said, "I will not write it for you and we have to protect the Qur'an. The Messenger of Allah, peace be upon him, used to speak to us and we would memorize. So memorize from us like we memorized from your Messenger."

Traveling to Learn Hadeeth:

The companions started the habit of traveling to collect and authenticate the ahadeeth. The companion Jabir ibn Abdullah traveled for a month to Syria to hear a hadeeth directly from the other companions who had directly heard it from Rasoolullah ﷺ. Abu Ayub Al-Ansari رضي الله عنه traveled to Egypt for one hadeeth, then he turned around and came back to madinah immediately after he heard it. Ibn Masood said, "If I knew that anyone had more knowledge than me regarding the Book of Allah, I would travel to him."

From the generation of scholars after the companions, Abi Al-A'lyia said: "In Basrah, we used to hear the narrations from the companions of Rasoolullah ﷺ, but we would not accept them until we traveled to them and heard from them directly." Muhammad ibn Sireen once said, "I came to Kufa, and there were four thousand people there as students of hadeeth." So when we pick up a book and read one hadeeth, we should remember and pray for the scholars who spent their lives traveling and collecting to make sure the ahadeeth were preserved for future generations.

Selected Story

Imam Al-Bukhari Rejects a Narration of a Man Who Lied to an Animal

It is narrated that Imam Al-Bukhari made a very tiring journey to meet a man who was a hadeeth narrator. He wanted to verify a hadeeth he heard that the man had memorized. When Imam Al-Bukahri arrived to the home town of the hadeeth narrator, he went immediately to his house and asked if he were available.

The imam was told that the man was not at home and he was out in the field trying to catch an animal that had run away from his farm. Imam Al-Bukhari followed the man and found him trying to trick his animal to come to him by pretending to have food. There was no food on him, so the Imam decided not to take the hadeeth from the man. He thought that if a person can lie to an animal, he may perhaps lie about a hadeeth. Imam Al-Bukhari returned to his faraway home without learning the new hadeeth.

Fast Facts

The most common books of hadeeth contain narrations from the first three generations of Muslims. About 7921 of the narration were from men, and 301 were women.

Overview of the History of Hadeeth:

As you learned earlier, in the first hundred years of Islam, the ahadeeth were mostly passed along by memory, and the chain of narration was preserved. In the second hundred years, scholars began to make collections of the ahadeeth that were available in their area. This is the time period when Imam Malik ibn Anas (93-179 A.H.) wrote his book Al-Muwatta' which contained the Hadeeth and prophetic knowledge that he collected in Madinah. It is probably the first full hadeeth book ever to be compiled.

During the third century of Islam, the major scholars of hadeeth traveled across the Muslim world making comprehensive collections of hadeeth. This was the time period during which Imam Al-Bukhari, Muslim, At-Tirmithi, Ibn Majah, An-Nasa'ee and Ahmad ibn Hanbal compiled their great collections of hadeeth. After these main collections of hadeeth were compiled, scholars spent the next 600 years analyzing, writing commentary, perfecting, and developing the different sciences of hadeeth. Then there was a period of stagnation in the science of hadeeth, up until the last hundred years.

Today, we are seeing scholars exerting new found energy by into simplifying the work that has been done making it more accessible to people. Work is also being done to write commentary and explanation for Ahadeeth to make them understandable to the modern audience. Modern technological advances have made access to Hadeeth very easy. We can use the Internet, CDs, and clearly typed, well printed books, with modern indexes. Modern science is also giving us a deeper appreciation of some of the things Rasoolullah ﷺ did, particularly from a medical perspective.

Categories of Books Written to Serve Hadeeth

There is nothing on Earth like the amount of work that has been put into serving and studying the hadeeth. The following list summarizes some of the different kinds of books written. In each of these categories, you can find between five and one hundred famous books:

1. There are books that are collections of only sound hadeeth. They include *Saheeh-ul-Bukhari* and *Saheeh Muslim,* among others.
2. The books that focus on collecting hadeeth relating to fiqh topics, and are called "Sunan." They include *Sunan Abu Dawood, Sunan-un-Tirmithi, Sunan-un-Nasa'ee* and *Sunan Ibn Majah*.
3. The books that organize the ahadeeth according to the companion who narrated it. The book posts the sahabi, and then it lists all of the ahadeeth that he or she narrated. These books are called a "musnad," like *Al-Musnad,* by Imam Ahmad Ibn Hanbal, that contains more than 30,000 ahadeeth.
4. Some books focus on collecting ahadeeth along with the opinions of the companions

and scholars from the following generations, like *Al-Muwatta* by Imam Malik Ibn Anas, and *Al-Musannaf* by Abd-ur-Razzaq Ibn Hammam.

5. There are books that include many ahadeeth even though the focus of the book was something else, like the books of tafseer and history. This is like "Tafseer-ut-Tabari."

6. There are books that focus only on a specific kind of hadeeth, like the Qudsi Hadeeth.

7. There are books that focus on collecting all of the Hadeeth pertaining to a specific topic, like the personal attributes of the Messenger of Allah, which are called "Ash-Shama'il". Other topics include "Jihad", "Al-Amwal: Money and Wealth," "Alamat-us-Sa'ah: The Signs of the Day of Judgment," "Ar-Raqaa'iq: Heart Softeners."

8. There are books that analyze a single hadeeth by collecting together all of the chains of narration and versions of that one Hadeeth.

9. There are books that focus on cataloging the narrators, strong and weak, of the different ahadeeth, like *Tahtheeb-ut-Tahtheeb* by Ibn Hajar Al-Asqalani.

10. There are books and commentaries that explain the vocabulary and terms found in the Hadeeth like *An-Nihayah* by Ibn-ul-Atheer.

11. There are books that collect all of the known fabricated Hadeeth, like *Al-Mawdoo'aat* by Ibn-ul-Jawzi.

12. There are books that merge and summarize a number of books of Hadeeth by removing the redundant Ahadeeth and grading the quality of the chain of narration like *Jami'-ul-Usool* by Ibn-ul-Atheer.

13. There are a few books that have attempted to collect all of the unique Hadeeth available from all of the books of Hadeeth. One book in this category, called *Kanz-ul-Ummal*, contains 46,624 different narrations which is a summary of about 93 books of Hadeeth.

So the lesson here is that Allah took care of protecting this religion by inspiring masses of scholars over the centuries who have worked day and night to protect and spread the Hadeeth of Prophet Muhammad ﷺ.

It is amazing that many imams and scholars of hadeeth and other subjects of Islam were not Arabs. However, they learned Arabic very well and became scholars of Qur'an, hadeeth, fiqh and other subjects of Islamic knowledge.

FAITH IN ACTION

★ Always work hard to seek good knowledge, like going to lectures, attending conferences and meeting with scholars and knowledgeable people. Do at least a fraction of what our great scholars used to do in the past.

CHAPTER REVIEW

Projects and Activities

1. Visit an Islamic library and browse through the books of hadeeth. Make a list of the hadeeth books that you see.
2. Create a time line showing the milestones of the recording of the Hadeeth.
3. Prophet Muhammad said "الأعمال بالنيات" (actions are judged according to the intention). This hadeeth is reported in Saheeh Bukhari and Sunan Abu Dawood. Do a search for the hadeeth and find out the similarities and differences between the mutoon and asaneed of the hadeeth that are cited in the two books.
4. Browse the hadeeth sections of the following sites:
   a. www.almeshkat.net/books
   b. www.al-islam.com/eng/

Stretch Your Mind

Last year, you learned how the Qur'an reached us through a fine documentation process. This chapter taught you how early Muslims documented the hadeeth. Create a table in which you compare and contrast how the Qur'an and Sunnah were documented. Make sure to compare and contrast the "when, where, who and how" elements of documentation in both cases.

Study Questions

1. Who was the first person ever to write the hadeeth?
2. Did many of the Sahabah write down the hadeeth? Explain why, or why not.
3. Describe how the ahadeeth were transmitted from one generation to another, or from one place to another, during the first century of Islam?
4. What was the name of the first compiled hadeeth book? Who compiled it?
5. What are the most well known books of hadeeth that were compiled during the third century of Islam?
6. List five types of hadeeth books that were written to preserve hadeeth? Include in your answer one title as an example of each type of book.

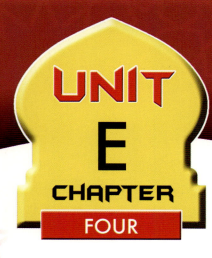

The Major Books of Hadeeth
(Part One)

CHAPTER OBJECTIVES

1. Recognize and learn about the most prominent books of hadeeth.
2. Gain a basic overview of the history of major hadeeth collectors.
3. Receive an introduction to the authors of the main books of hadeeth.

VOCABULARY

- Saheeh — صَحيح
- Sunan — سُنَن
- Musnad — مُسْنَد

PEOPLE TO REMEMBER

- Malik Ibn Anas — مالِك بن أنَس
- Muhammad Ibn Isma'eel Al-Bukahri — محَمَّد بن إسْماعيل البخَاري
- Muslim Ibn-ul-Hajjaj Al-Neesabouri — مُسْلِم بن الحَجَّاج النيسابوري
- Abu Dawood, Sulayman Ibn-ul-Ash'ath As-Sijistani — أبو داود، سُليمان بن الأشعَث السّجسْتاني
- Muhammad ibn Isa At-Tirmithi — مُحَمَّد بن عيسى الترْمِذي
- Ahmad Ibn Shu'ayb An-Nasa'ee — أحمَد بن شُعَيْب النَّسَائي

The most important books of Al-Hadeeth-us-Saheeh:

1. Al-Muwatta' of Imam Malik
2. Saheeh Al-Bukhari
3. Saheeh Muslim
4. Musnad of Imam Ahmed

Important Books of Al-Hadeeth-us-Saheeh

1. Muwatta' of Imam Malik:

Imam Malik Ibn Anas Al-Asbahi (93H to 179H) is one of the greatest scholars of hadeeth and Islamic law. His grandfather was a Sahabi by the name of Abu Amir Al-Asbahi. Allah has blessed our ummah with Imam Malik, who was one of the four major imams in Islamic history. He spent years collecting and perfecting his book "Al-Muwatta," meaning "the made easy," until it became one of the most authentic books of hadeeth of all time. Imam Shafi'ee said: "I don't know a book of knowledge that is more correct than the book of Imam Malik." In its entirety the book contains 4,319 ahadeeth, narrations and opinions of companions and scholars. Of this number, about 1,594 are ahadeeth of Rasoolullah ﷺ. If you remove the redundant hadeeth you get about 745 ahadeeth.

Some considered this book to be the first book of Saheeh Hadeeth. Others objected, pointing to the fact that the book is full of stories and narrations that have a disconnection in the chain of narration. However, all of the Hadeeth narrated in the Muwatta' can be assumed sound, because scholars afterwards collected the missing chains from other sources. It is also important to be aware of the fact that the main point of the book is to be an easy summary of the fiqh of Madinah. This is why Imam Malik wrote the first draft with around 10,000 narrations and then kept summarizing it year after year, until he refined it to its current form.

Al-Masjid An-Nabawi

Why doesn't the Muwatta' have connected chains of narration for every hadeeth?

The reason for this is that Imam Malik lived his whole life in Madinah. So he recorded many ahadeeth that were well known in the city of Madinah, even though he didn't always have a clear chain of narration for them. Also, we need to remember that many of the companions left Madinah and scattered across the world to perform jihad or to spread Islam. They took ahadeeth with them and taught them to people in those areas. Two centuries later, imams of hadeeth like Al-Bukhari, Muslim and others traveled around the Muslim world. Their aim was to collect sound asaneed, or chains of narration, for the mutoon of the ahadeeth that might have been well known in their areas.

Selected Story

The Khaleefah Al-Mansoor, of the Abbasid era, called Imam Malik to a meeting. Al-Mansoor told Imam Malik, "I decided to have your book, 'Al-Muwatta,' copied and distributed around the Muslim world. I will then command the people to stop studying anything else and only study and follow your book. I have come to the conclusion that the best knowledge of this religion comes from the people and scholars of Madinah."

Imam Malik said, "Oh Ameer-ul-Mu'mineen, please don't do this. The Sahabah have spread out to so many areas and taught the hadeeth of Rasoolullah everywhere. Every community accepted the knowledge that was brought to them and they follow it religiously. So the people have come to follow the differing opinions of the companions and later scholars. To force the people to change what they believe is correct is very difficult. So leave the people to follow what their choice of scholars favor and have adopted."

Al-Mansoor said, "I swear that if you ever change your mind, I will order it."

Quote from the Imam

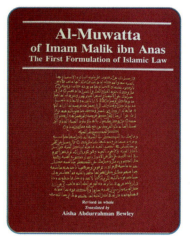

Imam Malik said, "I have met people in this city who, if they are asked to pray to Allah for rain, it would rain. They have also studied and learned many ahadeeth. I did not narrate a single hadeeth from them. They focused on fear of Allah and worship. This work (of hadeeth and fiqh) requires a person who fears Allah, protects himself, is usually very precise, and has strong knowledge and understanding. Such a person knows what he is talking about and can tell the difference between what he says today and what he hears tomorrow. An imprecise person who lacks understanding cannot be benefited from. He is not a reliable source of religious knowledge, and hadeeth is not to be taken from him."

2. Saheeh-ul-Bukhari:

Imam Muhammad Ibn Isma'eel Al-Bukhari was born in 194H in Bukhara, in today's Uzbekistan. He passed away in Samarqand at the age of 62 in the year 256H (810-870 A.D). Imam Al-Bukhari was an orphan, but showed signs of genius and possessed an amazing memory. He memorized the Qur'an and all of the ahadeeth available with the scholars in his area by the time he was only ten years old. Then he began his travels across the Muslim world to collect the hadeeth when he was sixteen. He traveled to Makkah, Madinah, Iraq, Syria, and Egypt to study with the great scholars of his time. His travels were inspired by the companions and great scholars, who journeyed long distances to find the strongest chains of narration for a hadeeth.

Bukhara

Imam Al-Bukhari Compiles the Hadeeth

The companion Jabir ibn Abdullah traveled for a month to visit another companion in Al-Sham (the area of Syria today) named Abdullah Ibn Unays. Jabir traveled this long distance because he had heard of a hadeeth that Abdullah had heard directly from the Messenger of Allah. So Jabir went to directly hear this one hadeeth to make sure of its authenticity. (Saheeh Al-Bukhari)

At the time of Imam Al-Bukhari, people had general collections of hadeeth. The scholars knew what was strong and what was weak based on their knowledge of the chains of narration. When the teacher of Imam Al-Bukhari saw his brilliance and precision, he suggested that he work on compiling a collection of only Saheeh Hadeeth in a small summarized book. Imam Al-Bukhari liked this idea and began writing his Saheeh when he was 23 years old. He then spent the next 16 years traveling, collecting, writing, analyzing and perfecting his book. He studied with over a thousand scholars of hadeeth, bringing together 600,000 different chains of narration for hadeeth. From all of these chains of narration, he selected about 2,607 of the very best to include in his Saheeh. He also presented it for review to many of the great scholars of hadeeth of his time. It didn't take long for the greatness of his book to be recognized and adopted by the scholars of our Ummah as the most perfect book after the Qur'an.

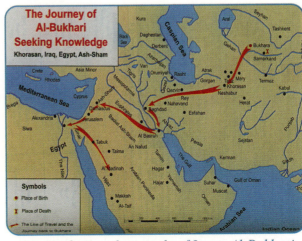
A map plotting the travels of Imam Al-Bukhari
Source: Dr. Shawqi Abu Khalil, *Atlas on the Prophet's Biography*, 2004 Darussalam.

They Loved Him!

Imam Muslim once said to Imam Al-Bukhari, "There are none like you in this world." He also said to him one time, "Please allow me to kiss your feet. You are the master of teachers and hadeeth scholars."

Layout of the Book

Imam Al-Bukhari was a brilliant scholar of Islamic law, in addition to being a scholar of hadeeth. So his book breaks up the hadeeth, or even sections of a hadeeth, based on the theme, law, or lesson that is learned from it. By contrast Imam Muslim put all of the different versions of a hadeeth together.

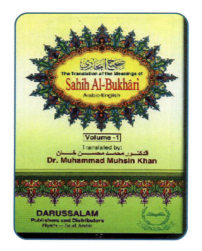

Because Imam Al-Bukhari breaks up and repeats the hadeeth in his book, the total numbers of narrations in the book are 7,563.

Selected Story
The Brilliance of Imam Al-Bukhari

In almost every city he visited, Imam Al-Bukhari was tested by the scholars from that city. He became prominent because he was proven to be a brilliant genius with incredible humility. Those who traveled with him said he would sometimes get out of bed between 15 and 20 times a night to continue his work on hadeeth.

When Imam Al-Bukhari came to Baghdad, the scholars prepared a hard test for him. They took one hundred hadeeth and scrambled their chains of narrations. They then gave ten Hadeeth each to ten people. Then they called for a gathering of the scholars and Imam Al-Bukhari attended. After the meeting began, one of the ten men got up and asked Imam Al-Bukhari about one of the hadeeth that he was given. Imam Al-Bukhari said, "I don't know it." Then the man asked him regarding the second of his hadeeth and Imam Al-Bukhari said, "I don't know it." The man continued with the rest of his ten hadeeth. Then the other nine men each got up asking about the hadeeth that they had one at a time. For each hadeeth, Imam Al-Bukhari did not say anything more than "I don't know it." When all ten men were finished presenting their 100 ahadeeth, the meeting became silent.

Then Imam Al-Bukhari turned to the first man and said to him, "As for your first hadeeth, you said... and the correct chain of narration is ... and as for the second hadeeth, you said... and the correct chain of narration is..." Imam Al-Bukhari continued with every hadeeth for each of the ten men, reminding them of what they had said, and then telling them what the correct narration was. When he finished he had corrected all 100 hadeeth. So the people were astounded by his brilliance and greatness. Later, Imam Al-Bukhari was nicknamed "Ameer-ul-Mu'mineen" of hadeeth, or the leader of the hadeeth knowledge.

3. Saheeh Muslim:

Imam Muslim Ibn Al-Hajjaj An-Nisaboori was born in 206A.H. in Neshabur, Iran and passed away in 261A.H. During his life, he became recognized as one of the greatest scholars of hadeeth. He traveled and studied with many scholars including Imam Al-Bukhari and Imam Ahmed Ibn Hanbal. He spent about 15 years compiling his Saheeh from a collection of about 300,000 chains of narration. After he completed his Saheeh he presented it to another great scholar of his time named Imam Abu Zar'ah Ar-Razi. When Imam Ar-Razi felt that a certain hadeeth had even a minor defect, Imam Muslim would remove that hadeeth from the book. In the end, Saheeh Muslim became accepted as one of the most authentic book of Hadeeth, second only to Saheeh Al-Bukhari. To understand why Saheeh-Al-Bukhari is slightly stronger overall, it could be said that Imam Al-Bukhari focused on collecting Hadeeth from "A+" narrators. Imam Muslim did not focus so exclusively on "A+" narrators, and included a lot of "A" narrators. Also, Imam Bukhari had a certain extra criterion that Imam Muslim didn't require for accepting narrations. According to Al-Bukhari, every narrator must have met his sheikh, or the scholar whom he learned the hadeeth from. Imam Muslim only required

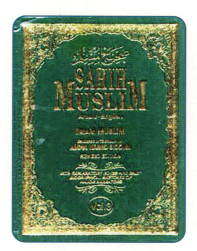

that the narrator and his sheikh have lived during the same time.

Layout of the Book

Saheeh Muslim does not focus on the fiqh lessons of the hadeeth, so Imam Muslim does not include opinions of companions or scholars. After the introduction, he only collected narrations attributed to Rasoolullah ﷺ. The focus of the book is to collect the different narrations and wordings of the same hadeeth in one place. So in total there are about 5,362 different narrations in the book. However, these narrations only represent about 2,846 different hadeeth.

4. Musnad of Imam Ahmed

Imam Ahmed Ibn Hanbal was born in 167H and passed away in 241H. He was one of the greatest scholars of hadeeth that this Ummah has ever produced. His collection of hadeeth dwarfs the other collections mentioned so far. His collection has about 27,363 chains of narration that can be summarized down to 9,339 unique, or unrepeated Hadeeth. However, the repetition is useful for scholars of hadeeth, who can compare the different chains of narration and the slight variations in wording to determine the strongest form of wording for the hadeeth. Imam Ahmed collected and organized all of these ahadeeth based on the narrator. His book, Al-Musnad, is so encompassing of all the documented hadeeth that some scholars would memorize his Musnad, instead of the other smaller famous books of hadeeth, because Musnad Ahmed doesn't miss many authentic hadeeth.

Imam Ahmed said he started with 750,000 chains of narration and then summarized and filtered them down to form his book. As a whole, his book turned out to be more authentic and of a higher quality than many of the other books of Sunan. Most of the ahadeeth in his collection are strong, or have mild weaknesses. Only a small handful of Hadeeth in the book have been assessed by some scholars as fabricated.

The Hadeeth scholar Abu Zar'ah was asked, "Which scholar that you met had memorized the most Hadeeth?" He said, "Ahmed Ibn Hanbal… The day he died, his books were collected and amounted to twelve camel loads. The books contained nothing but narrations and he had them all memorized."

Books of Imam Al-Bukhari

Al-Musnad means "the book of hadeeth that includes the proper chains of narration."

Quote from the Imam

Imam Ahmed was asked about the hadeeth, "A group from my ummah will always have the truth and will not be harmed by those who attack them until the Day of Judgment". He said, "If this group who remains victorious is not the people of hadeeth, then I do not know who they are."

Imam Ahmed was once asked about all of his travels to learn hadeeth, "If a man documents 30,000 ahadeeth isn't it enough for him?" The Imam was silent. The man said, "60,000?" The Imam was silent. The man said, "100,000?" Imam Ahmed said, "Then the person would know something."

This is how much knowledge one needed, at the time of the different chains of narration for each hadeeth to be sure of its authenticity. All praise is due to Allah, and may Allah bless all of our great scholars who have enabled us to follow our Prophet and study his ahadeeth with ease. They the work of collecting and categorizing the authentic narrations.

CHAPTER REVIEW

Projects and Activities

1. Visit an Islamic library and browse the four books of Hadeeth you learned about in this chapter.

2. Plot the routs of the journeys of one of the great imams whom you learned about in this chapter. Use a map which you have drawn or copied.

Stretch Your Mind

Write a paragraph about how each of the following imams has inspired you:
    a. Al-Bukhari
    b. Muslim
    c. Malik
    d. Ahmed Ibn Hanbal

Study Questions

1. List the eight books and their authors in chronological order.
2. Define: Saheeh; Musnad.
3. Describe briefly the following books:
    a. Saheeh-ul-Bukhari.   b. Saheeh Muslim.
    c. Saheeh Ibn Hibban   d. Musnad by Imam Ahmad.
    e. Muwatta'.
4. Are Saheeh Muslim and Saheeh-ul-Bukhari the only two books that carried the name "Saheeh" in their title? Explain your answer.

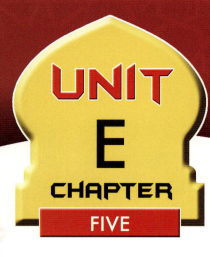

The Major Books of Hadeeth (Part Two)

CHAPTER OBJECTIVES

1. Recognize and learn about the Sunan books of hadeeth.
2. Gain a basic overview of the history of major Sunan book collections.
3. Receive an introduction to the authors of the main books of hadeeth.

The Other Important Collections of Hadeeth:

1. Sunan Abu Dawood — سُنَن أبو داود
2. Sunan Al-Tirmithi — سُنَن التِّرمِذي
3. Sunan An-Nasa'ee — سُنَن النِّسائي
4. Sunan Ibn Majah — سُنَن ابن ماجه

Books of Sunan

Quick Reminder

Remember that the compilers of the books of Saheeh only intended to collect Saheeh Hadeeth. In the books of Sunan the authors intended to collect both the Saheeh and Hasan Hadeeth. However, they will sometimes include narrations with minor to moderate weakness in their chains of narration.

1. Sunan-ut-Tirmithi سُنَن التِّرمِذي

The compiler of *Sunan-ut-Tirmithi* is Imam Muhammad Ibn Isa At-Tirmithi. He was born near Termez in present day Uzbekistan in the year 209 A.H. (824 A.D.). He passed away there in the year 279 A.H. (892 A.D.), when he was seventy lunar years of age. At-Tirmithi was a student of Imam Al-Bukhari, Muslim, and Abu Dawood. Later, he became a well-known and respected scholar of hadeeth. He was also known for his extreme fear of Allah, religious commitment, and precision. Imam Al-Bukhari used to admire him, and he once said to him, with great humility, "I benefited from you more than you benefited from me." It has been reported that towards the end of his life, At-Tirmithi lost his eyesight from crying so much out of the fear of Allah. It is sometimes difficult for us today to understand the amazing levels of piety that these great scholars of Islam had.

His collection of hadeeth incorporated a lot of different branches of the science of hadeeth. He did the following:

1. He carefully categorized the hadeeth based on its main theme.
2. He indicated any problems with the chain of the hadeeth.
3. He graded each hadeeth based on its overall strengths or weaknesses.
4. He clarified the names and nicknames of narrators.
5. He summarized what was said about strong or weak narrators.
6. He differentiated between narrators who actually met the Messenger of Allah, peace be upon him, and those who did not but narrated hadeeth directly to him.
7. He mentioned the opinions of scholars on different fiqh points like the opinions of Imam Ash-Shafi'ee, Malik, and Abu Haneefah.
8. He also summarized the number of chains of narration of a particular hadeeth, and whether it had other narrations that supported it.

Imam Al-Tirmithi did not repeat very many ahadeeth in his Sunan. Instead, he only mentioned the strongest hadeeth for each topic. He also mentioned how many other chains were available for the hadeeth. So the book is very comprehensive, containing about 3,965 hadeeth. When the repetitions are excluded, the number only drops to about 3,365.

Quote from the Imam

Imam Tirmithi said, "I wrote my book and presented it to the scholars of Hijaz (Madinah and Makkah), and they accepted it. And I presented it to the scholars of Iraq, and they accepted it. And I presented it to the scholars of Khurasan, and they accepted it. Whoever has this book in his house, it is as if he has a messenger from Allah talking to him."

2. Sunan Abu Dawood سُنَن أبو داود

The compiler of *Sunan Abu Dawood* is Abu Dawood Sulayman ibn Ash`ath al-Azdi As-Sijistani. Imam Abu Dawood was born in Sejstan, Afghanistan in 202 A.H. (817 A.D) and passed away in 273 A.H. (888 A.D.) at the age of 71. He was a student of Imam Al-Bukhari and Ahmed Ibn Hanbal. Imam Abu Dawood traveled to Iraq, Syria, Egypt, Makkah, Madinah, and Nisaboor (Nishaa'pur), among many other locations, to search for hadeeth and Islamic knowledge. After years of travel and study, he became widely recognized as one of the greatest scholars of hadeeth of his time. Imam At-Tirmithi and An-Nasa'ee were both counted among his students. He summarized his book from around 500,000 chains of narration to about 4,800 hadeeth. When repetitions are not counted, the number is around 3,784.

Quote from the Imam

Imam Abu Dawood said about his collection:

"I have collected in it (around) 4,800 Hadeeth. I mentioned the Saheeh Hadeeth and what comes close to it [Hasan]. It is enough for a person's religion to have four of them" (because most of the rules can be summarized in):
1. The Messenger of Allah, peace be upon him, said, "Actions are judged by the intentions."
2. And he said, "It is part of being a good Muslim to ignore that which does not concern you"
3. And he said, "A believer is not a believer until he wishes for his brother what he wishes for himself."
4. And he said, "What is permissible is clear and what is forbidden is clear, between them are unclear issues that not many people know (whether they are forbidden or not). So whoever avoids the unclear issues protects his honor and religion and those who fall into the unclear issues will fall into what is forbidden."

His book became widely accepted by scholars from all schools of fiqh.

3. Sunan-un-Nasa'ee سُنَن النَّسائي

Imam Ahmed Ibn Shu'ayb An-Nasa'ee was born in Nasa, Turkmenistan in 215 A.H (830 A.D.) and passed away in Palestine in 303H (915 A.D.). He traveled to Iraq, Syria, Makkah, Madinah, and Egypt, where he stayed for a long period of time. During his travels, he studied with many scholars including Imam Abu Dawood. He wrote many books about the grading of narrators of hadeeth, and was widely recognized as one of the greatest scholars of his time. He collected around 11,949 narrations in his collection called "Al-Sunan Al-Kubra." Then he was asked, "Is all of it sound?" He said, "No." So he was asked to summarize the strong hadeeth from it. He did so in a book called "Al-Mujtaba," which means "The Selected," where he documented 5,662 of the narrations. When repetitions are not counted, they number 2,515.

In his book he followed the example of Imam Al-Bukhari in categorizing and repeating Hadeeth to highlight the different lessons and rulings that can be inferred from them. He was also very careful to point out if there were any problems with a narration that were not clearly apparent.

Imam Ath-Thahabi once said, "No one memorized more Hadeeth than An-Nasa'ee at the start of the third century of Islam. He was comparable to Al-Bukhari."

Imam An-Nasa'ee was buried in Al-Quds, or Jerusalem

4. Sunan Ibn Majah سُنَن ابن ماجه

Imam Muhammad ibn Yazeed Ibn Majah was a great scholar of hadeeth in his time. He was born in the year 209 A.H. in Qazvin, Iran and he passed away in 273 A.H. In his book, he collected the Ahadeeth pertaining to the Sunnah of Rasoolullah ﷺ. His book is placed last among the famous books, because it contains a lot more weak hadeeth compared to the other books. The book is important because it contains a number of hadeeth that are not found in other books. There are around 4,341 ahadeeth in the book, of which 3,002 are narrated in the other five books of Hadeeth (Al-Bukhari, Muslim, Tirmithi, Abu Dawood, Nasa'ee). Imam Ibn Majah provides chains of narration that are often not found in the other books so his chains of narration act as supporting evidence. Of the rest of the ahadeeth:

1. 438 have sound chains of narration (Saheeh).

2. 199 have acceptable chains of narration (Hasan).

3. 613 have weak chains of narration.

4. 99 have weak chains of narration that might even include liars.

After seeing this breakdown, we should have a better idea of the importance of this book. The ahadeeth that are found only in this book have approximetly a 50% chance of being weak.

Fast Facts

The two main Saheeh books, and four Sunan are called الكتُبُ السِّتة Al-Kutub-us-Sittah," or "The Six Books." Some scholars have called all these books "الجماعة Al-Jama'ah," or "All."

Table:
Major Hadeeth Scholars

	Name	Dates of Birth and Death	Places of Birth and Death	Travels	Teachers	Main Hadeeth Book
1	Malik Ibn Anas	93 H- 179 H	Madinah	Stayed in Madinah	Shareek; Nafi', Rabee'ah Ibn Abdur-Rahman	Al-Muwatta'
2	Ahmed Ibn Hanbal	167 H- 241 H	Baghdad	Makkah, Syria, Yaman, Algeria, Morocco, and Persia	Imam Shafi'eee, Sufyan Ibn Oyaynah' Abu Yousuf	Musnad Ahmad
3	Muhammad Ibn Isma'eel Al-Bukhari	194 H - 256 H	B. Bukhara D.Samarkand	Makkah, Madina, Iraq, Syria, and Egypt	Abdullah Al-Humaydi, Ad-Dahhak Ibn Mukhlid	Saheeh-ul-Bukhari
4	Muslim Ibn Al-Hajjaj Al-Nisaboori	206 H-261 H	Neshabur (Iran)	Makkah, Madina, Syria, and Egypt	Ahmad Ibn Hanbal, Is'haaq Ibn Rahoyah Al-Bukhari	Saheeh Muslim
5	Abu Dawood, Sulayman ibn Ash`ath al-Azadi al-Sijistani	202 H-275 H	B. Sejstan D. Basrah	Neshabur, Iran, Iraq, Syria, Egypt,	Ahmad Ibn Hanbal, Yahya Ibn Ma'een Al-Bukhari	Sunan Abu Dawood
6	Muhammad Ibn Isa Al-Tirmithi	209 H - 279 H	Tirmith	Iraq, Makkah, Madina, Iran	Al-Bukhari, Muslim, Abu Dawood	Sunan-at-Tirmithi
7	Ahmed Ibn Shu'ayb An-Nasa'ee	215 H -303 H	B. Nasa D. Palestine	Makkah, Madina, Iraq, Syria, and Egypt	Abu Dawood, At-Tirmithi	Sunan-un-Nasa'ee
8	Muhammad ibn Yazeed Ibn Majah	209 H-273 H	Qazvin (Iran)	Makkah, Madina, Iraq, Iran, Syria, and Egypt	Abu Bakr ibn Abi Shaybah, Ali At-Yanafisi	Sunan-Ibn Majah

CHAPTER REVIEW

Projects and Activities

1. Visit an Islamic library and browse through the eight books of hadeeth you learned about in this chapter.

2. Plot the routes of the journeys of one of the great imam whome you learned about in this chapter. Use a map which you drawn or copied.

Stretch Your Mind

1. Write a paragraph about how each of the following imams inspired you:
    - At-Tirmithi
    - An-Nasa'ee
    - Ibn Majah
    - Abu Dawood
2. How many of the eight imams you have studied in this and the previous chapter come from "Arab" backgrounds. What lessons can you learn from this?

Study Questions

1 List the eight books and their authors in chronological order.

2 Define: Sunan; Al-Kutub-us-Sittah; Al-Jama'ah

3 Describe briefly the following books:
   a. Sunan Abu Dawood.
   b. Sunan-ut-Tirmithi.
   c. Sunan Ibn Majah.
   d. Sunan-un-Nasa'ee.

E35

UNIT F

Leading A Pure Life Style

Chapter One	Surat-ul-Hujuraat سورة الحجرات	F2
Lesson 1	Surat-ul-Hujuraat: Verses (1-5)	F2
Lesson 2	Surat-ul-Hujuraat: Verses (6-8)	F8
Lesson 3	Surat-ul-Hujuraat: Verses (9-10)	F16
Lesson 4	Surat-ul-Hujuraat: Verses (11-13)	F24
Lesson 5	Surat-ul-Hujuraat: Verses (14-18)	F32
Chapter Two	Alcoholic Beverages	F36
	The Mother of All Evils	
Chapter Three	Pork and Other Haram Meats	F46
Chapter Four	Gambling and Lottery	F54
Chapter Five	Other Addictions	F62

UNIT F
CHAPTER ONE
LESSON ONE

سورة الحجرات

Surat-ul-Hujuraat
(The Rooms of the Prophet)

Verses (1-5) The Etiquette of Visiting Elders and Speaking to Them

CHAPTER OBJECTIVES

1. Learn and memorize ayaat 1-5 of Surat-ul-Hujurat.
2. Internalize the ideal of applying the principles of the Qur'an and the Sunnah in issues of daily life before anything else.
3. Internalize the etiquette of speaking with elders in a polite tone.
   Learn the etiquette of visiting others and seeking permission to come in.

VOCABULARY

Al-Hujuraat   الحجرات

Introduction

This surah was revealed in Madinah. It contains 18 ayaat. Most of them address important aspects of Islamic human relations. Hujurat (الحجرات) the plural word of hujrah, means a room. In this case, hujurat refers to the rooms of the Messenger of Allah and his wives.

Understood Meaning

(49:1) O Believers, don't be in a hurry to make decisions without consulting Allah's (book) and His messenger. And fear Allah's (punishment so that you don't do anything without knowing you have Allah's permission). (Remember) Allah hears everything (you say) and knows everything (so Allah knows your intentions).

(49:2) O Believers, do not raise your voices over the voice of (the Messenger of Allah who was sent to you as a) warner. And do not talk loudly to him like you talk loudly to each other, so that you don't lose the reward of your good deeds without realizing it.

(49:3) Those who lower their voices are the ones whose hearts are purified by Allah so that they can have proper fear of Allah. They will be forgiven (for their past sins) and they will be given a great reward (in Paradise).

(49:4) Most of those who call you (O Muhammad) from behind the walls (of your room) are ignorant and they don't know better.

(49:5) If they had been patient and waited for you to come out by yourself, it would have been better for them. (Remind them) Allah is forgiving and merciful (so they should ask for forgiveness and thank Allah for not punishing them.)

Reason for Revelation

Ayah 1. A delegation came from the tribe of Bani Tameem to the Prophet Muhammad ﷺ to learn about and accept Islam. When it was time for them to go, Abu Bakr said to the Messenger of Allah, "Make Al-Qa'qaa' bin Ma'bad the leader for them." Then Omar said, "No, instead make Al-Aqra'a bin Ha'bis their leader." Both men were already important members of the tribe of Tameem. Then Abu Bakr said, "You only said that to disagree with me." And Omar said, "No I didn't want to disagree with you." So they started arguing and their voices got louder so Allah revealed these verses.

When the verse, "Those who lower their voice are the ones whose hearts are purified by Allah…" was revealed, Abu Bakr said, "I swear (by Allah) who sent down to you the Qur'an, O Messenger of Allah, I will only talk to you like someone telling you a secret until

I die." (Reported by Al-Hakim, sound hadeeth. It is also related in Bukhari that Omar Ibn Al-Khataab did the same. This shows how much respect they had, and how quick they were to obey the Qur'an.)

Imam Tabari reported another reason for revealing these ayaat. Some companions used to say, "If only Allah would reveal something about this or that topic." So Allah revealed this to tell them that this is bad manners; they should trust that Allah knows what He is doing in how He reveals the Qur'an.

Ayah 5. It is said that one reason they came was to ask the Messenger of Allah to free some captives. He decided to free half and ransom half, and if they had been patient, all of them would have been freed. (Fath Al-Qadeer)

Lessons Learned

1. Consulting with Qur'an and the Sunnah Before Making Decisions or Forming Opinions. Ayah 1 means, "do not make a decision in front of the Prophet Muhammad, peace be upon him, without consulting him". The meaning though is still the same. Even if we think we know what should be done, we must wait and consult the Qur'an and Sunnah, and the advice of scholars. Everything we do must follow the guidance that has been sent to us. If we make

decisions in a hurry, then we might do something against Islam without realizing it. This idea is reflected in the famous hadeeth of Sahabi Mu'ath Ibn Jabal, when he was sent to Yeman to serve as a leader there. This is the dialogue that went on between the Prophet and Mu'ath Ibn Jabal:

"How will you judge?"
"I will follow Allah's book."
"What if you don't find your answer?"
"Then I will judge by the Sunnah."
"What if you don't find your answer?"

F4

"I will work hard to come up with my own opinion."

Then Rasoolullah said, *"All praise is only due to Allah, who guided the messenger of the Messenger of Allah to what was accepted by the Messenger of Allah."* (Tirmithi)

2. Proper Etiquette of Visiting with Elders.

When the delegation from the tribe of Bani Tameem came to Madinah the Messenger of Allah was in one of the houses of his wives. Al-Aqra'a bin Ha'bis (one of the important people in the tribe of Tameem) yelled over the wall, "O Muhammad, come out to us." When Rasoolullah didn't respond Al-Aqra'a yelled some poetry,

"O Muhammad, if I praise someone then they look good [among the Arabs]

and if I put down someone then they become humiliated."

The Arabs back then liked to challenge each other with poetry to see who could show off the most. When this delegation first came they wanted to show off their importance. The Messenger of Allah answered,

"Actually it is Allah [whose praise and blame really matters and not yours]."

This incident of Bani Tameem yelling over the wall was the reason behind revealing ayah 2, according to Imam Ahmad.

This story shows how some inconsiderate people rudely approached Rasoolullah while he was in his home. According to some historians, these people came during the resting time of the Prophet, and they shouted at him by name. Islam teaches us to visit people in the proper times and to follow proper manners. A Muslim should avoid resting and private times and seek proper permission, like knocking at the door, ringing the bell or calling before coming. If the permission is not given, the visiting Muslim should not feel bad.

3. Muslims should not speak loudly, especially with their elders.

Ayah 3 tells that the Arabs of the time were used to talking loudly and yelling. So in these verses, Allah says that if they become respectful, Allah will purify their hearts.

When these verses were revealed, Thabit bin Qais (a Sahabi who had a loud voice) said to himself, "I am the one who used to raise his voice in front of Rasoolullah ﷺ . My good deeds are all gone. I am among those who are going to Hell." So he sat depressed and sad in his house. The Messenger of Allah missed him and sent someone to ask about him. When he found out why Thabit was so upset, he sent the man back to Thabit with good news saying, *"Go to him, and tell him he is not among the people going to Hell. He is among the people going to Paradise."*

(Reported by Al-Bukhari)

Related Story

As-Sa'ib was once lying in the masjid, and he felt a pebble hit him. So he looked up and saw Omar Ibn-ul-Khataab, who said to him, "Go get me those two people." When they came, he said to them, "Who are you?" They said, "We are from Ta'if." He said, "If you were from this city (Madinah) I would have you painfully beaten. How can you raise your voices in the masjid of the Messenger of Allah, may Allah's blessings and peace be upon him?" (Reported by Al-Bukhari)

This story shows us not to punish people in Islam if they don't know the rules. It also shows that the companions considered yelling in the masjid or near the grave of the Messenger of Allah as bad as if someone raising his voice in front of him.

FAITH IN ACTION

★ Always refer to Islamic law, the Qur'an, and the Sunnah before taking decisions in daily life, especially in matters that are addressed in the Qur'an and Sunnah.

★ Always talk about the Messenger respectfully and observe respectful manners toward him and other prophets.
Always recognize those who have more knowledge than you (including fathers, teachers and scholars) by asking their opinion before you rush to do things.

★ Always respect your teachers and elders by keeping your voice low and using a respectful tone when talking to them.

★ Always treat the hadeeth of the Prophet with great respect, by paying attention to them in a respectful manner.

CHAPTER REVIEW

Projects and Activities

1. Write a journal on the Islamic etiquette of speaking with others.

2. Prepare a Power Point presentation on the Islamic etiquette of visiting others, especially elders.

Stretch Your Mind

1. Which is more frightening Death, or the consequences of committing the major sin of disbelief in God? Explain your answer.

2. Why is it important to learn about death?

Study Questions

1. What is Al-Hujuraat?
2. What should a Muslim do when he is about to make a decision on an important matter? Support your answer with a hadeeth.
3. Discuss the importance of speaking respectfully with others, especially elders. Support your answer with an ayah and a story from the Prophet's time.

Surat-ul-Hujuraat:
سورة الحجرات
Verses (6-8) Verifying before Passing Judgment

UNIT F — CHAPTER ONE — LESSON TWO

CHAPTER OBJECTIVES

1. Learn and memorize ayaat 6-8 of Surat-ul-Hujurat.
2. Internalize the ideal of avoiding rushing into judgment against others without proper verification.
3. Understand the importance of obeying the authority of righteous leaders.
4. Learn what is nameemah, and become inspired to avoid falling into this evil habit.
5. Learn and memorize the du'aa' of the lesson.

VOCABULARY

Fasiq فاسق : Someone who is rebellious and extreme in disobedience, who commits major sins, and lies. In the above story, Allah called Al-Waleed fasiq, or disobedient, because he disobeyed Allah by accusing innocent people of serious wrong doing, and he did not verify his false thoughts.

nameemah نميمة : Slander. It usually refers to the act of carrying tales, especially evil ones, from one person to another in-order to instigate problems between two people or more.

Nammam نمّام : The slandering person who usually practices nameemah.

Understood Meaning

(49:6) O Believers, if a sinful person (fasiq) comes to you with some news, you must double check to make sure it is true. Do this so that you don't hurt someone, because you didn't know the whole story and then you will regret what you did.

(49:7) And remember that you have with you the Messenger of Allah (so do not say things that are untrue and do not be in a hurry to act on information before double checking.) If he followed you in everything you wanted, you would fall into difficulty, (and sin but he doesn't blindly follow you without double checking and making sure the best opinion is adopted.) But (remember) Allah has made you love belief (in Allah and His Messenger) and made (doing what you know is right, which is to listen and obey Allah and His Messenger) a beautiful thing in your hearts. And Allah has made you hate disbelief, rebellion against Allah, and disobedience. (Those who have these

characteristics are the ones who) are solid in following the straight path.
(49:8) (The feeling of loving for Islam) is from the extra good that Allah has given you and a blessing (so be thankful for this blessing). Remember Allah knows everything and is wise (in everything that He does, so trust Him).

Reason for Revelation

Verse 6-8: Al-Harith bin Durar Al-Khuza'ee said, "I came to Rasoolullah ﷺ who called me to accept Islam, and I did accept it. Then he called me to pray and give zakah and I accepted. Then I said, "O Messenger of Allah, I will go back to my people and call them to Islam and to pray and give zakah. From whoever accepts my call, I will collect their zakah and you can send me someone at such and such time to bring to you the zakah."

Then Al-Harith went back and called his people to Islam and collected the zakah from the Muslims. Then time passed and the appointment came and went without anyone coming from Madinah to collect the zakah. So he gathered together the leadership of the Muslims in that area and said to them, "Rasoolullah ﷺ told me that he would send someone at a given time to bring to him the zakah money I have collected. Rasoolullah would not break a promise, so I think the only reason he would not send someone is if we did something bad. So lets go and see why he did not show up."

The Messenger of Allah had sent Al-Waleed ibn Uqbahh to check on the Muslims in Al-Harith area and collect the zakah. When the man traveled part of the way, he got scared. There were bad feelings between Al-Waleed's tribe and Al-Harith's before Islam. It is said that the people came out to meet him and he thought they were coming out to attack him so he got scared. (Tabarani, Ibn

Jareer) Therefore, Al-Waleed Ibn Uqbahh went back to Madinah. He told the Messenger of Allah, "Al-Harith and his tribe refused to give me the zakah, and they tried to kill me."

Al-Harith was puzzled by the failure of the Muslim delegations to come to him. Therefore, he decided to go back to the Prophet in Madinah to deliver the zakah to him. Meanwhile, the Messenger of Allah sent out a small military expedition to go to double check, and if needed, to discipline Al-Harith and his tribe. When the two groups met on the road, Al-Harith asked the military group,

"Whom are you sent to?"

"To you," they said.

"Why?" He asked.

They said, "Rasoolullah ﷺ sent Al-Waleed ibn Uqbah to collect the zakah from you and he claimed that you refused to give it to him and tried to kill him."

Al-Harith then said, *"I swear (by Allah), Who sent Muhammad with the truth, I never saw him and he never came."*

Then the two groups went back to Madinah and Al-Harith repeated this to the Messenger of Allah and these verses were revealed."

(Reported by Ahmad)

Lessons Learned

1. Verify Before Passing Judgment. In verses (6-8) Allah addresses the main cause for disputes among people, which is misunderstanding. Misunderstanding happens when people get wrong information or interpret news or information in a wrong way. There are some people who spread wrong information on purpose and some who do so by accident. In these verses, Allah says there is no excuse for spreading false information that results in splitting the Muslim community and hurting innocent people.

Allah in these verses is calling anyone who acts on information without verifying it first, a fasiq, or someone being extremely disobedient. So if Al-Waleed, or anyone else whom we consider trustworthy, spreads information without strong proof to support it, then they are a fasiq for doing so. It then becomes our responsibility to verify the information before we act upon it. Al-Waleed saw the people coming out to him and he assumed that they were coming out to kill him. Instead of coming back to the Messenger of Allah and saying what he said, he should have double checked the situation himself before accusing the people of serious aggression against Muslims.

2. Nameemah, or Slander is Prohibited in Islam. Nameemah, or slander usually refers to the act of carrying inaccurate or false tales, especially evil ones, about one person to another, to instigate problems between two people or more. This is usually done intentionally or unintentionally by speaking, writing, nodding, hinting, or signaling. Al-Waleed Ibn Oqbah probably didn't intentionally convey inaccurate news to the Prophet in order to cause harm to Al-Harith's tribe. However, his seriously inaccurate news could have caused a disaster to Al-Harith and his tribe. Nevertheless, this story conveys several lessons, including the harm of nameemah, or nameemah - like actions.

{ وَيْلٌ لِكُلِّ هُمَزَةٍ لُمَزَةٍ ۝ } الهمزة: ١

Allah says in Surat-ul-Humazah, "Woe to every slanderer and backbiter." (104:1)

The Prophet ﷺ is reported to have said: "Shall I tell you about the most evil ones from amongst you?" They said, "Of course." He said, "Those who go around with nameemah. They make enmity between friends and they seek problems for the innocent."
(Reported by Imams Ahmad and Al-Bukhari in Al-Adab Al-Mufrad)

عن حذيفة رضي الله عنه قال: قال رسول الله:

"لَا يَدْخُلُ الْجَنَّةَ نَمَّامٌ"

رواه البخاري ومسلم

Hudhaifah (RA) reported that the Prophet ﷺ said: *"A nammaam will never enter Paradise."*
(Al-Bukhari and Muslim)

"The Nammaam, or the slanderer is a greater evil than an evil witch-craft. The Nammaam does in one hour what an evil witch cannot do in one year." It was also said, "The acts of Nammaam are more harmful than the acts of Shaytan. Shaytan acts by evil whispering, while the Nammaam acts face-to-face and openly."

Nameemah, then, is haram in Islam and it is actually considered one of the greatest sins by Allah. It has also been said that one-third of the torture in the grave is because of nameemah. Allah سبحانه وتعالى has prohibited going about with nameemah because it causes enmity and hatred amongst the Muslims.

If a slanderer comes to you and starts to spread gossip the evilness, do not believe the evil. Stop the nammam and advise him of the punishment of Allah. A Nammam should also not be trusted and is not a good friend. Many people are so busy spreading the slander they hear that they do not even stop to think if it is true or not. Mus'ab Bin 'Umair (RA) said: "We believe that accepting the tale is worse then telling it. Telling it is carrying the news, but accepting it is approving of it and the act, so be aware of the person conveying tales. Even when he tells the truth, he is actually mean, because he did not observe the honor of his brother nor did he cover his brother's faults."

Al-Hasan Ibn Ali Ibn Abi Talib (RA) said: "Whoever carries nameemah to you, will carry one about you."

The Nammam is Never Truthful

A man came to Sulaiman Bin Abdul-Malik and Sulaiman reportedly said to him: "I was told that you have said bad things about me." The man said, "I have not done or said anything." Sulaiman then said, "The one who told me is truthful." Upon that Az-Zuhari, who was in the company of Sulaiman said, "The nammaam is never truthful." Sulaiman then said, "You are right." And then he said to the man, "Go in peace."

3. Follow the guidance of the Prophet and the righteous leaders.

Although we do not have the Prophet with us now, we still have the Qur'an and the teachings of Rasoolullah with us. Therefore, along with this wealth of guidance we should be careful and respectful to consult scholars before rushing to do things. Verse 7 teaches us that, as followers, we must be prepared to follow the leader, even if he doesn't go with our opinion. If the leader were to follow every opinion of his followers, it would lead the community to chaos, hardship and possibly sin. Imagine what would have happened if the Muslims fought Al-Harith and his tribe before knowing the accurate information! A leader has the responsibility of listening to all available opinions and then weighing them to find the best opinion. The followers' duty is to advise the leader and then follow his guidance, even if some of them don't agree with the leader's decision, unless the decision is to commit a sin.

4. Love Allah and hate disobedience and disbelief.

Allah tells us why the Muslims were not punished for following the words of Al-Waleed. Allah explains that they were protected from falling into a terrible problem. The situation could have resulted in a battle and Muslims would have been killing Muslims. Allah protected the Muslims in that incidence because of their true love of Islam. In other words, even though it was a mistake in judgment to accept the words of Al-Waleed at face value, the Messenger of Allah and his companions were doing their best out of a love for Islam. This teaches us that even if the sincere leader and followers somehow commit a mistake, Allah will protect them from being seriously harmed by it because of their love of Allah and their strong faith in Him.

FAITH IN ACTION

★ Always double check stories and things people tell you before acting on them.

★ Always avoid falling in nameemah situations, by conveying news to create problems and enmity between innocent Muslims.

Du'aa'

اللهُمَّ حَبِّبْ إلَيْنا الإيمانَ وَزَيِّنْهُ في قُلوبِنا وَكَرِّهْ إلَيْنا الكُفْرَ والفُسوقَ والعِصْيانَ واجْعَلْنا من الرّاشدين

Prophet Muhammad would always look for ways of incorporating the Qur'an into du'aa'. It is related, with a good chain of narration that the Messenger of Allah included verse 7 in a dua saying, "O Allah, make us love our belief, and make it beautiful in our hearts, and make us hate kufr, fusooq (rebellious disobedience), and sin, and make us among those who are on the right path." *(Ahmad)*

CHAPTER REVIEW

Projects and Activities

1. Write a personal story in your journal describing a situation through which your learned the importance of verifying before passing judgment on others.
2. Write and act out a sketch with your classmates on the importance of verifying and double checking before rushing to judgment.
3. Create piece of artwork or a poster for the du'aa' of this lesson.

Stretch Your Mind

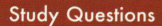

1. Can a Sahabi make a serious mistake? Support your answer with at least two stories from the time of the prophet.

2. Should we disrespect a Sahabi because of a mistake he made? Why, or why not?

Study Questions

1 What is a fasiq?

2 What should a Muslim do when he or she hears a negative story, or report about another Muslim? Support your answer with an ayah and a story from the Prophet's time.

3 What is nameemah, and what is the Islamic rule on it? Support your answer with an ayah and a hadeeth.

UNIT F
CHAPTER ONE
LESSON THREE

سورة الحجرات

Surat-ul-Hujuraat
Verses (9-10) Muslims Are Brothers, and They Should not Fight

CHAPTER OBJECTIVES

1. Learn and memorize ayaat 9-10 of Surat-ul-Hujurat.
2. Internalize the ideal of brotherhood and sisterhood in Islam.
3. Understand the importance of keeping peace among Muslims, and avoiding disputes and conflicts.
4. Learn what should happen when Muslims fight each other.
5. Learn and memorize the ahadeeth of this lesson.

VOCABULARY

Ukhuwwah   أخوّة
Sulh   صلح

Understood Meaning

(49:9) If two groups of believers fight each other, then make peace between them (by calling them to solve their dispute according to the Qur'an and Sunnah). Then if one side continues in an unjust manner (fighting the other side and refusing to submit to Allah's judgment, all the Muslims must) fight against them, until that group comes back from its position and submits to having the dispute solved according to Allah's law (the Qur'an and Sunnah). Then if they do come back (and submit), the Muslims should solve the dispute between the two groups in a just way. And do your best to aim for a just solution. Remember Allah loves those who aim for a just solution.
(49:10) (Remember) only the believers share a brotherhood (under Islam) so solve the disputes between your two (groups of) brothers. (Remember) to fear Allah (and do not be unjust) so that Allah will be merciful with you (and heal the bad feelings between the two Muslim groups that were fighting)

Reason for Revelation

It was said to the Messenger of Allah, "Why don't you go to Abdullah ibn Ubai (the leader of the Munafiqeen, or hypocrites) to try talking to him." So the Messenger of Allah took off on his donkey across an area that doesn't grow plants with a group of Muslims. When he got there, Abdullah said, "Get away from me. The smell of your donkey is bothering me." One of the Ansar said, "I swear by Allah, the donkey of Rasoolullah ﷺ smells better than you!" So men from the tribe of Abdullah felt insulted by this and a fight broke out. The two sides were hitting each other with sticks, hands, and shoes. So Allah revealed this verse. [Reported by Al-Bukhari]

Other incidents are also related as the reason for the revelation. Scholars of Qur'an say that Allah sometimes sent down some verses to answer several incidents that happened in the Muslim community.

These other incidents include:

1. Two Muslims had a dispute about something one of them owed the other. Then one of them said he was going to take it by force, because he had a strong tribe to help him. The other one said they should go to the Messenger of Allah to solve the dispute. The first person refused and a fight broke out. [Reported by Imam Tabari]

2. A man got into a fight with his wife, (Um Zaid), and he closed her into a second story room. Her family came to help her and his tribe came to help him and a fight broke out. Then Messenger of Allah came and solved the dispute. [Reported by Imam Tabari].

Lessons Learned

1. Believers are brothers and sisters in Islam.

Ayah 10 is a very famous ayah on أُخُوَّة Ukhuwwah, or brotherhood and sisterhood in Islam. The Muslim Ummah is distinctive with the qualities of love and brotherhood. Islam teaches that brotherly affection adorns the hearts and smiles beautify the faces. The principles among the believers are those of brotherhood and good friendship. Allah said in ayah 10 of this surah: "The believers are nothing else than brothers." [49:10]

Prophet Muhammad has many beautiful Ahadeeth on brotherhood and sisterhood in Islam.

Among the first things the Prophet did in Madinah at the time of Hijrah is building the masjid and establishing brotherhood between Al-Muhajireen and Al-Ansaar.

Hadeeth Shareef

عن أبي هريرة رضي الله عنهُ قالَ: قالَ رسول الله ﷺ:
"المُسْلِمُ أخو المُسْلِمِ..."
رواه مسلم

Abu Hurayrah narrated that the Prophet said,
"A Muslim is the brother of the Muslim." (*Reported by Muslim*)

عن ابي هريرة – رضي الله عنه قال– عن النبي صلى الله ﷺ:
"...الله في عون العبد ما كان العبد في عون أخيه"
رواه مسلم

Abu Hurayrah narrated that the Prophet said,
"Allah will help his slave (meaning Muslims) as long as the slave of Allah helps his brother." (*Reported by Muslim*)

عن أبي موسى الأشعري رضي الله عنه قال: قال رسول الله ﷺ:
"المؤمن للمؤمن كالبنيان يشد بعضه بعضا وشبك بين أصابعه"
متفق عليه

Abu Musa Al-Ash'ari narrated that the Prophet said,
"The believer's relationship to the believer is like a building; the different parts of it support each other." And he intermined his fingers together. (*Reported by Muslim*)

عن أنس بن مالك رضي الله عنه قال : قال رسول الله ﷺ:
"لايؤمن أحدكم حتى يحب لأخيه ما يحب لنفسه"
رواه البخاري

Anas Ibn Malik narrated that the Prophet said,
"None of you will have [complete] faith till he wishes for his [Muslim] brother what he likes for himself." (*Reported by Al-Bukhari*)

2. Muslims Must Not Dispute or Fight. Since Muslims are brothers and sisters, they must not hate nor feel anger toward each other. Obviously, they must avoid all kinds of disputes and fights. Allah has prohibited the believers from anything that might induce enmity and hatred among them. Obviously, Shaytan loves it when Muslims divide among themselves and fight. Allah says,

﴿ إِنَّمَا يُرِيدُ ٱلشَّيْطَٰنُ أَن يُوقِعَ بَيْنَكُمُ ٱلْعَدَٰوَةَ وَٱلْبَغْضَآءَ ﴾

النساء: ٩١

"Shaytan just wants to instigate among you enmity and hatred." [Surat-un-Nisaa' 5:91]

It was narrated that Abu Hurayrah رضي الله عنه said that Rasoolullah ﷺ said: "Whoever has wronged his brother with regard to his honor or anything else, let him seek his forgiveness today, before there will be no dinar and no dirham, and if he has any good deeds to his credit they will be taken from him in a manner commensurate with the wrong he did, and if he has no good deeds, then some of his counterpart's bad deeds will be taken and added to his burden."

However, companions were humans and they made mistakes like all humans do. What made them great in history was that they always turned to the Qur'an and Sunnah to heal the problems in their society and so Allah made them into a great community.

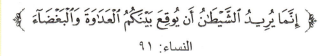

Hadeeth Shareef

عن عبد الله بن مسعود رضي اللهُ عنهُ قال: قالَ رسول الله ﷺ:
"سِبابُ المسْلِمِ فُسوقٌ وقِتالُهُ كُفْرٌ"

رواه الترمذي وقال حديث حسن صحيح

Abdullah Ibn Mas'ood narrated that Rasoolullah said, "Swearing at Muslim is an act of disobedience and fighting him is like committing an act of disbelief."

(Reported by At-Tirmithi)

3. Muslims Should Avoid Fighting, and Must Reconcile Whenever They Fight.

By Allah saying, "If two groups of believers fight… ," it shows us that believers should not fight each other. Conflicting Muslims must always strive to end their differences and conflicts. They should not allow Satan and their self pride to keep them apart from each other. Allah will not forgive the conflicting Muslims until they reconcile. Allah says in Surat-un-Nisaa',

﴿ وَالصُّلْحُ خَيْرٌ ﴾ النساء: ١٢٨

"Reconciliation is good." [4:128]

عن أبي أيوب الأنصاري أن النبي صلى الله عليه وسلم قال: "لا يحل لمسلم أن يهجر أخاه فوق ثلاث يلتقيان .. فيعرض هذا ويعرض هذا وخيرهما الذى يبدأ بالسلام"

رواه البخاري ومسلم

Abu Hurayrah narrated that Rasoolullah said,

"It is prohibited for a Muslim to abandon his Muslim brother for more than three days and to avoid each other when they meet. The best of them is the one who greets his brother."

[Reported Al-Bukhari andMuslim]

4. Allah Orders His True Servants to Mediate to End Disputes and Fights Among Muslims.
If a conflict or fighting erupts between two Muslims or two Muslim groups, it is obligatory on the rest of the Muslims to step in and try to resolve the dispute. Reconciling the relations of two Muslims, or two Muslim groups is one of the greatest achievements a Muslim must work for.

عن أبي هريرة رضي اللهُ عنهُ قال: قالَ رسول الله صلى الله عليه وسلم: "مـا عـمـل ابـن آدم شـيـئـاً أفضل مـن الصـلاة ، وصلاح ذات البين، وخلقٍ حسن"

رواه البيهقي

Abu Hurayrah narrated that Rasoolullah said,

"The best deeds the son of Adam can do are prayer, reconciling between fighting Muslims, and having good manners."

Another important lesson from this verse is that, as big a sin as it is for Muslims to fight each other, it doesn't take them out of Islam. This reinforces our belief that a Muslim who commits a major sin is still a Muslim, and will eventually come out of Hell if Allah chooses to punish him there for a while.

Al-Hasan Ibn Ali: A Role Model in Ending Disputes

The Messenger of Allah once said about his grandson, Al-Hasan Ibn Ali Ibn Abi Talib رضي الله عنه, "This son of mine is a leader, and maybe Allah, the Most High, will use him to reconcile between two big groups of Muslims." (Bukhari). Thirty years after the Messenger of Allah passed away, this prediction came true. Al-Hassan reunited the Muslims in the Syria area with the Muslims in Iraq after they had been through a series of battles. The way this happened was that Al-Hassan became the Khaleefah and the people of Iraq swore allegiance to him (so he was the fifth Khaleefah). Then he stepped down as Khaleefah, transferring it to Mu'awiyah, who was the leader of the Muslims in Sham (Syria). In making this sacrifice he brought unity to the Muslims, and he ended he the fighting among Muslims.

Sulh (Reconciliation) the Prophet's Way

Reconciliation is the process of getting two or more disputing sides to work together. One or both sides of the dispute will give up some of what they are asking to reach a peaceful solution. The only thing one can't do when trying to make reconciliation is to approve something Allah made forbidden. When two men were arguing over some inheritance, the Messenger of Allah told them to follow this plan to solve their dispute:

1. Split up the parts you both agree go to one side, or the other.

2. Then split by a lottery system (In other words, if there are two items of equal value they might flip a coin, or do something similar, to see which item goes to which person.) Another opinion is for one person to split the disputed property into two piles, and the other side picks the pile he wants to take.

3. Then once you are close to a solution, both sides should forgive the other for the little things that are still in dispute. (Reported by Abu Dawood)

Hadeeth Shareef

عن أبي هريرة رضي اللهُ عنهُ قال: قالَ رسول الله ﷺ :
" تفتح أبواب الجنة يوم الاثنين ويوم الخميس فيغفر لكل عبد لا شريك بالله شيئا إلا رجلا كانت بينه وبين أخيه شحناء فيقال : أنظروا هذين حتى يصطلحا ، أنظروا هذين حتى يصطلحا ، أنظروا هذين حتى يصطلحا " [رواه مسلم]

Abu Hurayrah narrated that Rasoolullah said,
"The gates of Heaven open every Monday and Thursday, when Allah forgives everyone who does not take partners with Allah, except a man who is conflicting with his Muslim brother. Allah will then say, hold on these two until they reconcile, hold on these two until they reconcile, hold on these two until they reconcile." [Reported by Muslim]

F22

CHAPTER REVIEW

Projects and Activities

1. Write a 500 word essay on the importance of brotherhood and sisterhood in Islam.
2. Write and act out a sketch with your classmates on a dispute and reconciliation between two Muslim brothers or sisters.
3. Create a piece of artwork, or a poster, for the du'aa' of this lesson.

Stretch Your Mind

What are the similarities and differences between brotherhood relationships in families and in Islam.

Study Questions

1. What is the nature of the relationship between two Muslims? Support your answer with an ayah and a hadeeth.
2. Is it allowed for two Muslims or Muslim groups to dispute or fight? Support your answer with an ayah and a hadeeth.
3. What should happen when two Muslims dispute? Support your answer with an ayah and a hadeeth.
4. What is nameemah, and what is the Islamic rule on it? Support your answer with an ayah and a hadeeth.

UNIT F
CHAPTER ONE
LESSON FOUR

سورة الحجرات

Surat-ul-Hujuraat
Verses (11-13) Do Not Hurt Others' Feelings

CHAPTER OBJECTIVES

1. Learn and memorize ayaat 11-13 of Surat-ul-Hujurat.
2. Learn the types of behavior a Muslim is prohibited to do toward other Muslims.
3. Internalize and become inspired to abandon bad attitudes toward other Muslim brothers and sisters.
4. Learn and memorize the hadeeth of this lesson.

Understood Meaning

(49:11) O Believers, It is forbidden for any group (of men) to make fun of another group because you don't know. Maybe that the group, you are making fun of, is better than you (with Allah). And it is forbidden for women to make fun of women because you don't know. Maybe they are better than you (with Allah). And do not point out (your Muslim brothers) faults (in any way, directly or indirectly, because if you do you are pointing out your own bad character). And do not label each other with bad names. It is terrible to call someone a Fasiq (disobedient sinner) after they have become believers (and because it would be terrible for you to become a Fasiq because of this behavior after you became Muslims). Those who do not repent (by stopping this bad behavior and fixing the harm they have done to their fellow Muslim brothers, should know that Allah considers them) unjust (and so they will be severely punished for this).

(49:12) O Believers stay away from having a bad opinion of Muslims, because having a bad opinion of good Muslims is a sin. And do not spy (to try to uncover the mistakes and problems of people.) And do not talk about each other in a way that the other person would not like (backbiting). Would one of you like to eat from the body of your dead Muslim brother? As you would hate to do this (you should hate backbiting.) And fear Allah's punishment (by immediately stopping any of these sins that you are doing immediately). (Remember) Allah is the only one who accepts peoples' repentance and Allah is continuously merciful (so turn to Allah and ask for forgiveness.) (49:13) O People, I created all of you from a male and a female (Adam and Ha'wa and each one of us also has a mother and a father) and I made you nations and tribes so that you would recognize each other (and not for you to claim one group is better than another). The best of you with Allah are those who fear Allah the most (and no other standard really matters about who is better than who.) Allah knows everything (so Allah knows what in your hearts) and Allah knows the true reality of everything you do (so you can't deceive Him).

Reason for Revelation

Verse 11. It is said that a group from Bani Tameem (the same group talked about at the beginning of the Surah) made fun of some of the poor Muslims including Bilal, Salman, Ammar, Khabbab, Suhaib, Ibn Faheera, and Salim Mawla Abi Huthaifa. (Reported in Fath Al-Qadeer and Musnad Ibn Abi Hatim)

Verse 11. Before Islam, people used to have two or three nicknames. Once Prophet Muhammad, peace be upon him, called a man by his nickname, and someone said to him, "O Messenger of Allah, that man hates it." So Allah revealed, "And do not label each other with bad names." (Reported by Al-Hakim)

Verse 13. It is said that this verse was revealed when Bilal climbed on top of the Ka'bah to call the athan, when the Muslims liberated it during Fateh Makkah. Some people looked down on him and called him a black slave. (Reported in Fath Al-Qadeer and Musnad Ibn Abi Hatim)

Lessons Learned

1. Allah Prohibits Mockery and Name Calling of Others.

Allah continues to deal with the bad habits people have that harm or even destroy the community. Bad traits like mockery, gossip, backbiting, spying, and thinking you are superior to another group cause bad feelings and even fighting with other Muslim brothers and sisters in the society. In Islam, it is haram, or prohibited, to mock or debase others, whether by words, deeds, or indications. These behaviors usually spread hatred among Muslims in the society. Therefore, Allah forbids all of these bad attitudes and tells people to be humble to each other and compete in their obedience to Allah.

The second section of the verse literally reads, "and do not point out your own faults." This can be explained in two ways:

1. The Muslim community is one body, and, if you hurt some Muslims, it is hurting the community, which in turn hurts you.

2. By pointing out the faults of others, we are showing our own bad character.

Name calling is common among people, especially during the teen years. Islam prohibits exchanging bad names and labeling. Allah says, "do not exchange (bad) nicknames." An example of this would be calling a Muslim: a kafir, a stupid, a donkey, or a pig, etc. The reason Allah said, "exchange" is because usually, when people start name-calling, they get called similar bad names back.

Prophet Muhammad ﷺ used to give and call his companions by good nicknames. He used that to highlight their good qualities; therefore, this is a Sunnah of the Messenger of Allah. Some of the good nicknames of the companions include: Khalid ibn Al-Waleed, who was called Sayf-ullah, or the sword of Allah. 'Othman Ibn Abbas was called Thun-Noorayn, or the one with the two lights (because he married two of the Messenger of Allah's daughters). Finally, Omar Al Khattab was called Al-Farooq (which means the one who distinguishes truth from falsehood).

Related Story

One time, Abu Tharr Al-Ghifari and Bilal Ibn Rabah had a dispute. Both of them became truly aggravated. In the heat of the moment, AbuTharr called Bilal a bad name. Bilal become extreme furious, but he refrained from calling Abu Tharr with a bad name back. Instead, he went to the Prophet and complained about what Abu Tharr had done. Rasoolullah was disappointed, but he kept patient until Abu Tarr came and admitted what he did. The Prophet then said to Abu Tharr, "You did an act of the pagans of Jahiliyyah." Abu Tharr felt very bad and he deeply regretted what he had said to Bilal. Abu Tharr then laid down on the ground and called on Bilal to step on his face. Bilal refused to do what Abu Tharr had told him to do, and he informed Abu Tharr that he had forgiven him.

2. Allah Prohibits Hurting People Based on False Thann, or Assumption.

"Thann" means non-verified thoughts and assumptions. This word can mean different things, depending on the sentence. It can be used to mean "doubt." Some thann should not be followed. For example, if you look for the bad in people, you might start collecting a lot of reasons to have a bad opinion of some good Muslims. This kind of opinion is a sin because we are required to have a good opinion of Muslims until clear evidence to the contrary comes to us. The Messenger of Allah said, "Don't you dare adopt (bad) opinions (of your Muslim brothers, it will lead to fighting and splitting the community) because those inner discussions you have about people are the most common places for lies."

What the Messenger of Allah is protecting us from is the whispers of the Shaytan. The Shaytan wants to tear Muslims apart, so he will do his best to give people bad ideas about each other and try to get them to keep thinking about those bad ideas. If you keep thinking of those bad ideas, you might adopt them as a bad opinion of your Muslim brother or sister. When you have a bad opinion of people it makes you more likely to misunderstand them and then fight with them.

3. Spying Is Haram in Islam.
Some people fall into the major sin of Tajassus, or spying against others and spreading their secrets. Rasoolullah once said in a speech, "O people who only say they believe, but belief hasn't really entered their hearts. Do not look

to uncover the mistakes (and problems) of the Muslims. Whoever looks to uncover the mistakes of the Muslims will have his own secrets and weaknesses exposed by Allah, even if he hides in his house." [Reported by Abu Dawood] This hadeeth tells us that spying on people, and trying to publicly humiliate them, is what hypocrites do, so we should not do it.

In contrast, Allah loves those who protect the secrets of other people and refrain from exposing their faults. Uqbah ibn Amir narrated that Rasoolullah said,

"Whoever covers the faults of a believer is like one who has brought to life a female child buried alive." [Reported by Sunan Abu Dawood]

4. Gheebah is Common, But It Is a Major Sin.

At dinner time in the Siraj family home the following dialogue went on between Sarah and her mother.

Mrs.Siraj: Sarah, what's wrong? You have barely eaten any of your food. Are you sick?
Sarah: No, Mama, I'm fine. I just keep thinking about lunch today.
Mr.Siraj: What happened?
Sarah: Some of my friends were saying bad things about my other friend Leena when she wasn't there. They said that the dress she was wearing was ugly, and that she shows off about her good grades.

Mrs.Siraj: It's sad that when many Muslims meet their friends, their talk only hurts other people. Islam is a religion of peace and love. Hurting others leads to hatred among our Ummah. Gheebah is just one way of hurting people and is a major sin, because they did not respect the honor and reputation of Leena.

Bilal: What is gheebah?
Mr.Siraj: Gheebah is the Arabic word for backbiting. It is to talk badly about a person without them being present, about moralities, appearance, or personality.

Mrs.Siraj: One time, the Prophet Muhammad asked: "Do you know what gheebah (backbiting) is? They said, "Allah and His Messenger know best." He said, ""You mentioning your brother with something about him that he dislikes [being spoken about]."

Mr.Siraj: And then someone asked, "How about if my brother has that attitude or the characteristic which I am mentioning?" He replied, "If he possesses that which you mention, then you have [indeed]been backbiting him. And, if he does not have that which you say (which is even worse), then you have slandered him."

[Reported by Muslim]

What To Do When You Hear Gossip?

A Muslim must not sit with those who insist on backbiting others. He or she should advise those who gossip and commit gheebah and defend their victims. "Whoever is present while a Muslim is humiliated before him, and is able to assist him [and yet does not], Allah will humiliate him before [all of] creation."

[Reported by Ahmad in Al-Musnad]

At the very least you should refuse to listen to the gossip. Say "I don't want to hear about this." Keep saying this until the gossiping person stops the gossip.

How To Be Forgiven from Slandering and Backbiting?

First of all, you have to understand that backbiting and gossip are major sins in Islam. The only way of being forgiven for backbiting, or any sin that hurts others, is to do the following:

1. Pray for the forgiveness of Allah. You have to sincerely repent for the sins and you have to feel and regret the guilt in front of Allah.

2. Ask for the forgiveness of the person who was talked about or was hurt. And that is, of course, the difficult part.

If the backbitten person forgives, you will be forgiven. If not, you will be questioned about the backbiting incident in the Hereafter. If the person is dead, then ask Allah for forgiveness. But if the information has not reached the person, just pray for forgiveness, and make du'aa' for him, and speak well of him in his absence, just as you spoke against him. Also, if telling him will provoke more hatred, then just make du'aa' for him and pray for forgiveness.

Hadeeth Shareef

عن أبي هريرة رضي اللهُ عنهُ قال: قالَ رسول الله صلى الله عليه وسلم: "إيـاكـم والـظـن فإنَّ الـظَنَّ أكـذبُ الحَديث. لا تجسسـوا ولا تحسسـوا ولا تحاسَدوا وَلا تَباغَضوا وَلا تَدابَروا، وَكونوا عِبادَ اللهِ إخْوانا كما أمركم الله عز وجل. المُسْلِمُ أخو المُسْلِمِ، لا يَظْلِمُهُ، ولا يَخْذلِهُ، وَلا يَحْقِرُهُ. التَّقْوى ها هُنا وَيُشيرُ إلى صَدْرِهِ ثَلاث مَرّات. بِحَسْبِ امرئٍ مِنَ الشَّرِّ أنْ يَحْقِرَ أخاهُ المُسْلِمَ.

"كُلَّ المُسْلِمِ عَلى المُسْلِمِ حَرامٌ دَمُهُ، وَمالُهُ وَعِرْضُهُ"" رواه مسلم

Abu Hurayrah narrated that Rasoolullah said,
"Beware of doubting each other, for doubting and assuming is falsehood. Do not spy. Do not be jealous of each other. Don't hate each other.
Don't abandon each other. Don't spoil the sales of each other. O servants of Allah, be brothers and sisters. A Muslim is the brother of the Muslim; he is not unjust to him and he doesn't turn his back on him (when he is in need). He does not oppress, nor abandon, nor humiliate, nor lie to him. Piety is here [and the Prophet pointed to his heart]. The worst thing a Muslim can do is to humiliate his Muslim brother [or sister]. A Muslim is forbidden to hurt his Muslim brother's life, wealth or family."

Reported by Al-Bukhari and Muslim

5. The Unity of Mankind. Verse 13 of this Surah is a great, divine declaration that all people are brothers and sisters. We are all descendants of Adam, and yet Allah has for example, made us into nations and tribes (Caucasian, African, Asian, European.) This ability to differentiate ourselves is a blessing, because the verity of human experience provides people the opportunity to learn from each other, develop unique ideas, and share them. This blessing is also a test, because people can use this difference and make it into a reason to feel superior and arrogant over other people. So Allah gives us the cure for the disease of arrogance by calling us to fear Allah. If we fear Allah, we do not look down on some of Allah's creations because Allah created them shorter or taller, or in various ways.

6. Taqwa Is the Best and Most Honorable Thing a Muslim Can Do in Islam. Taqwa is the love of Allah and the fear of displeasing Him. This attitude pushes us to do the things leading us to Jannah, and it help us avoid being punished by Allah. In ayah 13, Allah explains that the best of people are those who demonstrate Taqwa, or piety. Therefore, we should value people according to their spiritual and moral behavior, not based on their looks, ethnicity, or racial backgrounds.

CHAPTER REVIEW

Projects and Activities

1. Write a personal story in your journal describing a situation when you or another person were a victim of backbiting or mockery, and how you dealt with this situation.

2. Write and act out a sketch with your classmates about the importance of the evil effects of mockery, backbiting, and/or spying.

Stretch Your Mind

1. Assuming and doubting others leads to many evil behaviors, like backbiting and spying. Do you agree with this statement? Defend your answer.

2. Prophet Muhammad gave Abu Hurayrah this famous nickname. Do research and figure out how this positive nickname came about.

Study Questions

1. What does Islam say about mocking and ridiculing others?
2. What is thann? Why did Allah prohibit it?
3. What should a Muslim do when he or she gossips about another Muslim? Support your answer with an ayah and a story from the Prophet's time.
4. What is gheebah and what is the Islamic rule on it? Support your answer with an ayah and a hadeeth.
5. How did Allah portray the sin of gheebah to make Muslims hate falling into it?
6. What can a backbiter do to be forgiven?
7. Who is the best and most honorable among people? Support your answer with an ayah.

UNIT F — CHAPTER ONE
LESSON FIVE

سورة الحجرات

Surat-ul-Hujuraat
Verses (14-18) The True Faith in Islam

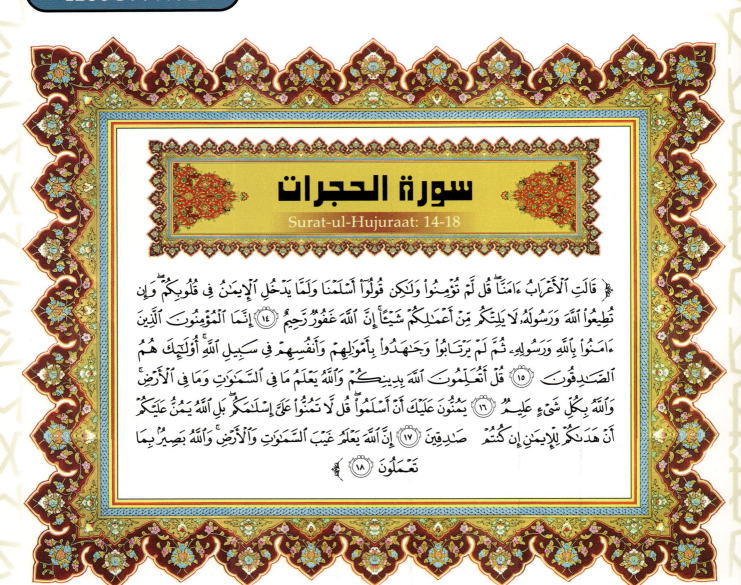

Understood Meaning

(49:14) Some of the Arabs said, "We have believed." Tell them, "You do not have complete belief so instead say we submit". Belief has not yet entered into your hearts. But if you obey Allah and His Messenger (with pure intentions, making your actions match what you believe in your hearts) nothing will be lost from your good deeds. (Remember) Allah is forgiving and merciful (so ask for forgiveness for your sins and ask Allah for help.)

(49:15) The believers are only the ones (meaning anyone who doesn't have these characteristics does not have true belief) who believe in Allah and His Messenger (a sincere true belief) and after that they never have doubt in their belief. And then they work hard, giving their money and their lives for the sake of Allah's (religion of Islam). Only those who do both of these things are truthful (in saying they are believers 'Muminoon').

(49:16) Say, "Are you trying to tell Allah what you believe? When Allah knows about everything in the Heavens and on Earth (so how do you expect to trick Allah?) And Allah knows everything (so Allah knows that your hearts have not submitted to Him)."

(49:17) They then act like becoming Muslims was a favor they did for you. Say, "Don't act like your Islam is a favor to me. Actually it is Allah who reminds you of His favor to you that He guided you to belief (in the truth), if you are really telling the truth (that you have become Muslims).

(49:18) (Remember) Allah knows everything hidden and unseen in the Heavens and Earth and Allah sees everything you do (and will reward you, if it is good or punish you, if it is bad).

Reason for Revelation

Verse 17, A group of Arabs (Bedouins) said, "O Messenger of Allah, we became Muslim and we didn't fight you like such and such tribe did." So Allah revealed this verse. (Tabarani with an acceptable chain of narration)

Lessons Learned

1. The Difference Between Islam and Iman. Why did Allah describe some of the Arabs at the time of the Prophet as Muslims, but not yet mu'mins, or believers? Allah told this group of Arabs that they do not really believe yet. Their faith was not strong enough to affect their actions and behavior. They had submitted themselves to obey Allah mostly because they were afraid of having to fight the Muslims. So they were only one step above the hypocrites, who submit to Allah in public and privately they work against the Muslims.

Allah knows what is in the hearts of people, something humans cannot tell. Iman, or faith, is what people believe and may hide in their hearts. They may believe in something and show of the opposite to the surrounding people, like what the munafiqeen, or hypocrites, used to do. Islam is the spiritual and moral actions people do, like prayers, Hajj, charity, honesty and other good actions. Therefore, Allah was telling those tribes that they might be acting as Muslims, but they still needed to work harder on faith and hearts. He wanted them to become more sincere, and not fall in the mistakes of the hypocrites. In conclusion, iman is the belief in the heart and mind, while Islam is the good actions a person physically does, based on his or her beliefs.

2. Iman Must Be Proven Through Good Actions. Muslims must believe in all of the Arkan-ul-Iman, or the six core beliefs in Islam to become believers. From this perspective, a person is either a believer or not. So when we talk about the purity of belief, we mean how much the belief affects actions. We all believe in the Day of Judgment. A person of weak belief believes that there is a Day of Judgment, but this doesn't stop him from doing bad deeds. A person with a strong belief will be unable to do bad deeds, because his belief is so strong it generates a fear that prevents him from being tempted to disobey Allah.

Related Texts

﴿ وَٱلۡعَصۡرِ ۝ إِنَّ ٱلۡإِنسَٰنَ لَفِى خُسۡرٍ ۝ إِلَّا ٱلَّذِينَ ءَامَنُوا۟ وَعَمِلُوا۟ ٱلصَّٰلِحَٰتِ وَتَوَاصَوۡا۟ بِٱلۡحَقِّ وَتَوَاصَوۡا۟ بِٱلصَّبۡرِ ۝ ﴾ العصر

{1} By (the Token of) Time (through the ages),
{2} Verily Man is in loss,
{3} Except such as have faith, and do righteous deeds, and (join together) in the mutual teaching of Truth, and of Patience and Constancy.

Imam Al-Hasan Al-Basri said,

"ليس الإيمان بالتمني ولا بالتحلي ولكنه ما وقر في القلب وصدقه العمل"

"Iman cannot happen to you by wishful thinking and it is not something for show. Rather, it is what you deeply believe in your heart and is proven through your actions."

لا إيمان بلا عمل ولا عمل بلا إيمان

Imam Malik said,

"Iman is not complete without good action, and action will not be acceptable without iman."

وعن أبي هريرة عبد الرحمن بن صخر رضي الله عنه قال : قال رسول الله ﷺ :
"إن الله لا ينظر إلى أجسامكم ، ولا إلى صوركم ، ولكن ينظر إلى قلوبكم"
رواه مسلم

Abu Hurayrah narrated that Rasoolullah said,
"Allah doesn't look at how you look or your wealth, (Allah) looks at your hearts and at what you do." (Reported by Muslim)

CHAPTER REVIEW

Projects and Activities

Create a poster explaining the Pillars of Islam and the Pillars of Iman.

Stretch Your Mind

Compare and contrast Islam and Iman.

Study Questions

1. Why did Allah tell some Arab tribes that they were Muslims but not believers yet?
2. What proves that a person is a true believer? Support your answer with ayaat, hadeeth, and other quotations.

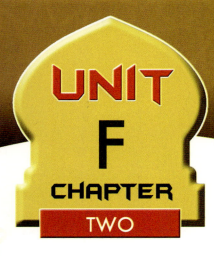

Dangerous Life Styles I
Alcoholic Beverages: The Mother of All Evils

CHAPTER OBJECTIVES

1. Learn that alcoholic beverages are harmful, and therefore haram.
2. Understand the evil effects of alcoholic beverages, or khamr.
3. Learn that khamr is the mother of evil lifestyles.
4. Understand how intoxicants destroy human societies.
5. Become more motivated to warn others against the devastating effects of intoxicants.

VOCABULARY

Al-Khamr   الخمر

Introduction

No other substance has caused nearly the amount of death, chaos, crime, and pain as alcohol. Alcohol is an intoxicant that functions like a poison to the human body and mind. It is also brings an addictive and destructive lifestyle to every human society. Intoxicating drinks or substance are called in Arabic "khamr."

During the early days of Islam, drinking alcohol was very common. In the beginning, alcohol was not haram, or prohibited, for the early Muslims. Finally, Allah سبحانه وتعالى made it absolutely haram to all. It is now a major sin to drink, serve, buy or sell alcoholic beverages Intoxicating substances.

Hadeeth Shareef

عن عبد الله بن عمر رضي الله عنه قال : قال رسول الله ﷺ :
"كل مسكر خمر وكل خمر حرام ، ومن شرب الخمر في الدنيا فمات وهو يدمنها لم يشربها في الآخرة"

سنن الترمذي – الألباني/باب شارب الخمر

Abdullah Ibn Omar narrated that Rasoolullah said:
Every intoxicant is Khamr and every Khamr is Haram. And whoever drinks Khamr in this life and dies while he is addicted to it will never drink it in the hereafter.

(Reported in Saheeh Muslim)

"Muhammad, can you please go get the mail?" the mother requested.
"Just a minute Mama. I'm almost finished with this leve," Muhammad replied, as he was playing his video game.
"Muhammad, please go now, before it gets too dark!"
"Okay, I'm going."
Muhammad walked out the door towards the mailbox, and he saw a car speeding in all directions. Muhammad stopped from fear and watched as the car almost hit his mailbox. Muhammad watched as the car sped down the road, and he went back inside the house forgetting about the mail.
"Did you get the mail Muhammad?" His mother asked.
"Mama, a car almost hit our mailbox."
"Oh?? Are you okay?!" Muhammad's mom went over to him and gave him a hug.
"I'm fine, Alhamdulillah. I'm afraid that car will hit someone, Mama. It was driving really fast and going in weird directions."
"Do you want to report it? Do you remember how the car looked like?"
"It was a small blue car".
Muhammad's mother went to another room to get the phone. She called the police station and told them about the small blue car. The operator thanked Muhammad's mom.

Later in the evening Muhammad was watching the television. Suddenly, he saw something shocking. He immediately called his mother,
"Mama look! That's the car that almost hit our mailbox!"
"Oh, ya Allah. He hit a tree?"
"Yes, the driver was taken to the hospital…they are saying he was a drunk driver. What does that mean?"
"That means he drank a lot of alcohol and became drunk."
"Oh, drinking alcohol makes you drive like that?"
"Yes, it makes the mind unsteady"
"Then why would anyone want to drink alcohol?!"
"I am not sure, but Allah سبحانه وتعالى, the All Wise, forbade His believers to drink alcohol."
"That is the smart choice. Plus, we are obeying Allah سبحانه وتعالى."
"Exactly, Alhamdulillah that we are Muslims."
"Alhamdulillah"
"Now can you please go get the mail?"

F37

Why Do People Drink Alcohol?

Some say that it helps them to relax. Others use it to celebrate and many drink it to become unconscious and run away from their problems. There are many reasons people make up to drink. But alcohol is dangerous, and there is no good enough to drink it. Drinking alcohol makes people lose their common sense and spoil their minds. Alcohol can make you dizzy. Large amounts can blur your vision and make you lose your balance. Too much alcohol can even cause death.

Alcohol has caused many problems. Drinkers have lost their jobs and their families. Most traffic accidents are caused by people who drive under the influence of alcohol. As a matter of fact, drinking under the influence of alcohol is number one reason of fatal accidents on America's highways.

Drinking Alcohol Is Haram

Alcohol is a chemical that has some benefits, but causes great harms. Alcohol is widely used in hospitals, clinics and homes to clean wounds and fight bacteria. However, Alcohol is still a dangerous substance if it is consumed as a drink, or used with food. Alcohol is sometimes referred to as a drug because of its harmful effect on the human body, mind, and society.

Alcoholic drinks can be produced from anything: fruits, flowers, rice, honey, palm, and even barley. The ancient Arabs, during the time of Jahiliyyah (Before Islam), used to make alcoholic drinks from dates and grapes. Allah says in Al-Qur'an:

﴿ وَمِن ثَمَرَٰتِ ٱلنَّخِيلِ وَٱلْأَعْنَٰبِ تَتَّخِذُونَ مِنْهُ سَكَرًا وَرِزْقًا حَسَنًا إِنَّ فِي ذَٰلِكَ لَءَايَةً لِّقَوْمٍ يَعْقِلُونَ ۝ ﴾ النحل: ٦٧

"And of the fruits of the palms and the grapes-- you obtain from them intoxication and goodly provision; most surely there is a sign in this for a people who ponder." [16:67]

Common modern alcoholic drinks such as champagne and wine use grapes. Nevertheless, whatever fruit or food used to produce such drinks, alcohol is haram.

Some intoxicating drinks have only small amounts of alcohol, and people who drink them do not usually get drunk unless they consume a large amount of it. Beer is a clear example of this type of alcoholic drink which is also prohibited in Islam.

Hadeeth Shareef

عن جابر بن عبد الله رضي الله عنه قال : قال رسول الله ﷺ :
"ما أسْكَرَ كثيرُهُ فقليلهُ حَرام."

رواه أصحاب السُّنن أبو داوود والترمذي وإبن ماجه والنسائي

Jabir Ibn Abdullah narrated that Rasoolullah said:

"If a large amount of substance causes intoxication, then even a small amount is forbidden."

Reported in Sunan Abu Dawood, At-Tirmithi, Ibn Majah and An-Nasa'i

The above hadeeth means that a Muslim is prohibited to drink even a small amount of alcohol. Therefore, drinking a can of beer or even one sip of it is totally prohibited in Islam.

Allah سبحانه وتعالى also warns us to stay away from dealing with intoxicants in any shape or form. For example, it is haram to serve, sell, buy, trade, and/or produce wine, beer, or any other alcoholic beverages. Even if you did not drink from it, it is still haram to serve or make such substances. This shows that Allah سبحانه وتعالى really wants His believers to stay away from alcohol as much as possible.

60-70% of all crimes involve alcohol or other intoxicating drugs

Hadeeth Shareef

عن عبد الله بن عمر رضي الله عنه قال: قال رسول الله ﷺ:
"لعن الله الخمر وشاربها وساقيها وعاصرها ومحضرها وبائعها ومبتاعها وحاملها والمحمولة إليه وآكل ثمنها."

رواه أصحاب السنن أبو داوود والترمذي وإبن ماجه والنسائي

Abdullah Ibn Omar narrated that Rasoolullah said:
"Allah cursed wine and whoever drinks, serves, sells, buys, produces, delivers or receives it."
(Reported in Sunan Abu Dawood, At-Tirmithi, Ibn Majah and An-Nasa'i)

How Alcohol Become Haram

During the early days of Islam, drinking alcohol was very common. In the beginning, alcohol was not haram for the early Muslims. However, Prophet Muhammad ﷺ always stayed away from it. He never drank khamr in his life. One day, a group of the Sahabah brought up the evils of alcohol to Prophet Muhammad ﷺ. Then Allah  revealed the following verse:

﴿ يَسْأَلُونَكَ عَنِ ٱلْخَمْرِ وَٱلْمَيْسِرِ ۖ قُلْ فِيهِمَآ إِثْمٌ كَبِيرٌ وَمَنَـٰفِعُ لِلنَّاسِ وَإِثْمُهُمَآ أَكْبَرُ مِن نَّفْعِهِمَا ﴾ ۲۱۹ ﴿البقرة: ٢١٩﴾

"They ask you about intoxicants and games of chance. Say: In both of them there is a great harm and means of profit for men, and their harm is greater than their profit."[2:219]

The above verse was the first verse in a series of verses leading to the absolute prohibition of alcohol. This verse presents advice for the early Muslims. Allah سبحانه وتعالى is telling the Muslims that because there is more harm than good in alcohol, they should stay away from it. Since it did not prohibit alcohol completely, some Muslims continued to drink it. Shortly afterwards, one incident changed the situation. One day, Abdul Rahman ibn Awf had invited some Sahabah for a gathering and alcoholic drinks were served. Soon, it was Maghrib time and the Sahabah wanted to perform the salah. Most of these Muslims were drunk, including the imam. While the imam was leading the salah, he made several errors in his recitation of Surat-ul-Kafiroon. After this incident, Allah سبحانه وتعالى revealed in the Quran:

﴿ يَـٰٓأَيُّهَا ٱلَّذِينَ ءَامَنُوا۟ لَا تَقْرَبُوا۟ ٱلصَّلَوٰةَ وَأَنتُمْ سُكَـٰرَىٰ حَتَّىٰ تَعْلَمُوا۟ مَا تَقُولُونَ ٤٣ ﴾ النساء: ٤٣

"O you who believe! Do not go near prayer when you are drunk until you know (well) what you say." [Surat-un-Nisaa' 4:43]

This verse tells the Muslims that it is now haram for them to drink alcohol when it is nearing the salah time. Still, it did not prohibit alcohol completely. Some Muslims continued to drink. Another incident occurred that brought an end to drinking alcohol completely. Uthman ibn Malik invited some companions for a meal. After the meal, alcohol was served. After a few drinks, the Muslims were drunk. They began singing and reciting poetry loudly. They sang about themselves and about their tribes. As they became excited, they teased and insulted Muslims who were not part of their tribe. Uthman ibn Malik particularly insulted the Muslim Ansar in Madinah with his singing. There was a young Ansari in the group who got very angry when he heard this. The young Ansari threw a bone at Uthman ibn Malik and injured his head. The next day, Uthman ibn Malik went

> **Almost 78% of assaults (and beatings) involve the influence of alcohol.**

to the Prophet ﷺ, complaining to him about what happened the night before. Prophet Muhammad ﷺ made du'aa':

"Oh Allah! Grant us a clear-cut guidance regarding alcohol."

In response, Allah سبحانه وتعالى revealed in the Qur'an:

﴿ يَـٰٓأَيُّهَا ٱلَّذِينَ ءَامَنُوٓا۟ إِنَّمَا ٱلْخَمْرُ وَٱلْمَيْسِرُ وَٱلْأَنصَابُ وَٱلْأَزْلَـٰمُ رِجْسٌ مِّنْ عَمَلِ ٱلشَّيْطَـٰنِ فَٱجْتَنِبُوهُ لَعَلَّكُمْ تُفْلِحُونَ ٩٠ إِنَّمَا يُرِيدُ ٱلشَّيْطَـٰنُ أَن يُوقِعَ بَيْنَكُمُ ٱلْعَدَٰوَةَ وَٱلْبَغْضَآءَ فِى ٱلْخَمْرِ وَٱلْمَيْسِرِ وَيَصُدَّكُمْ عَن ذِكْرِ ٱللَّهِ وَعَنِ ٱلصَّلَوٰةِ فَهَلْ أَنتُم مُّنتَهُونَ ٩١ ﴾ المائدة: ٩٠-٩١

"Oh you who believe! Intoxicants (alcohol and drugs) and gambling are forbidden...it is of Satan's handwork. Avoid such thing so you may prosper...Satan's plan is to create hatred and tension among you, with intoxicants and gambling, and hinder you from the remembrance of Allah, and from prayer: will you not then abstain?" [Surat-ul-Ma'idah 5:90-91]

As you learned earlier, Allah سبحانه وتعالى first declared that alcohol has more harm than good. This made some Muslims stop drinking alcohol. Then Allah سبحانه وتعالى prohibited alcohol during Salah times. This caused more Muslims to stop drinking.

Finally, Allah سبحانه وتعالى made it absolutely haram, or forbidden. It is now a major sin to drink or deal with alcohol. When a person drinks, they have allowed Satan to do his dirty work. Satan enjoys seeing Muslims forgetting about salat, and not remembering Allah سبحانه وتعالى. Satan enjoys seeing Muslim brothers and sisters to fight one another. This is why it is very important to stay away from alcohol. A Muslim who drinks alcohol is very sinful. The Prophet Muhammad ﷺ said:

عن عبد الله بن عمر رضي الله عنه قال قال رسول الله صلى الله عليه وسلم :
"من شَرِبَ الخمر لم تُقْبَل لهُ صلاة أربعين ليلة، فإن تاب تاب الله عليه."

رواه أحمد وابن ماجه

Abdullah Ibn Omar رضي الله عنه narrated that Rasoolullah said:

"If anyone drinks any alcoholic drinks, God will not accept his prayer for forty days, but if he repents Allah will accept his repentance." *Reported in Ahmad and Ibn Majah*

Alcohol Is The Mother of All Evils

The Prophet Muhammad ﷺ referred to alcohol as the 'mother of all sins'.

عن عثمان بن عفان رضي الله عنه قال: قال رسول الله صلى الله عليه وسلم :
"اجتَنِبوا الخَمْرَ فإنَّها أمُّ الخَبائِثِ"

رواه النسائي

Othman narrated that Rasoolullah ﷺ once said:

"Avoid drinking wine for it is the mother of all sins."

Reported in An-Nasa'ee

This is because after drinking alcohol, the mind is not steady. The mind becomes blurry and a person cannot think clearly. This may cause the person to commit other sins without realizing it. For example, one day, a pious man was forced to drink. He eventually got drunk. The next day, he found out that after he got drunk, he had committed murder and adultery. The alcohol caused him to commit twoother major sins without him realizing it. This shows how dangerous alcohol is. Indeed, alcohol is the "mother of all sins." Every day, police investigators in America and around the world encounter many crimes that were committed under the influence of alcohol.

The Haram of Alcohol:

1. Causes the stomach to gradually loses its ability to function properly.
2. Causes loss of appetite.
3. Makes one age quicker.
4. Weakens and reduces the ability to think and speak properly.
5. Causes heart failure.
6. Creates fights and tension between people.
7. Leads toward great sins, such as adultery and murder.
8. Wastes money.
9. Causes liver damage.
10. Causes road accidents, and the loss of innocent lives.

CONCLUSION

No other substance has caused nearly the amount of death, chaos, crime, and pain. Alcohol is like a poison to the human body and mind. It is also a poison to society. Alcohol is also dangerous because it is addictive. Once a person begins to drink alcohol, it is very hard to stop. Allah سبحانه وتعالى warns us to stay away from alcohol, and places that serve it. Allah سبحانه وتعالى gives us such instructions because He is All-Knowing. Everything in Islam has a good reason behind it. Some reasons we know, and others we don't. Allah سبحانه وتعالى knows what we don't know. We also know that Allah wants what is best for His believers. This is why we should trust Allah and obey him in every way.

The Long-Term Health Effects of Alcohol

Central Nervous System (brain and spinal cord)
- impaired senses
  — vision, hearing, dulled smell and taste, decreased pain perception
- altered sense of time and space
- impaired motor skills, slow reaction
- impaired judgment, confusion
- hallucinations
- fits, blackouts
- tingling and loss of sensation in hands and feet
- early onset dementia (alcohol related brain damage)
- Wernicke's Syndrome and psychosis (delirium)
- mood and personality changes
- feeling anxious or worried

Circulatory System
- high blood pressure
- irregular heart beat
- damage to the heart muscle
- increased risk of heart attack and stroke

Liver
- swollen, painful inflamed
- cirrhosis
- cancer
- fluid build up (oedema)
- increased risk of haemorrhage
- liver failure, coma and death

Pregnancy and Babies
- fetal alcohol syndrome/fetal alcohol effects
  — small head, possible brain damage, retarded growth and development

General Body
- weight gain
- headaches
- muscle weakness

Gastrointestinal System
- stomach lining inflamed and irritated
- ulcers of the stomach or duodenum
- inflammation or varicose veins of the oesophagus
- loss of appetite, nausea, diarrhoea and vomiting
- cancer

Pancreas
- painful, inflamed, bleeding.

Intestines
- irritation of the lining
- inflammation and ulcers
- cancer of intestines and colon

Reproductive System Male and Female
- reduced fertility
- impaired sexual performance
- impotence
- decreased sperm count and movement
- increased risk of breast cancer in females
- early onset of menopause
- irregular menstrual cycle

CHAPTER REVIEW

Projects and Activities

1. Write an essay about the medical harms of drinking alcohol.

2. Learn a story about a crime committed by someone who was under the influence of alcohol. Share this story with your classmates.

Stretch Your Mind

1. Compare and contrast the behavior of someone getting drunk, and someone being really angry.

2. "Khamr and crime are friends." Explain this statement, and prove your points.

Study Questions

1. What is the Islamic ruling on khamr?
2. Describe how Allah gradually prohibited drinking wine.
3. Determine if the following statements are true or false:
4. Khamr may be halal if someone drinks only a little bet.
5. Drinking khamr is absolutely haram whether the drinker become drunk or not.
6. It took a while before Allah prohibited drinking wine.
7. Write three reasons for the prohibition of alcoholic drinks in Islam.
8. Who said that "Khamr is the mother of all sins?" Explain why he thought so.
9. Prophet Muhammad cursed six types of people who deal with khamr; who are they?
10. How would Allah punish the person who drinks wine in this life. Support your answer with a hadeeth.
11. Describe one type of punishment awaiting Alcohol drinkers in the Hereafter. Support your answer with a hadeeth.
12. What are some social harms of drinking alcohol.
13. In Surat Al-Maidah, Allah mentioned that Shaytan makes people have three incorrectbehaviors after drinking alcohol. What are those incorrect actions?

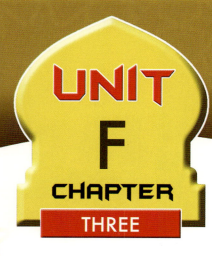

Dangerous Life Styles II Pork and Other Haram Meats

CHAPTER OBJECTIVES

1. Recognize the gifts of food and nutrition that Allah gave to us.
2. Understand that Allah made the good food permissible to people.
3. Understand that Allah made harmful food prohibited.
4. Learn that pork products are all Haram, or prohibited to eat.
5. Understand reasons behind the prohibition of pork in Islam.

VOCABULARY

Khinzeer خنزير

Allah blessed us with many of His gifts and favors. Food and drinks are among the most important favors of Allah. Look around, and you will see that Planet Earth is full of Allah's bounties, and God made it all available for our consumption.

Allah says in Surat Luqman

﴿أَلَمْ تَرَوْا أَنَّ ٱللَّهَ سَخَّرَ لَكُم مَّا فِي ٱلسَّمَٰوَٰتِ وَمَا فِي ٱلْأَرْضِ وَأَسْبَغَ عَلَيْكُمْ نِعَمَهُۥ ظَٰهِرَةً وَبَاطِنَةً﴾ ﴿لقمان: ٢٠﴾

"Do you not see that Allah has made what is in the Heavens and what is in the Earth available to you, and He bestowed upon His seen and unseen favors." [Surat Luqman 31:20]

﴿يَٰٓأَيُّهَا ٱلنَّاسُ كُلُوا۟ مِمَّا فِي ٱلْأَرْضِ حَلَٰلًا طَيِّبًا وَلَا تَتَّبِعُوا۟ خُطُوَٰتِ ٱلشَّيْطَٰنِ إِنَّهُۥ لَكُمْ عَدُوٌّ مُّبِينٌ﴾ ﴿البقرة: ١٦٨﴾

"O mankind! Eat the lawful and good things out of what is in the Earth, and do not follow the footsteps of the Shaytan; surely he is your open enemy." [Surat-ul-Baqarah 2:168]

F46

By the mercy of Allah and His kindness towards us, Allah has permitted us to eat all good things, and He has not forbidden anything but that is impure and unhealthy. Allah has prevented us from eating certain kinds of harmful meats, like pork and the meats of predators and dead animals.

He says concerning the mission of the Prophet ﷺ,

﴿ وَيُحِلُّ لَهُمُ ٱلطَّيِّبَٰتِ وَيُحَرِّمُ عَلَيْهِمُ ٱلْخَبَٰٓئِثَ ﴾ الأعراف: ١٥٧

"He will make lawful for them all good things and prohibit for them what is unhealthy and unwholesome." [7: 157]

Food and drinks have a direct effect on our health. That is why Islam has prescribed regulations about what we put inside our bodies. Allah سبحانه وتعالى wants His believers to be in the best health, physically, psychologically, and spiritually.

When Muslims are healthy, a healthy Muslim society can be easily established. Allah has forbidden eating the meats of pigs, wild animals and birds, and the flesh of dead animals. Muslims show their obedience to Allah by abstaining from pork and other Haram meats and food. Allah even prohibited overeating and all kinds of Israaf, or wasting..This obedience brings us the blessings of Allah and helps them maintain a healthy and happy Muslim society.

Allah Prohibits Pork and other Unhealthy Meats

Allah سبحانه وتعالى prohibits the consumption of pork in no fewer than four different places in the Qur'an. Allah orders us in the Qur'an not to consume the flesh of swine and dead animals.

﴿ حُرِّمَتْ عَلَيْكُمُ ٱلْمَيْتَةُ وَٱلدَّمُ وَلَحْمُ ٱلْخِنزِيرِ وَمَآ أُهِلَّ لِغَيْرِ ٱللَّهِ بِهِۦ وَٱلْمُنْخَنِقَةُ وَٱلْمَوْقُوذَةُ وَٱلْمُتَرَدِّيَةُ وَٱلنَّطِيحَةُ وَمَآ أَكَلَ ٱلسَّبُعُ إِلَّا مَا ذَكَّيْتُمْ وَمَا ذُبِحَ عَلَى ٱلنُّصُبِ وَأَن تَسْتَقْسِمُوا۟ بِٱلْأَزْلَٰمِ ۚ ذَٰلِكُمْ فِسْقٌ ۗ ٱلْيَوْمَ يَئِسَ ٱلَّذِينَ كَفَرُوا۟ مِن دِينِكُمْ فَلَا تَخْشَوْهُمْ وَٱخْشَوْنِ ۚ ٱلْيَوْمَ أَكْمَلْتُ لَكُمْ دِينَكُمْ وَأَتْمَمْتُ عَلَيْكُمْ نِعْمَتِى وَرَضِيتُ لَكُمُ ٱلْإِسْلَٰمَ دِينًا ۚ فَمَنِ ٱضْطُرَّ فِى مَخْمَصَةٍ غَيْرَ مُتَجَانِفٍ لِّإِثْمٍ ۙ فَإِنَّ ٱللَّهَ غَفُورٌ رَّحِيمٌ ﴿٣﴾ المائدة: ٣

"Forbidden to you is: an animal which died by itself, blood and flesh of swine, and what is slaughtered by names other than that of Allah, and animals that were strangled, beaten to death, killed by a fall, or by being smitten with the horn, that which wild beasts have attacked, except what you slaughter before they die, what is sacrificed on stone altars (idols) and that you divide by the arrows. All that is a transgression." [5: 3]

F47

This day have those who disbelieve despaired of your religion, so fear them not, and fear Me. This day have I perfected for you your religion and completed My favor on you and chosen for you Islam as a religion; but whoever is compelled by hunger, not inclining willfully to sin, then surely Allah is Forgiving, Merciful. [Surat-ul-Ma'idah 5:3]

In the above verse, Allah says that dead animals, blood, the flesh of swine and animals slaughtered for idols are all prohibited. In another verse [6: 145], Allah describes these meats as filthy. Therefore, these meats are unfit for human consumption and we must stay away from them. For Allah forbids only that which is impure and harmful.

It should be noted that all pork products are prohibited and not only the meat. Lard, which is the pig's fat, is prohibited too. It is unfortunate that food factories use it in processing many kinds of food, deli, sweets and even hygiene products like soap and tooth paste. Muslims should always try their utmost best to avoid all foods that include all pork products.

...and Unlawful Meats

In contrast, the following meats are described by Allah and the Prophet as unlawful meats:

1. Pork products (Pork, ham, bacon and lard).
2. Wild animals that feed on other animals (Lions, tigers, wolves, hyenas etc.).
3. Dead animals, including those dead because of accidents like falling, or being suffocated, hit or preyed on by a wild animal.
4. Dogs
5. Donkeys and mules
6. Mice and rats
7. Worms and insects, except locust.

There is enough evidence to show that the flesh of swine is not at all good for human consumption.

Harmful Effects of Eating Pork, Blood and Dead Animals

When you go to the food store and pass by the meat department you see many kinds of meat. You always see beef, lamb, chicken, fish and seafood. You will not see dog, cat, and donkey or mule meats, because almost all people believe it is prohibited or find it disgusting. However, in America and many other countries you can easily see pork. Pork is pigs' meat and many people, especially Christians, like to eat it. However, in Islam, pork products are strictly prohibited and considered Haram. It is a major sin for a Muslim to eat pork or any pork products.

The fact that eating pork is prohibited in Islam is well-known. The main reason for this is because Allah سبحانه وتعالى prohibits this particular meat in the Qur'an. Prophet Muhammad ﷺ also ordered Muslims not to eat pigs' meat or fat nor sell it to others.

Medical experts have recently discovered the harms of pork meat and research shows that eating pork can cause many health risks. Allah سبحانه وتعالى tells us to take care of our bodies, and avoid anything that may damage it. Pig's bodies contain many toxins, worms and latent diseases. Although some of these infestations are found in other animals, modern veterinarians say that pigs are far more subject to these illnesses than other animals. This could be because pigs like to hunt and will eat any kind of food, including dead insects, worms, rotting carcasses, excrement (including their own), garbage, and other pigs.

Eating pork can cause no less than seventy different types of diseases. A person can have various Helminthes, like roundworm, pinworm, hookworm, etc. One of the most dangerous is Taenia Solium, which is also called "tapeworm." It stays in the intestine and is very long. Its eggs enter the blood stream and can reach almost all the organs of the body. If it enters the brain it can cause memory loss. If it enters the heart it can cause heart attack and if it enters the eye it can cause blindness. If it enters the liver it can cause liver damage. It can damage almost all the organs of the body.

One can also say the same about the harms of the meat of dead animals and other prohibited meats. Harmful bacteria and sometimes deadly ones can quickly grow in dead animals' flesh and blood. It is dangerous and completely unhealthy to consume such things and that is why Allah made them prohibited.

You might be puzzled to see Allah prohibiting eating blood. You may ask are there people around who consume blood? The answer is yes. There are people in certain parts of our world who use blood in their food. While they see that as sensible, Muslims believe it is unlawful food. Prophet Muhammad explained that blood is haram, however, the spleen and liver of the lawful animal is halal. Most of the components of these two organs are made of blood turning into flesh.

Hadeeth Shareef

عن عبد الله بن عمر رضي الله عنه قال: قال رسولُ اللهِ ﷺ:
" أُحِلَّتْ لنا مَيْتَتان ودَمان ، فأما الميتتان فالحوتُ والجَرادُ ، وأما الدَّمان فالكَبِدُ والطِّحال."

رواه أحمد وابن ماجه

Abdullah Ibn Omar (R) narrated that Rasoolullah said:
"Two kinds of dead animals and two types of blood were made lawful to us; the two dead animals are fish and locust and the two bloods are liver and spleen."
Reported in Ahmad and Ibn Majah

Is Pork Forbidden Only to Muslims?

Islam is not the only religion in which pork is prohibited. Other religions teach the same rule also. For example; In Judaism, pork consumption is forbidden. The Jews believe in the Old Testament. It is clearly stated:

"And the swine, though he divided the hoof, and be clovenfooted, yet he cheweth not the cud; he is unclean to you. Of their flesh shall ye not eat, and their carcass shall ye not touch; they are unclean to you. "Leviticus (11:7-8).

Also, "And the swine, because it divideth the hoof, yet cheweth not the cud, it is unclean unto you: ye shall not eat of their flesh, nor touch their dead carcass." Deuteronomy (14:8).

Many Christians believe that this verse was directed only at the Jews. But Jesus himself says during the Sermon on the Mount;

"Think not that I am come to destroy the Law, or the Prophets: I am not come to destroy, but to fulfill."

Some Christians say that, after a vision by St. Peter, God cleansed all animals and made them fit and lawful for human consumption. If ALL animals are cleansed by Peter's vision, this includes dogs, cats, vultures, and rats. But you just don't see people getting excited

about a cat-meat sandwich like they do over barbecued pork or bacon. Others say that it was Paul who rescinded the law forbidding pork to humans, in order to appease the Romans, who enjoyed the taste of pig-meat. Many excuses have been given, but none are very sound.

Many Far Eastern traditions also discourage the eating of pork. The 3,000 year old Confucian Book of Rites says,

"A gentleman does not eat the flesh of pigs and dogs."

Although many Chinese are avid eaters of pork today, physicians of ancient China recognized pork-eating as the root of many human ailments. Buddhists, Jains and Hindus usually avoid eating any kind of meat.

Kindness to Animals

It must also be remembered that just because eating pig meat is haram that does not mean we should hate pigs. There are many other animals that we can't eat like cats, dogs, eagles, lions, cheetahs and tigers to mention a few. Does that mean we should hate or hurt them? They are Allah وتعالى سبحانه's creations, and we should always show kindness to all animals, except in case of self defense.

Every creature was created by Allah for a purpose. The Prophet always encouraged us to be kind to animals. Although we should not eat the meat of the pig, it doesn't mean that we should hate pigs. We should show them the same kindness as any other animal, and not abuse or torture them. Pigs score high on tests devised to determine animal intelligence; in other words, they are very smart. It is ironic that people in Europe believed that pork would taste better if the pigs were kept in a state of filth, but this is not the natural inclination of the pig. When left to their own devices, it is said that pigs do not like to soil their sleeping quarters. As for their tendency to wallow in mud, that is done mainly to keep cool.

Conclusion

Even if we did not know about the harmful effects of eating pork and other unlawful foods, this would not change our belief that it is haram at all. We must follow Allah's orders even if we cannot understand fully the wisdom behind them. When Prophet Adam (peace be upon him) was expelled from the garden, it was because he ate from the forbidden tree. We do not know anything about that tree, and Adam did not need to ask why he was forbidden to eat from it. Rather it was sufficient for him, as it is sufficient for us and for every believer, to know that Allah has forbidden it. It is not required of the believer to always find a scientific justification for divine prohibitions. However, if they look and find it, they must share the information, that will increase people's faith. However, lack of confirmation should not allow anyone to question the authenticity of the Qur'an. We believe that all the Qur'an's statements are true, and if science has not confirmed some of them yet, it will do so in the future.

Related Literature

Dr. E. Kazim. M.D. in his article "Medical Aspects of Forbidden Foods in Islam" (July 1981 issue of Muslim Journal) has described diseases carried or caused by the flesh of the swine. He writes:

"The pig is a scavenger. It is an omnivorous animal. It eats everything. There are many diseases carried from swine to man, particularly parasite infestations. Lately extensive research has been focused on senility-old age is characterized by hardening of inner lining of the blood vessels of the heart, brain etc., a process called atherosclerosis. When a clot forms, it results in coronary thrombosis, or a heart attack, or cerebral thrombosis or stroke.

Different dietary factors are responsible for atherosclerosis. Gross atheroma may be produced in rabbits by feeding them with cholesterol, but when you add lard (derived from hog fat) to the cholesterol, the incidence of atheroma is increased and thus you would produce coronary thrombosis, and myocardial infraction.

Besides, lard contains 2800 units of vitamin D per 100 grams and no vitamin A at all. Lately Vitamin D has been held responsible for atheroma, by causing increased absorption of calcium in the blood vessels. In human beings, serum cholesterol is not dependent on the intake of cholesterol in the diet, but depends upon the proportion of animal fats in the diet, which elevates the beta-lipo protein level in the blood. Animal fats contain saturated fatty acids and these saturated fatty acids have been found to be as one of the causes of atheroma in man. Medium fat bacon contains 25% proteins and 55% fat.

According to medical research, the fat content in pork is more than in any other meat, (beef, lamb etc.) and it takes longer to digest. Dr. M. Jaffer, (January 1997 issue, Islamic Review, London has listed 16 kinds of harmful germs which have been discovered in pork in modern research and the diseases which could be caused by them. The number of patients suffering from tapeworm disease is the highest in the world among pork eating nations. Other diseases attributed to pigs are caused by tri-chinelia spirates and intestinal worms."

Dr. Glen Shepherd wrote the following on the dangers of eating pork in *Washington Post* (31 May 1952).

"One in six people in USA and Canada have germs in their muscles - trichinosis 8 from eating pork infected with trichina worms. Many people who are infected show no symptoms. Most of those who have it recover slowly. Some die; some are reduced to permanent invalids. All were careless pork eaters."

He continued, "No one is immune from the disease and there is no cure. Neither antibiotics nor drugs or vaccines affect these tiny deadly worms. Preventing infection is the real answer."

After reading the statement of Dr. Shepherd, one can realize that there is no real guarantee of safety when eating pork that one would not be affected by the trichina worm. That is why modern doctors advise three prohibitions during illness: no liquor, no pork and no smoking.

Muslims follow the divine law which is much higher than medical advice. The Glorious Qur'an says, "So eat of the lawful and good food which Allah has provided for you, and thank the bounty of your Lord if it is Him you serve. He has forbidden for you only carrion and blood and swine-flesh and that which has been immolated in the name of any other than Allah; but he who is driven thereto, neither craving nor transgressing, Lo! then Allah is Forgiving, Merciful." [Surat-un-Nahl 16:114-115)

The above is the order from the Creator of the universe and the Supreme Law-Giver. All Muslims are under the obligation to obey it. This is a plain and straightforward answer to those who usually ask why Muslims abstain from eating pork. Nevertheless, there is no sin, if a Muslims is forced by famine or starvation, to eat pork in order to save his life.

http://www.miraclesofthequran.com

FAITH IN ACTION

★ Always avoid eating pork and its products like bacon, ham and lard.

★ Always be careful to check the food ingredients of sweets and other foods before you eat. Lard, which is pig's fat, is commonly used in many deli, sweets, and other types of food.

CHAPTER REVIEW

Projects and Activities

Write an essay about the medical harms of pork.

Stretch Your Mind

1. What is more harmful to society, addiction to alcohol, or eating much pork?

2. In Islam, Muslim wine drinkers get punished, but not pork eaters. Why?

Study Questions

1. What are the main kinds of meat that Allah made unlawful to eat?
2. Why did Allah prohibit certain types of meat?
3. What dead animals are we allowed to eat? Support your answer with evidence from Al-Qur'an or the Sunnah.
4. What do other religions say about pork? Support your answer with a quotation from their holy books.
5. Describe some of the medical harms of eating pork products.
6. Can a Muslim sell pork products, and other haram food as long as he or she does not eat it? Support your answer with a hadeeth.

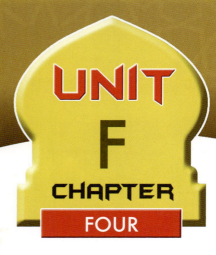

Dangerous Life Styles III
Gambling and Lottery

CHAPTER OBJECTIVES

1. What is gambling?
2. Types of gambling.
3. Gambling: haram or halal?
4. What are the harms of gambling?

VOCABULARY

Maysir مَيْسِر

Qimaar قمار

Rihan رهان

Before Islam, gambling was a social evil. When Islam came, Allah strictly forbade all forms of gambling, including betting, lottery, and other games of chance. Gambling has unfortunately become an acceptable practice in Muslim society due to its wide scale promotion by the media. Many governments legalize and even organize gambling and lottery activities. In some cases, they devote portions of the lottery profits to charity.

Islam forbids gambling in all ways and forms. Any money gained through gambling is considered haram.

Taking someone else's money by winning a game of chance is distasteful to Islam. It is a basic principle of Islam that a person should not take money which he has not earned or worked for or exchanged it with halal product. This is for reasons of fairness and justice. Maysir is the Arabic word for gambling in the Qur'an. It is derived from a root word that literally means "easy" and "something attained easily with almost no effort." Qimaar is another Arabic word for gambling.

Traditional gambling involves games of chance, like rolling dice or playing cards. If the player happens to roll or pick the right numbers on the dice or cards, he would simply win. But if he misses, he will lose his money in a matter of minutes or even seconds.

Rihan, or betting, was another ancient form of gambling. In old times people used to bet money on horse races, fights and other games and sports. In this case, a person would bet his money on a horse to win the race or a knight to win the fight. If he bet on the winner, he will double or triple his money, but if he loses, his money is totally gone.

Every transaction in which gain and loss is due to mere luck and chance is considered gambling in Islam. When gambling is involved, it means that the winner takes the money of the loser without having lawfully earned it. Islam teaches us to follow the proper practice in earning money through our halal work and effort, not relying on mere chance. Consequently, gambling was declared unlawful. Today gambling has taken many forms, such as betting and lottery. These are among the most well known forms of gambling.

Gambling Today

In every era and every land, gambling is practiced in a variety of ways. Gambling today takes countless different forms. Nevertheless, gambling in all its forms is prohibited. Here are the most common kinds of gambling available today:

F55

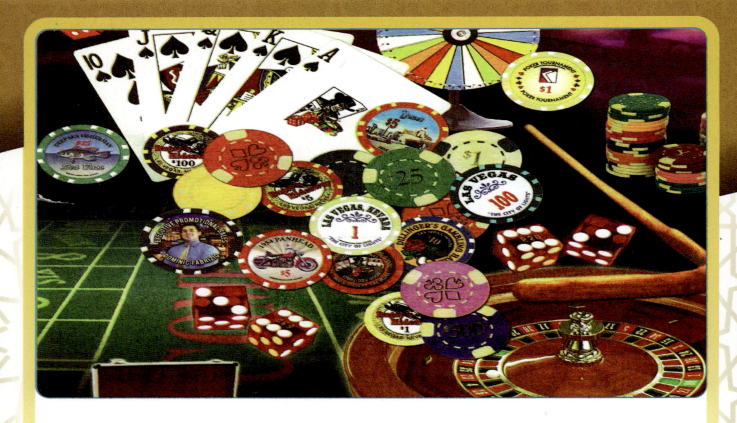

Games of Chance

Among the most widespread practices today are slot machines, jackpots, roulettes, cards games, Bingo and many other games. Casinos in Las Vegas and elsewhere in America and around the world provide thousands of ways for some gamblers to win and millions of others to lose their money.

Betting

Betting on the outcome of horse and dog races, rodeo, boxing, wrestling matches and other prize fights have become popular forms of gambling. Even very popular sports like soccer, baseball, football, basketball, and hockey have unfortunately become subjects for betting and gambling. Attempts on the part of professional gamblers to fix the outcome of such games have caused numerous problems. Other common forms of gambling include roulette, card and dice games, and bingo. Take the case of two persons competing in a race on the condition that the loser pays the winner $100; or that a person says, "If it rains today, I will give you $100, and if it does not rain, you will have to give me $100." Since one party gains and the other loses in a mere game of chance, it falls under the definition of gambling.

The Lottery

You probably heard about some people who won millions of dollars in lottery. How can the lottery companies afford to give out these huge prizes? You know that millions of people buy lottery tickets hoping that they will win the grand prize, but they don't. Over 99% of those who buy lottery tickets or involve in other forms of gambling lose their money to lottery and gambling companies.

Lottery is just one of the most popular forms of gambling today. Every kind of lottery is included within gambling and is prohibited. The lottery business has now reached an international level. Usually, lottery is conducted through a big corporation. This corporation makes business selling lottery tickets to its customers. With a lottery, you buy numbers that are usually on a ticket, and different prizes are given to the winning numbers. The purchaser of a lottery ticket does not buy the ticket with the intention of just buying it, but he or she buys it on the basis of it being a possible winner. That is the reason why this is not merely trade or business venture, but rather it is an act of sin to buy these or even to sell them. When few people win millions of dollars in lottery, millions others lose their money. This is a waste of wealth that Islam strongly prohibits.

Are Free Draws Haram?

No. Various companies and organizations sometimes do promotions for their products and services by making free draws. People don't have to pay money, they only have to fill out forms or write their names on cards to qualify for certain prizes like cars or air tickets. Then the company officials draw one or more forms that carry winners' names and grant them different prizes. This kind of free draw is not haram, as long as you don't have to pay money and the prizes are halal.

Prohibition of Gambling

In the jahiliyyah era, the time before Islam, a person would gamble away his wealth, possessions, and even his wife. When losing them, he would go so disappointed at his quick and unexpected loss that his anger would be inflamed. He would be angry to see his belongings suddenly in the hand of the winner. This situation created much hatred between people so much that fights and quarrels would erupt between different individuals. Often, these fights would involve an entire tribe, and it would last for many years. Arabian history tell us that a war erupted and continued for forty years as a result of horse race between two hoses called "Dahis" and "Al-Ghabraa."

In Islam, gambling is strictly prohibited. In the Glorious Qur'an, we see that gambling is mentioned while being associated with wine (khamr). Wine, games of chance, idols and dividing arrows are Satan's handiwork. In the early days of Islam, the Prophet ﷺ was questioned regarding the permissibility of gambling and alcohol. God describes maysir, which we often translate as "games of chance" or gambling, as "an abomination devised by Satan" which all Muslims should avoid at all costs. The first verse that was revealed regarding this, is in Surah Baqarah:

﴿ يَسْأَلُونَكَ عَنِ الْخَمْرِ وَالْمَيْسِرِ قُلْ فِيهِمَا إِثْمٌ كَبِيرٌ وَمَنَافِعُ لِلنَّاسِ وَإِثْمُهُمَا أَكْبَرُ مِن نَّفْعِهِمَا ﴾ البقرة: ٢١٩

"They ask you concerning wine and gambling. Say, 'In them is great sin and some benefit for people; but the sin in them is greater than their benefit.'" [2:219]

F57

In the above ayah, the permission to deal with wine and gambling is not clarified. Soon after understanding this verse, the highly ranked companions of the Holy Prophet ﷺ abstained from them. The general public, however, were still involved in them and the Prophet ﷺ had not said anything that indicated their prohibition, until Allah revealed the following verse:

﴿ يَٰٓأَيُّهَا ٱلَّذِينَ ءَامَنُوٓا۟ إِنَّمَا ٱلْخَمْرُ وَٱلْمَيْسِرُ وَٱلْأَنصَابُ وَٱلْأَزْلَٰمُ رِجْسٌ مِّنْ عَمَلِ ٱلشَّيْطَٰنِ فَٱجْتَنِبُوهُ لَعَلَّكُمْ تُفْلِحُونَ ﴿٩٠﴾ ﴾ المائدة: ٩٠

"Oh believers! Intoxicants and gambling, worshipping stones and divination by arrows are impure, of Shaytan's handiwork: refrain from such abomination that ye may prosper." [5:90]

In the above verse, the total prohibition of alcoholic drinks and gambling has been clearly revealed. As you can see, alcohol and gambling have always been associated together. This is true in almost every society that offers gambling as a form of entertainment. Getting drunk and gambling have many things in common. Both are created for the temporary pleasure and they allow us to lose focus on more important things, such as the remembrance of Allah سبحانه وتعالى and worshipping Him. There are many ahadeeth that speak of different games often used for gambling, showing that they are all forbidden to play.

Fiqh Matter

Suppose that a Muslim committed the sin of gambling, and he won some money or a lot of it. Then he or she realized that this was an awful thing to do. What should he or she do with the money he or she won?

Contemporary scholars of Islam have said that it is haram for the winner of lottery, betting or any other forms of gambling to keep the money and use it. Scholars advise the person to give it to poor people or charity organizations. Some scholars, however, recommend that poor people or charity organizations should be told not to use this money for buying food or spending on spiritual matters like buying copies of the Qur'an, prayer rugs, or going to Hajj. The wisdom behind that is to prevent people from eating food or worship Allah the use haram money. This type of money, they say, should be used in paying utility bills, buy gas for the car, buying appliances and other household items, repairing broken machines, buying travel tickets, or these kinds of activities.

Gambling Statistics

What is unique about the current gambling situation is the speed at which it has gone from an undercurrent in American society, to a high-profile, socially recognized activity.

The gambling industry has grown tenfold in the U.S. since 1975.

Thirty-seven states now have lotteries.

15 million people display some sign of gambling addiction.

Two-thirds of American adults have placed some kind of bet every year.

Gambling profits in casinos are more than $30 billion, while lotteries are about $17 billion annually.

"Players" with household incomes under $10,000 bet nearly three times as much on lotteries as those with incomes over $50,000.

In 1973, state lotteries had $2 billion in sales. By 1997, the revenues reached $34 billion.

Gambling among young people is on the increase: 42 percent of 14-year-olds, 49 percent of 15-year-olds, 63 percent of 16-year-olds, and 76 percent of 18-year-olds participate in gambling.

There are now approximately 260 casinos on Indian reservations (in 31 states and with $6.7 billion in revenue).

Internet gambling has nearly doubled every year since 1997 – in 2001 it exceeded $2 billion.

The Internet boasts 110 sport-related gambling sites.

According to the American Psychological Association, the Internet could be as addictive as alcohol, drugs, and or gambling.

After casinos opened in Atlantic City, the total number of crimes within a thirty-mile radius increased 100 percent.

The average debt incurred by a male pathological gambler in the U.S. is between $55,000 and $90,000 (it is $15,000 for female gamblers).

The average rate of divorce for problem gamblers is nearly double that of non-gamblers.

The suicide rate for pathological gamblers is twenty times higher than for non-gamblers (one in five attempts suicide).

Sixty-five percent of pathological gamblers commit crimes to support their gambling habit.

Evil Effects of Gambling

Some people claim that they gamble just for fun and don't spend a lot of money. Such people are making a great sin, because they are not avoiding gambling, but instead they are using it for entertainment. This may eventually drag them to become addicted to gambling and over the years they lose so much money on this insanity. Gambling indeed is a very addictive entertainment.

Gambling entails religious, social, moral and economic harm:

1. Gambling distracts those who partake the game from the remembrance of Allah and prayer. When a gambler sits continuously for hours together, he is so absorbed in it that he forgets everything around him; rather he becomes unconscious of his own self. He forgets his households and family. How, then, can he take care of his prayer?

2. Gambling sows the seeds of disputes and quarrels among the gamblers which ultimately assume hatred among them. This point is made clear in the following verse:

﴿ إِنَّمَا يُرِيدُ ٱلشَّيْطَانُ أَن يُوقِعَ بَيْنَكُمُ ٱلْعَدَاوَةَ وَٱلْبَغْضَاءَ فِي ٱلْخَمْرِ وَٱلْمَيْسِرِ وَيَصُدَّكُمْ عَن ذِكْرِ ٱللَّهِ وَعَنِ ٱلصَّلَوٰةِ ۖ فَهَلْ أَنتُم مُّنتَهُونَ ﴿٩١﴾ ﴾ المائدة: ٩١

"Only would Satan sow hatred and strife among you, by wine, and games of chance and turn you aside from the remembrance of Allah, and from prayer. Will you not, therefore, abstain from them?" (5:91)

3. The sin of gambling is greater than its benefit.

4. It corrupts morals, making people sluggish waiting to get wealthy by luck and chance. It turns their heads away from hard work and production through agriculture, industry, and business, the foundation stone of social living and human prosperity.

5. It enslaves the gambler, who becomes a mute slave in the hands of gambling and seldom succeeds in abandoning it. When he earns some benefit, his greed for gambling increases and when he loses the game, even then his interest in the games of chance increases to make good the loss. In this way, he remains very engaged in gambling until he becomes poor.

6. It brings about sudden chaos in many countries, due to sheer waste of wealth when gamblers lose.

7. It usurps the wealth of towns and transfers it to the hands of the mischief-mongers within and outside the country. Thus gambling is a root-cause of countless economic evils, reducing many rich people to poverty and ultimately forcing them to commit suicide.

8. Gambling is usually associated with theincrease of crime, suicide, divorce, and other major epidemics in society.

We seek refuge in Allah from gambling and its ancillary sins.

FAITH IN ACTION

Always avoid:
- ★ Being part of betting and gambling.
- ★ Buying lottery tickets.
- ★ Spending money on games of chance.
- ★ Watching gambling related shows or activities.

CHAPTER REVIEW

Projects and Activities

1. Develop a list of gambling games that people do in current times.
2. Share a story with your classmates about the harms of gambling.

Stretch Your Mind

1. What are the reasons behind the prohibition of gambling?
2. Compare and contrast gambling and trade. Explain why Allah prohibited gambling while He permitted trade.
3. What are the similarities of drinking khamr and gambling, in terms of harming people?

Study Questions

1. Define: a. Gambling b. Lottery c. Betting
2. What are the Arabic words for gambling and betting?
3. What is the Islamic ruling on gambling? Support your answer with evidence from Al-Qur'an.
4. List four harms in gambling.
5. Suppose you made a mistake and won some money in gambling, or from a lottery ticket. What should you do in this case?

F61

Mental Drugs

UNIT F CHAPTER FIVE

CHAPTER OBJECTIVES

1. Learn about the things that waste time and energy.
2. Recognize that games and entertainment can be other addictions addictive.
3. Realize that "other addictions" can distract people's attention away from worship, studying, and other serious things in life.

In the previous lessons on "alcohol" and "drugs," you learned about their harm and danger to us. However, harm doesn't stop there. In this lesson, you will learn about other kinds of "drugs," that are not necessarily intoxicants. Let us learn about some harmful habits and addictions that can hurt you like the addictive substances do.

Muhammad Learns Many Lessons

Teacher Hiba walked into the Eigth grade inside the classroom. "Assalamu Alaykum class," she greeted the class.

"Wa'alaykum As-Salam," the class cheerfully responded.

"Everyone, please get out yesterday's homework and place it on your desks.

I will come around to check them," the teacher said.

As soon as everyone placed their notebooks on their desks, Teacher Hiba began walking through the class checking. Muhammad was nervous. He hadn't done his homework. He couldn't stop playing his video game until he finished at least the fifth level.

"Muhammad?" Sr.Hiba interrupted his thoughts.

"Yes, Teacher Hiba?" Muhammad was scared.

"Your notebook is empty," Teacher Hiba said confused.

"I know Teacher Hiba, I'm sorry, I promise, this will be the last time," Muhammad said apologetically.

"You're a good student Muhammad; I don't expect this from you. Stay after class so we can talk about it," Teacher Hiba said.

"Yes Teacher Hiba." Muhammad said.

Teacher Hiba continued to check around for homeworks. Layan was getting nervous. She only half-completed the homeworks assignment. Layan had been up late watching television. She thought she could wake up early in the morning and do her homework quickly. But the homework was a lot longer and harder than expected.

"Layan?" Teacher Hiba called her.

"Yes, Teacher Hiba?" Layan said nervously.

"You did not complete your assignment." Teacher Hiba said confused.

"Yes, I know. I'm sorry. I..umm..it was hard," Layan explained.

"I know you're a good student. But I will have to ask you to stay after class for a talk." Teacher Hiba said.

"Yes, Teacher Hiba" Layan said with guilt. When class was over, all the students left the classroom. Muhammad, Layan, and Omar stayed behind.

"Why are you still here Omar"? Layan asked.

"Teacher Hiba saw my cd-player in my bag."

"Oh, why would you bring that to school?" Mohammad asked.

"I guess I got addicted to this one song. I wanted to listen to it during my break."

"Is that so?" Teacher Hiba was coming back after running an errand.

"Sr.Hiba!" all three exclaimed.

"I'm sorry, I did not mean to eavesdrop. But I'm glad I heard that. Take a seat you three." Teacher Hiba said kindly. Muhammad, Layan, and Omar sat on their chairs.

"About the music, you said it was addictive?" Teacher Hiba asked Omar.

"Well, one song is..kind of.." Omar said.

"Right…so addictive that you were willing to break the school policy about bringing the cd-player to school?" Teacher Hiba asked.

Omar didn't have anything to say. Sr. Hiba continued. "Do you know one big reason why alcohol and drugs are dangerous?"

"Because they are addictive?" Layan answered.

"Yes, you don't want to stop. Anyone who takes drugs will get addicted to it. If he/she did not have the money to buy it, he/she might go steal money to get it. Addiction is a powerful. This is also why it's dangerous. It's hard to control. You might commit a crime, rr break a school rule, like you did Omar." Teacher Hiba explained.

"I'm so sorry…" Omar couldn't look up to the teacher, he was so ashamed.

"Now, Muhammad and Layan." Teacher Hiba said.

"Yes Teacher Hiba?" Muhammad and Layan both responded.

"Do you have a good reason for not completing the homework assignment?"

Neither Muhammad nor Layan knew how to respond.

"This is a concern for me. It has been a pattern. You were doing excellent at the beginning of the year." Teacher Hiba said worried.

"Are our grades getting lower?" Layan asked worriedly.

"I hate to say this, because I know you are good students. But your grades have been affected. Whatever it is that's causing these distractions should be stopped immediately. I suggest that the instant you go home, you start on the important activities. Don't let any 'other addictions' become a distraction. I will give you two another chance to make-up last night's assignment," Teacher Hiba said smiling.

"Thank you so much Teacher Hiba." Muhammad and Layan said gratefully.

Muhammad went home thinking about what Teacher Hiba said. Video games are definitely not worth getting bad grades in school. As soon as Muhammad got home, he went straight to his room. He got his books and homework out, and started to work on it. It took Muhammad an hour to do it. Finally, he was done. "Alhamdullilah, I am done with my homework,"Muhammad said, satisfied. He looked at the clock. It was 20 minutes till Salatul-Asr. He had some time left to finish level six on his new video game.

Muhammad turned on the video game and began playing. Before he knew it, he was on level seven. Muhammad's mother was calling him; "Muhammad, dinner's ready."

Muhammad did not hear his mother calling him. He was too involved with the game. Muhammad's mother sent his brother HAni to get him.

"Muhammad!!" Hani shouted. "What?!" Muhammad said, eyes on the television screen..

"We've been waiting for you, Come on, I'm hungry."

"Okay, okay..wait.."

Muhammad paused the game, washed up, and went for dinner. After dinner, Muhammad's mom said, "Everyone go make wudoo', It's almost time for Maghrib."

Muhammad gasped. He had totally forgotten about Salat-ul-Asr.

"What's wrong Muhammad?"

"I missed Salatul Asr!"

"But I asked you earlier if you prayed Asr, and you nodded your head.."

"You did?"

"Yes, were you not listening to me? You were playing that video game of yours. I suppose that is more important than listening to your parents. And now, missing your salah? How could you?!" Muhammad's mother said angrily.

"Oh..I'm so sorry. I was planning to pray.." Muhammad tried to explain.

"Yes and the video game changed your plan to pray? Should I take away this video game away from you Muhammad? Ever since you've been playing it, you have been more distant with your family. You are not listening to me when I talk to you. Don't you see what's happening? This video game is interfering with your responsibilities. How can you miss your salah?!" Muhammad's mother was getting extremely angry.

"I'm sorry," Muhammad said ashamed.

"Don't be sorry to me, you have committed a crime against Allah سبحانه وتعالى.

Go make wudoo' and ask forgiveness from Allah سبحانه وتعالى."

"Oh mama, I feel so bad." Muhammad couldn't stop saying.

"I realize how dangerous it is. Like Teacher Hiba said, I have turned the video game into a "Another addictions." Astaghfirallah, how can I miss my prayers.

I'm going to go make up Salat-ul-Asr and repent to Allah سبحانه وتعالى. Inshallah, I'll never let anything become more important than praying to Allah سبحانه وتعالى." Muhammad told his mother.

Immediately, Muhammad made wudoo' and prayed. After he finished, he looked at the clock. One more hour until Isha prayer. Normally, he would have thought about going to the next level on his video game. But now, he went and got a copy of the Holy Qur'an and started to recite verses.

The next day, Muhammad met Omar at school.

Omar said to Muhammad, "I decided not to let the Internet ruin my life."

"How is that?" Muhammad asked.

"Every day I spend around three hours on it. Some nights I go to bed, but I can not sleep, so I sneak back to the computer and stay up very late. I find some school friends up late too chatting like me. A few times, I get to see bad stuff! Astaghfirullah, sometimes I let myself go with it, but afterward I feel so bad I did. If I did not stop myself, I would get addicted to wasting my life on the Internet, without much good out of it," Omar explained.

"You know Omar, I am not into the internet, but I almost got addicted to the video games. This made me forget about salah, schoolwork, my family and other important things. I also decided to be balanced. I am learning now to love worship, knowledge and family more than games and entertainment," Muhammad said.

"I know. We sometimes say we love Allah more than anything else but, astaghfirullah, we inside love playing games more than reading Qur'an or praying," Omar complained.

"That is Shaytan. He encourages us to get hooked on these "Other Addictions" as teacher Hibah said. He makes us give more time to games and TV than to worship, knowledge and other important things. This way he sets us apart from loving Allah and worshipping him as we should."

Other Addictions

Examples of Other Addictions Are Too Much of the Following:

1. Video games
2. T.V. shows
3. Internet
4. Comedy; jokes
5. Celebrities and athletes' news, pictures and fashions
6. Movies
7. Chatting
8. Music, songs, and dancing
9. Bad pictures and videos
10. Arcade games

FAITH IN ACTION

★ Always give your full attention to worshipping Allah, obeying and helping your parents, studying, and other serious daily life matters.

★ Always avoid becoming addicted to watching TV, video games, and other time wasters.

Hadeeth Shareef

عن أبي برزة الأسلمي رضي الله عنه قال: قال رسول الله ﷺ:
" لا تزول قَدَما عبدٍ يومَ القِيامة حتى يُسْألَ عن عُمُرِه فيما أفناه ، وعن عِلْمِه فيمَ فعل وعن مالِهِ من أين أكْتسَبَهُ وفيمَ أنفَقَهُ وعن جِسْمِهِ فيما أبلاه " رواه الترمذي والدارمي

Abu Barzah Al-Aslamiy narratated that Rasoolullah said: "The servant's feet would not move during the Day of Judgment until he is questioned about:
1. What he did during his lifetime
2. How he used his knowledge
3. How he earned his money and where he spent it
4. And how he utilized his body.

Lessons Learned

Allah gave you life, time, knowledge, money, a body, and many other gifts in this life. He wants you to use them all in the best manner possible. He wants you to spend your life worshipping Him, doing good deeds, and being good to people and the environment. Shaytan, on the other hand, wants you to waste your life and everything God gave you, in doing bad deeds and avoiding good work. During the Day of Judgment, Allah will ask us all about how we used our time, our brains, our wealth, and our bodies. Shaytan will not help us there; he will betray us. If we are into bad habits and during this life, we will be regretful on the Day of Judgment. If we used God's gifts as Allah wishes, we will enjoy a happy life here, and Jannah in the other life.

Projects and Activities

1. Create a list of the things that may distract you from worship, studying, and other important duties in your life.

2. Write a poem about "Other Addictions."

Stretch Your Mind

Why is time a very important element in your life?

Study Questions

1. What are some of the things that distract your mind away from worshipping Allah, studying, and other important daily life matters?
2. How can games, movies, and chatting negatively influence your daily life?
3. What will every person be asked about during the Day of Judgment? Support your answer with a hadeeth.